T0224303

Customizing Dynamics 365

Implementing and Releasing Business Solutions

Sanjaya Yapa

Apress®

Customizing Dynamics 365: Implementing and Releasing Business Solutions

Sanjaya Yapa
Kandy, Sri Lanka

ISBN-13 (pbk): 978-1-4842-4378-7   ISBN-13 (electronic): 978-1-4842-4379-4
https://doi.org/10.1007/978-1-4842-4379-4

Managing Director, Apress Media LLC: Welmoed Spahr
Acquisitions Editor: Smriti Srivastava
Development Editor: Matthew Moodie
Coordinating Editor: Shrikant Vishwakarma

Cover designed by eStudioCalamar

Cover image designed by Freepik (www.freepik.com)

Distributed to the book trade worldwide by Springer Science+Business Media New York, 233 Spring Street, 6th Floor, New York, NY 10013. Phone 1-800-SPRINGER, fax (201) 348-4505, e-mail orders-ny@springer-sbm.com, or visit www.springeronline.com. Apress Media, LLC is a California LLC and the sole member (owner) is Springer Science + Business Media Finance Inc (SSBM Finance Inc). SSBM Finance Inc is a **Delaware** corporation.

For information on translations, please e-mail rights@apress.com, or visit www.apress.com/rights-permissions.

Apress titles may be purchased in bulk for academic, corporate, or promotional use. eBook versions and licenses are also available for most titles. For more information, reference our Print and eBook Bulk Sales web page at www.apress.com/bulk-sales.

Any source code or other supplementary material referenced by the author in this book is available to readers on GitHub via the book's product page, located at www.apress.com/978-1-4842-4378-7. For more detailed information, please visit www.apress.com/source-code.

Printed on acid-free paper

Table of Contents

About the Author

Sanjaya Yapa currently works as a Microsoft Dynamics 365 consultant in Melbourne, Australia. He has more than 12 years of experience in the industry and has been working with various Microsoft technologies since 2005. He possesses a wealth of experience in software design, development, team leadership, product management, and consultancy. He specializes in solution design and development with Microsoft Dynamics 365 and the application life cycle management with Azure DevOps. Sanjaya was the coauthor of *Effective Team Management with VSTS and TFS* (www.apress.com/us/book/9781484235577). Find him on @sanjaya_yapa and at techjukebox.wordpress.com and almbox.wordpress.com.

About the Technical Reviewer

 **Scott Durow** is an experienced software architect and technologist with a passion for enabling business transformation through Microsoft technologies.

Scott is a Microsoft Business Applications MVP specializing in Dynamics 365. He is also the author of the Ribbon Workbench and SparkleXRM.

Find him on Twitter as @ScottDurow, and read his blog at scottdurow.develop1.net.

Acknowledgments

A special thanks must go to Chaminda Chandrasekara, who has been the encouraging influence for me to move into this amazing world of authoring technical content. Also, I am thankful to Scott Durow for providing valuable technical reviews in order to make this book a success. I am extremely grateful for all my mentors who have encouraged and helped me during my carrier and provided me with so many opportunities to gain the maturity and courage required to write this book.

Last, but in no way least, I owe a huge debt to my family, not only because they have put up with late-night and weekend typing, research, and my permanent air of distraction from them for the past eight months. My heartful gratitude is offered to them for all the encouragement and the help to make this wonderful dream come true. Finally, I would also like to express gratitude to my friends for cheering me on.

Introduction

The objective of this book is to introduce the reader to the features of Dynamics 365 for Customer Engagement, provide examples, and show how release management can help to increase productivity when delivering software to users. The platform has a ton of features, and it is growing extremely fast; in fact, it is difficult to condense such a plethora of features into a book of this size. Therefore, this book covers the features that are used primarily to design and develop solutions using the platform and gives references for further reading. This book can be used by intermediate to advanced programmers with Dynamics 365 knowledge. The topics covered in this book are ideal for both technical and functional consultants.

Specifically, Chapter 1 will set the stage for the book by introducing you to the evolution of the platform and by explaining how to capture requirements using Azure DevOps. This chapter will also introduce you to the example scenario, which will be used to explain the platform features in the upcoming chapters. Chapter 2 is all about setting up a development environment and configuring release automation. Chapters 3 and 4 cover how to customize the platform to implement the requirements using form customizations, autonumbering, business rules, workflows, and business process automation. These chapters will also introduce you to using TypeScript instead of JavaScript and to Microsoft Flow.

Advanced customizations are introduced from Chapter 5 onward, starting with plug-ins and custom workflows. In Chapter 6, you will gain knowledge about Azure integrations including WebJobs, Functions, and Logic Apps. Reporting is covered in Chapter 7, which highlights a wide range of features and configurations. The commonly used features are described, and additional reading references are given. Like Chapter 7, Chapter 8 covers another mammoth feature, the Dynamics 360 portals for external user interactions. Since this is a bulky topic, this chapter introduces the feature and gives additional references. The book concludes in Chapter 9 with the discussion of data migration along with design tips and best practices.

This book will serve as your reference for your Dynamics 365 for Customer Engagement implementation needs. I hope it will be your go-to reference when faced with an implementation challenge.

CHAPTER 1

Getting Ready

In the current business world, competition is growing every minute of the day, and every business must find intuitive ways of staying ahead of the competition. One of the primary challenges businesses face is to establish better customer relationships in order to provide better service to their clients. In such a competitive and demanding environment, the requirement for customer relationship management software is increasing.

Dynamics 365 for Customer Engagement is a powerful and highly adaptable platform that has been around since 2003. As shown in Figure 1-1, the product has evolved gradually throughout the years. The platform was first released with contact management and e-mail marketing tools aimed at the small business market. Today, it is known as Dynamics 365 for Customer Engagement. You can customize the product to meet almost any business need, and with every release, new features and integrations are being introduced. Needless to say, with all these new enhancements, the platform is growing rapidly and gaining popularity among the business crowd. Many industries such as energy, insurance, people management, and health have adopted Dynamics 365 as their primary platform for serving their clients.

© Sanjaya Yapa 2019
S. Yapa, *Customizing Dynamics 365*, https://doi.org/10.1007/978-1-4842-4379-4_1

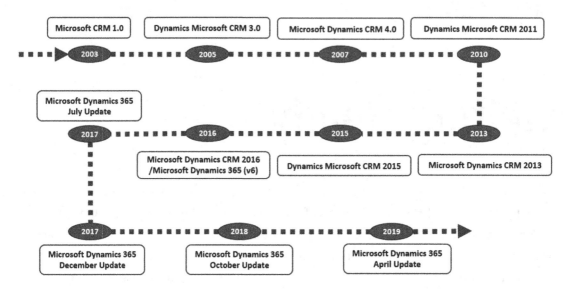

Figure 1-1. *Dynamics history and evolution*

To provide all these features the newest invension is the Microsoft Power Platform which brings all your data into one common data model. It consolidates the powerful capabilities of PowerApps, Microsoft Flow, and Power BI into one powerful business application platform that opens up a whole new domain of application development and data insights. Each part of the Power Platform is dynamic and built into Common Data Service for Apps, which is the heart of the Power Platform.

Common Data Service for Apps is an Azure-hosted database that comprises standard entities, such as accounts, contacts, and leads; it can be extended by adding new entities or new fields to the existing entities. Even business rules can be configured to apply validations and to show and hide fields. Microsoft Flow allows you to create automated workflows that can generate notifications, update data, synchronize files, and more. The analytical part of the Power Platform is Power BI, which can be used to develop descriptive reports and dashboards. Another part of the Power Platform is PowerApps, which enables developers to create standard business applications based on Common Data Service. The Power Platform is gaining popularity among the community, and it will take the Dynamics 365 ecosystem to a new era.

How This Book Is Structured

This book will cover how to develop a solution using the Dynamics 365 online platform for the membership management domain. And it will guide you from designing through developing to releasing a solution to clients. On this journey, you will discover how to use the out-of-the-box customizations, advanced customizations such as workflows and plugins, and integrations with cloud technologies such as Azure—all to build a membership management system. Also, it will guide you with best practices and show how to automate the build and release management process to establish DevOps.

Note   One important thing to remember is that all these examples are based on the Dynamics 365 for Customer Engagement online version.

The Case Study Domain

As it may sound like, membership management is not a simple domain. Many governments, nongovernment organizations, private organizations, and clubs have membership management requirements. This book will present a midrange membership management solution.

At a high level, the Small Business Members Association (SBMA) is a nonprofit organization. It has about 5,000 medium to small business owners throughout the country, and this number is growing. The association is set up to provide a wide range of benefits to the businesses owned by the members. The association is renowned for helping out the members when they face critical issues with finance, marketing, selling, and so on. It also organizes events throughout the year to educate the members to stay competitive in the market. One of the key benefits the association provides to its members is finance, marketing, and sales consulting through individual and group sessions with professionals in each domain.

Many small to medium businesses want to join the association, which is not that easy. The business owners must provide evidence of the business, for which SBMA is dedicated to safeguard. To provide these services, SBMA charges a subscription to each of their members depending on the size and annual revenue of the business.

Also, the representatives of SMBA reach out to prospective members around the country, and their objective is to increase the number of memberships. For every prospect a representative has converted, SMBA will pay a commission, which is a percentage of the annual membership fee.

Management has decided to get rid of their legacy desktop application and invest in a new feature-rich solution that improves customer engagement and provides better service to the members.

The Case Study Requirements

As an initial step, the business analysts have identified the list of requirements of the business, and they have entered them into Azure DevOps. They have used the Agile template as the project template because the end users want the project to be executed with Agile practices.

With Dynamics CRM projects in the past, source control has been a problem. But now the situation is different because there are so many advanced source control options available. As we all know, Azure DevOps supports Git and Team Foundation Server as version control options. In this book, since we are using Visual Studio Team Services (VSTS) now renamed as Azure DevOps for capturing the requirements, we will also be using it for source control, which will be explained in detail later. This must be selected when creating the project in Azure DevOps. See Figure 1-2.

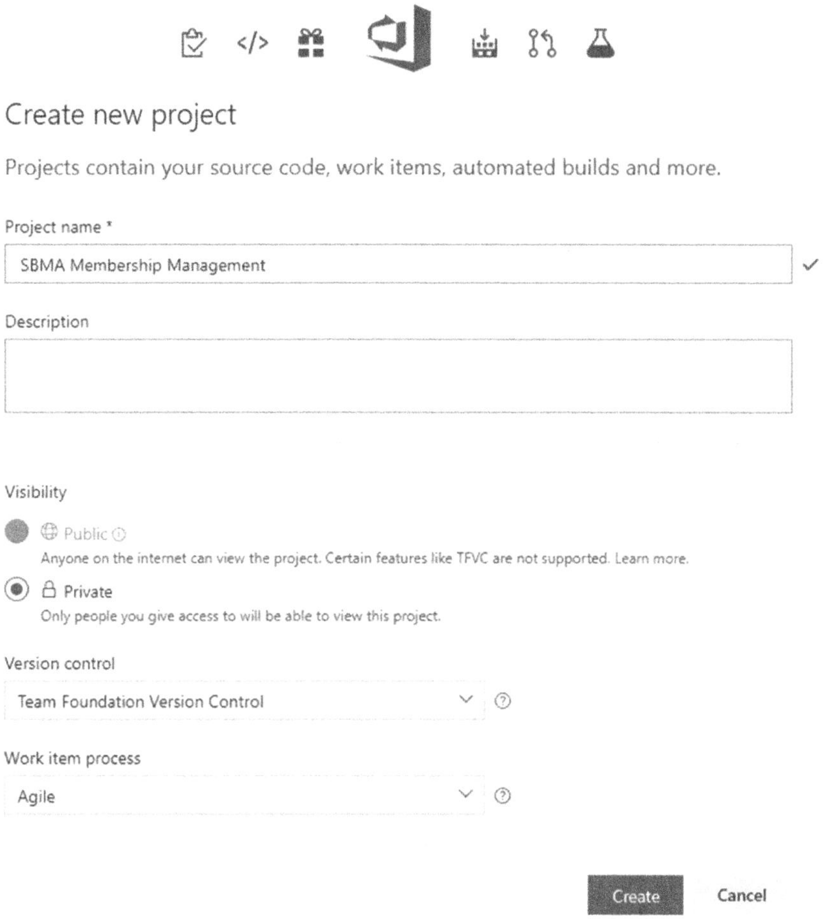

Figure 1-2. *Azure DevOps "Create new project" screen*

By default Azure DevOps enables only two levels of work items: features and user stories to create the backlog. For this particular scenario, the business analysts also want to have an epic work item, as shown in Figure 1-3. Epics are the highest level of workitems which will be used to define the Modules of the system. You can find more details at `https://docs.microsoft.com/en-us/vsts/work/customize/select-backlog-navigation-levels?view=vsts`.

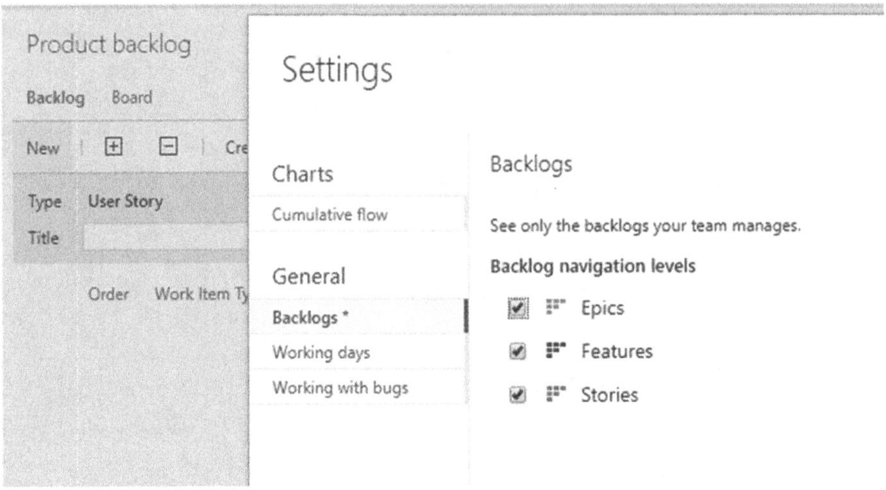

Figure 1-3. *VSTS Settings page to enable epics*

The primary objective of using Agile practices is to see the results quickly. During the analysis phase, the business analysts identified that there are high-level modules, and each module will have unique features. As the first step, they have extracted the modules. After entering the epics, the backlog looks like Figure 1-4. Epics are used mainly for future improvements of each module. The SBMA application will continue to evolve, and each module will be expanded with new features in the future.

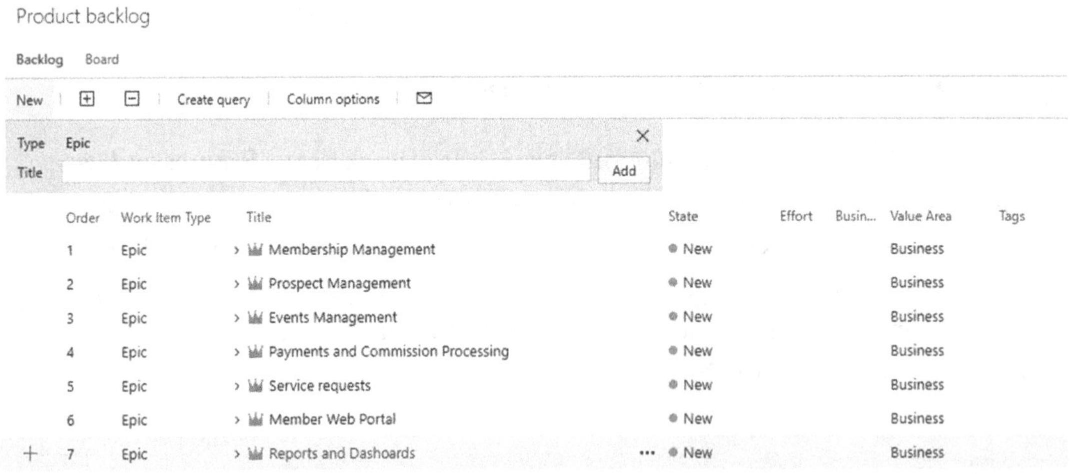

Figure 1-4. *Project backlog with epics (system modules)*

Next, the business analysts have created the features identified for each of the epics (see Figure 1-5).

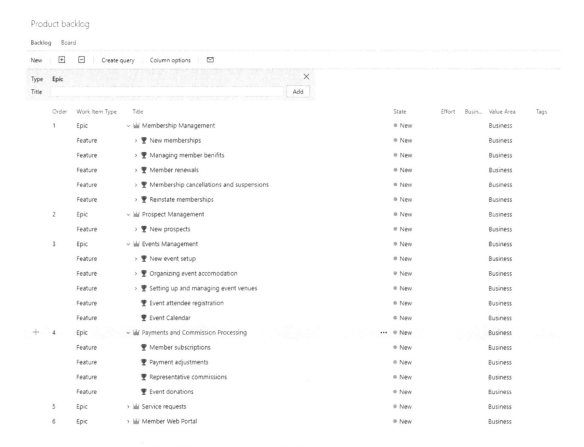

Figure 1-5. *Project backlog with module features*

The business analysts completed the backlog for the application by entering the user stories, as illustrated in Figure 1-6.

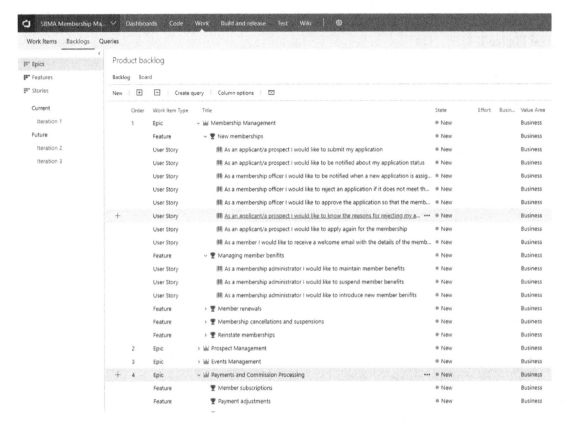

Figure 1-6. *Completed project backlog with user stories*

Now that the requirements have been captured, the next step is to select the platform to build the application. The next section will guide you through why SBMA has decided to use Dynamics 365 as the platform for its application.

Why Use Dynamics 365 as the Platform?

The next big challenge is to select the primary platform to develop the application. There are two options to consider.

- **Developing an application from scratch:** Since the application components are developed from scratch, the development team will have more control over the application development. But the downsides are the cost and the time they have to spend building the application. SBMA is more concerned about the security aspects of the data and its operations. The usability and maintainability of the application are also major concerns. In this approach, the development team may have to spend time reinventing the wheel. It is not impossible, but these issues should be considered before taking this path.

- **Using an existing platform and configuring it:** The other avenue is to buy a platform and configure it, which is inexpensive in the long run and can save loads of time because the developers are not reinventing the wheel. The usability, security aspects, document management, integrations, and so on, are just a matter of configurations and customizations.

Therefore, the conclusion is to use a platform that has already been developed and configure and customize it to the business's needs. Among the many platforms available, the online version of Dynamics 365 is the preferred platform for these reasons:

- **Flexibility:** Dynamics 365 can be customized to the way the company is working. It can be extended with simple as well as advanced customizations.

- **Usability:** The new interface is easy to use and has the highest user adoption.

- **Seamless integration:** Dynamics 365 integrates seamlessly with many other platforms such as SharePoint integration for document management, Microsoft Flow, Azure Logic Apps, and much more.

- **Powerful reporting with Dynamics 365 and Power BI:** Dynamics 365 offers powerful reporting features using FetchXML and even extends the reporting capabilities by integrating with Power BI.

- **Regular updates:** Microsoft invests heavily in Dynamics 365, and as a result, the platform is constantly being updated. These updates are also known as **Waves**. With every update/wave the application improves, meaning that the solutions implemented on top of the platform will also benefit from these improvements.

- **Pricing:** Last but not least, the pricing is affordable when compared to the other platforms, especially given the benefits the company will be getting.

The next section will guide you through some of the key requirements and why Dynamics 365 is the ideal platform to implement them.

Implementing Features with Dynamics 365

The following are a few of the high-level business requirements that are mapped to features of Dynamics 365.

Creating a Membership

Member registration is one of the primary business processes of the application. This workflow consists of several steps. When an application is submitted, a prospect record is created. At this point, the application is not approved, but the membership officer is notified with a task to review the application. The application can be approved or rejected. For the application to be successful, SBMA has several business rules that must be met. If any of the application information fails to meet any of the rules, then the application is considered to be failed/rejected. When the application is approved or rejected, the prospect should be notified via e-mail.

The Dynamics 365 workflow engine is ideal for implementing such requirements. The requirements can be configured to automatically trigger when the prospect record is created. Also, they can trigger child workflows as required. For instance, in simple terms, a workflow can be configured to create a task and can be assigned to a membership officer for review. This workflow will move the prospect record to a Dynamics 365 queue where the membership office will select the record for further processing.

If the application is approved, the prospect will be converted to a member, and a welcome e-mail will be generated, which can be easily configured with the Dynamics 365 workflow engine. Figure 1-7 shows a typical workflow configuration window.

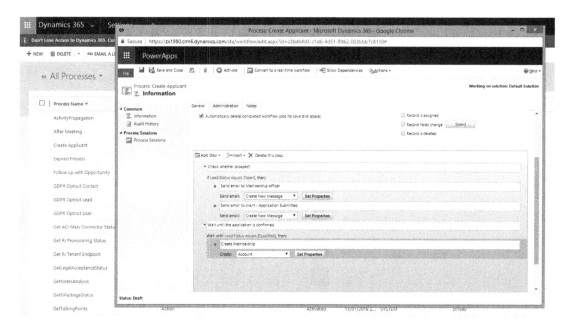

Figure 1-7. *Dynamics 365 workflow configuration window*

In addition to typical workflows, Microsoft Flow, which is also part of the Power Platform, is an attractive option for some scenarios. The graphical designer of Flow makes it easier to create workflows in no time with less training (see Figure 1-8).

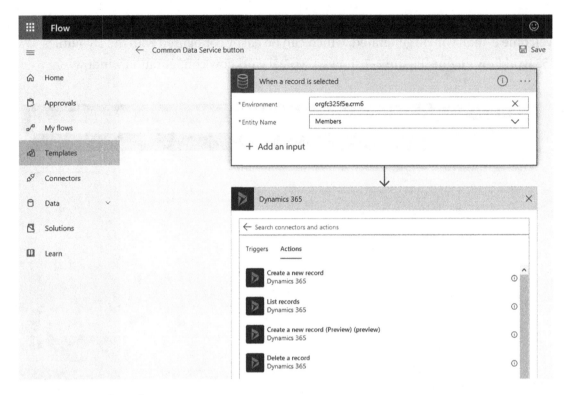

Figure 1-8. *Flow designer*

Submitting the Required Documents

As part of the member registration, the applicants must submit several documents, such as bank statements, business registration documents, and so on. These documents must be saved securely, and members should be able to update the documents from time to time.

You might know that SharePoint is an ideal document management solution, and Dynamics 365 can be integrated with SharePoint easily. Once SharePoint is configured, the documents will be saved and mapped to Dynamics 365 records seamlessly. Figure 1-9 displays documents that are saved to the SharePoint library and attached to a Dynamics 365 record.

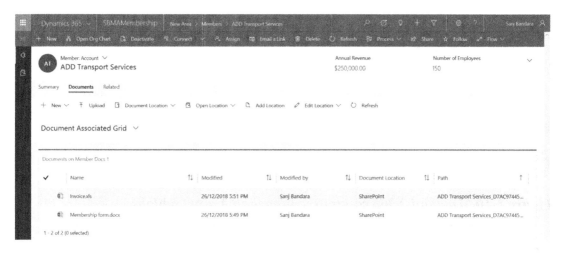

Figure 1-9. *Dynamics 365 grid display of documents from a SharePoint repository*

This book will demonstrate the server-based integration, which is the basic integration type between Dynamics 365 and SharePoint. It is suitable for most document management requirements, but if you need anything specific, you have the option to create a custom solution.

Generating a Member Subscription

When members are created, every member must pay a subscription annually. These subscription records should be raised automatically. The challenge is that the subscription dates for the members will not fall on the same day. A batch process must execute in the background to select the members on a daily basis, create the next subscription record, and notify the client automatically when the subscription is created.

This is where the Azure integrations come into play. Ideally, an Azure web job can be utilized as the background process to pick up a batch of records and create the subscription. When generating the e-mail, there are two options; either you can use a plug-in or you can use a workflow. Figure 1-10 is a theoretical illustration of the connection between Azure WebJobs and Dynamics 365. This topic will be covered in detail later in this book.

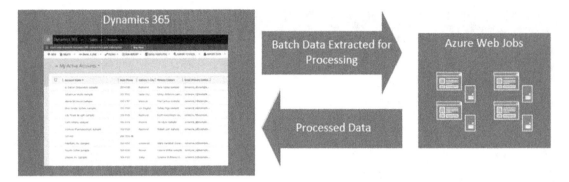

Figure 1-10. *Dynamics 365 communicating with Azure WebJobs*

Generating Reports

Dynamics 365 provides reporting and dashboards for management to review their data. Out of the box, a few dashboards are available, and you can also create your own. These dashboards can be shared with different users of the system. See Figure 1-11.

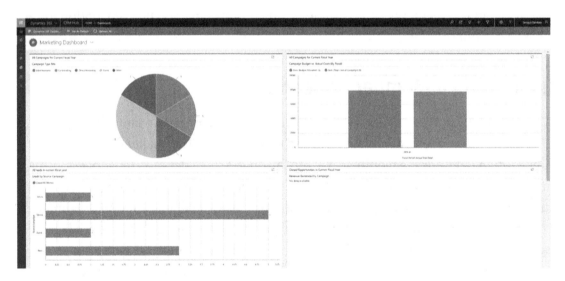

Figure 1-11. *Dynamics 365 dashboard*

Similar to dashboards, there are a few out-of-the-box reports under the Marketing section of the main menu of Dynamics 365. You can use the Report Wizard to create simple reports, or you can use FetchXML for advanced reports. Dynamics 365 online does not support SSRS reports. Figure 1-12 shows the Report Viewer.

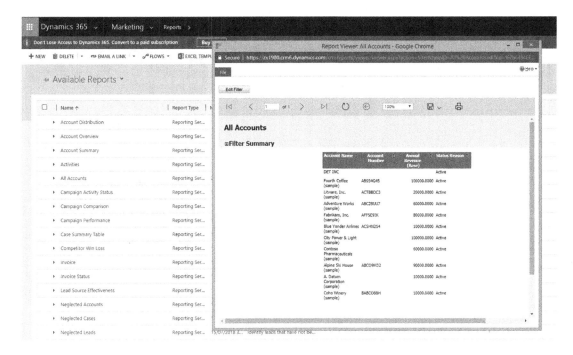

Figure 1-12. *Dynamics 365 reports*

Sometimes the reporting requirements are overwhelming, and these tools may not be enough to satisfy the information cravings of management. In such situations, you can use Power BI to meet more complex demands. Connecting with Power BI is simple, and you can find a detailed explanation of this topic in Chapter 7. The Power BI design view, as shown in Figure 1-13, extracts data from Dynamics 365 online.

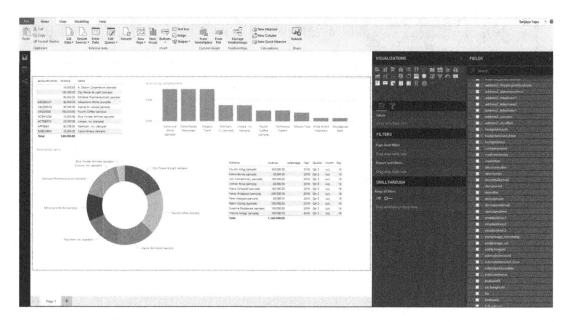

Figure 1-13. *Power BI desktop editor connected to Dynamics 365*

Processing Direct Debit Payments

Processing payments is one of the key requirements of SBMA because some of the members will be paying their subscriptions via direct debit. When a member selects direct debit as the payment method, their subscription will be deducted directly from the bank and deposited into SBMA's account. To process these payments, the association must send the list of payments due for the month to the direct debit payment system as a CSV file. The application should create this file and drop it into a shared folder in the cloud where the finance manager will send the file to the direct debit system.

Then the system will send back a processed CSV file that contains the successful and failed transactions with the relevant code. The system should read the file and update the member subscriptions with successful payments as well as generate reminders to the members with unsuccessful payments.

The integration with Azure Logic Apps is an ideal solution to process this file on a monthly basis, as shown in Figure 1-14. This is the most reliable and cost-effective approach to processing direct debit transactions.

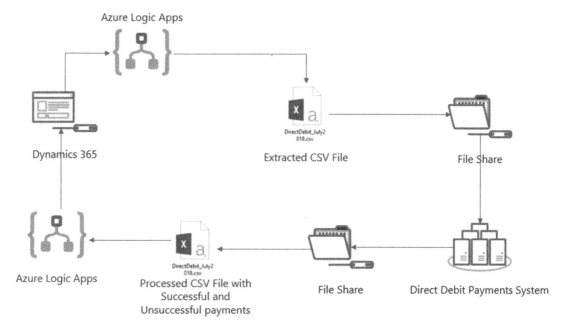

Figure 1-14. *Dynamics 365 using Azure Logic Apps for data processing*

This book will describe all these requirements with detailed implementations later in this book. As you can see, Dynamics 365 is the ideal platform for the implementation. Next we will look at the data model of the proposed application.

The Entity Model

It is time to look at the high-level entity model of the application. Table 1-1 lists the entities identified based on the requirements captured. This is just a simple model that will not cover all the aspects of membership management. Figure 1-15 illustrates the high-level data model of the application. As shown in Figure 1-15, the data model is representing the data in relation to the business terms.

Table 1-1. *Entities of the Proposed System*

Entity	Description
Member	This is the primary entity that holds the member information. A member is actually a business.
Prospect	This is a potential member entered by a representative or an applicant awaiting his or her application to be approved by the membership officer.
Contact	As per the requirements of SBMA, every member must have a primary contact who is responsible for dealing with the membership. Also for a given member, there can be one or more contacts.
Representative	Representatives are SBMA staff in different states of the country looking to increase the number of members of the association. Based on the number of members and the size of the member business, they will be paid a commission.
Knowledge Base	This entity will hold the details of service request resolutions, which can be used by the staff to solve similar issues raised by the members in the future.
Service Requests	These are the cases or issues raised by the members. A contact from the member organization will raise a service request, and it will be processed by the membership staff.
Member Subscriptions	Subscriptions are the yearly payments done by the members to the association. These subscriptions can be paid via direct debit or credit cards.
Member Benefits	The member subscription is determined by the benefits a member is registered for. Different benefits will have different features. Members can add benefits to their membership based on the size of their business.
Member Payments	Member payments are recorded against the subscriptions, which are used to track the member payments. There will be credit card payment records as well as direct debit payment records.
Events	Events are organized by the association for the members.
Event Accommodation	If the member representatives are coming from different states, they should be provided with accommodations, which will be part of the event registration. Members have the option to buy their own accommodation as well.
Event Registrations	This entity will record the event registrations for a given event. An event registration should always be a contact of the member.

(*continued*)

Table 1-1. (*continued*)

Entity	Description
Event Programs	Every event will have a defined program targeting different business verticals. Members can decide to go for these programs based on the schedule. There could be events with only one program.
Program Location	Within the event venue, there are different locations for the programs.
Event Venue	This is the venue where the event will be held, and there are several venues where the association will always organize events.
Commission	Commission is paid to representatives for bringing in new members. Based on the annual revenue of the business and the size of the business, the commission percentage will be decided.

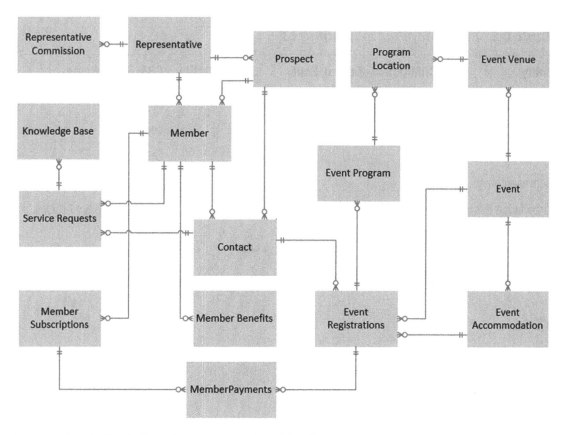

Figure 1-15. *High-Level entity-relationship diagram*

In general, if you are using any platform to provide a solution, it is always a good idea to use the out-of-the-box features as much as possible, before even thinking of any customizations. This is a fundamental best practice that applies to Dynamics 365. Out of the box, Dynamics 365 comes with several entities that can be used, and others have to be created.

Note   Dynamics 365 online is also comprised of virtual entities, which you can directly connect with external data sources, and during runtime, this external data will be available in the system. For more information, please visit `https://docs.microsoft.com/en-us/dynamics365/customer-engagement/customize/create-edit-virtual-entities`.

Table 1-2 maps the entities from Table 1-1 to the Dynamics 365 entities.

Table 1-2. *Entity Mapping to Dynamics 365*

Entity	CRM Out-of-the-Box Entity	Custom Entity	CRM Entity Name
Member	√		Account
Prospect	√		Lead
Contact	√		Contact
Representative	√		Users
Knowledge Base	√		Knowledge Base Articles
Service Requests	√		Case

(continued)

Table 1-2. (*continued*)

Entity	CRM Out-of-the-Box Entity	Custom Entity	CRM Entity Name
Member Subscriptions		√	
Member Benefits		√	
Member Payments		√	
Events		√	
Event Accommodation		√	A new custom entity must be created
Event Registrations		√	
Event Programs		√	
Program Location		√	
Event Venue		√	
Commission		√	

Summary

In this chapter, you briefly looked at how Dynamics 365 has evolved into an extremely powerful platform that can be used to provide business solutions. This chapter set the stage for this book and briefly explained the problem domain that will be used as an example to explain the customizations and integrations of Dynamics 365. The chapter also demonstrated how to use Azure DevOps to capture requirements and organize the backlog. Then the chapter described the primary reasons to use Dynamics 365 as the platform to provide a solution to the problem. Finally, the chapter illustrated the high-level data model and the mapping to the Dynamics 365 entities. The next chapter will guide you through setting up the development environment.

CHAPTER 2

Setting Up the Development Environment

This chapter will guide you through setting up your development environment to start the project. To recap, in Chapter 1 we captured the requirements in Azure DevOps (formaly known as VSTS), created the data model, and mapped the entities to Dynamics 365 entities. Now it is time to commence development. But before doing that, we must decide what tools are required for the implementation and how to configure them.

Dynamics 365 Online vs. On-Premises

Dynamics 365 is available in two flavors, online and on-premises. The decision of which one is best for the solution is totally dependent on the organizational requirements. Some organizations highly value their customer and transaction data, and they have policies to safeguard the privacy of that data. In such scenarios, they will hesitate to put the data online and prefer to maintain an on-premises server farm to host the application. So, Dynamics 365 on-premises is the ideal solution for such organizations. The most notable drawback of the on-premises version is that updates are not released frequently compared to the online version.

The Dynamics 365 online version is regularly updated, and issues are fixed promptly. Additionally, since Microsoft has data centers on every continent, it guarantees the security of the data. Still, sometimes more traditional people will want to stay on-premise with their data. Even though this book is based on the Dynamics 365 online version, all the examples are compatible with the on-premise version as well.

© Sanjaya Yapa 2019
S. Yapa, *Customizing Dynamics 365*, https://doi.org/10.1007/978-1-4842-4379-4_2

Before commencing any development work, you must download the latest SDK. Needless to say, you will be needing the XrmToolBox as well. In the Dynamics 365 development world, XrmToolBox provides you with a wealth of plugins to develop and troubleshoot your work. Make sure that you have the latest version downloaded to your development environment.

Setting Up a Dynamics 365 Development Environment

When setting up a development environment, if you already have enough licenses and extra instances for development, testing, user acceptance testing (UAT), and production, then things will be much easier. But we all cannot have this kind of perfect environment. The easiest option is to create a 30-day trial of Dynamics 365. The following are the steps to create a 30-day trial:

1. Navigate to `dynamics.microsoft.com`, and locate the Start Free option (see Figure 2-1). Click it.

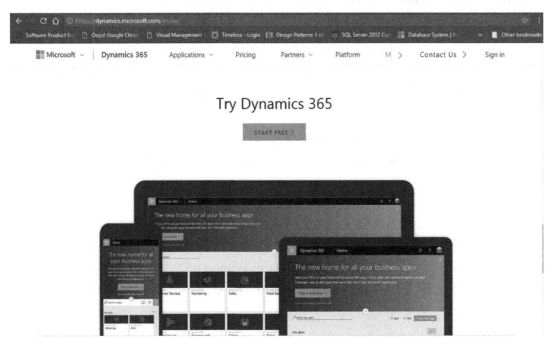

Figure 2-1. *Start Free option to create the trial*

2. As shown in Figure 2-2, select the Sales option. By default, this is
   selected.

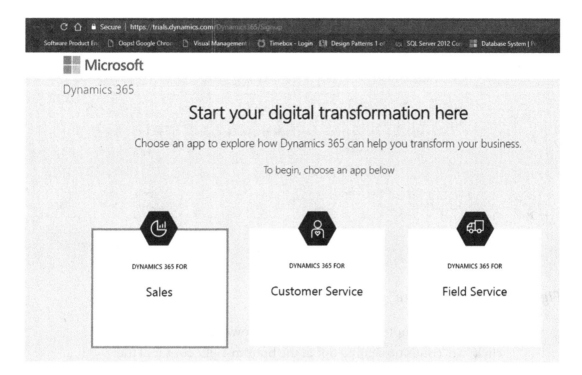

Figure 2-2. *Selecting the app*

3. Scroll down to the bottom of the page, and click the "Sign up here"
   link (see Figure 2-3).

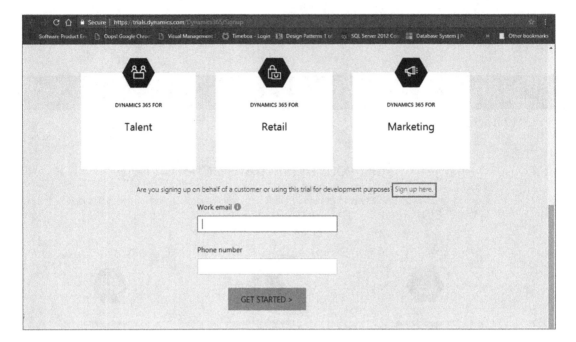

Figure 2-3. *"Sign up here" option*

4. You will be prompted with the message shown in Figure 2-4. Just click "No, continue signing up" at the bottom-right corner of the message box.

Figure 2-4. *Sign-up confirmation for partners and Microsoft employees*

5. On the next screen, fill in your details and click the Next button, and you will be prompted to enter your account details. The details provided here will be used to create the Dynamics 365 URLs. Once you have populated the account details, click "Create my account" at the bottom of the page. See Figure 2-5.

Figure 2-5. *Creating an account*

6. On the next screen, you will be asked to enter the phone number, and Microsoft will send you a text message containing a code if the "Text me" option is selected. See Figure 2-6.

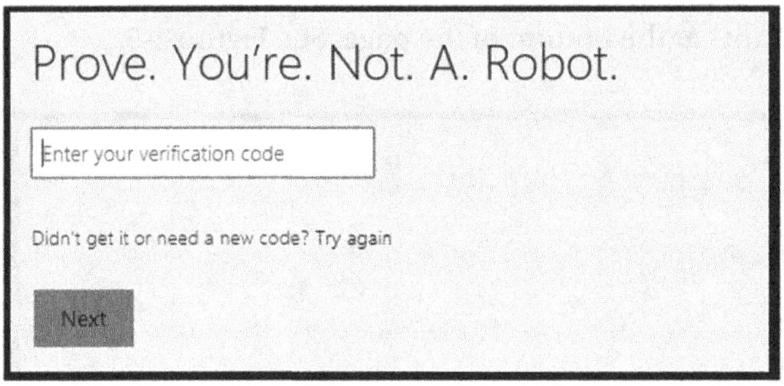

Figure 2-6. *Entering the security code*

7. Now that your account has been created, save the account details somewhere. They will also be e-mailed to the business e-mail address you provided. Now click the Set Up button, and you will be redirected to select the scenario that is right for you. For the purposes of this book, we will be selecting "None of these. Don't customize my organization." Even though this option is selected, you will be getting the Customer Engagement scenario as your base. So, it doesn't matter whether you select any of these options. But, if you select "Field services" or "Project service automation," there are some specific components that will be installed to your Dynamics 365 instance. See Figure 2-7.

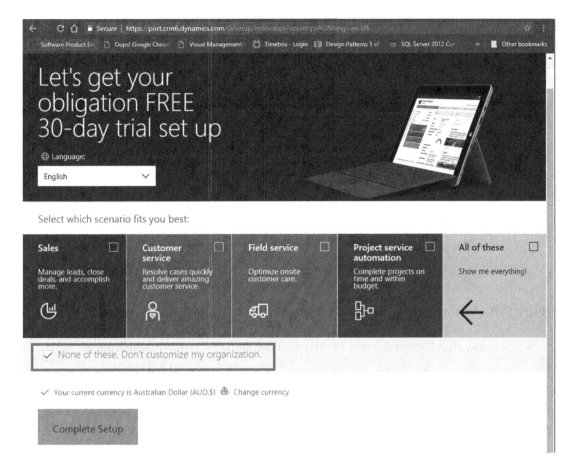

Figure 2-7. *Selecting the organizational scenario*

8. Click the Complete Setup button, and your organization will be created in a few minutes.

Setting Up Visual Studio for Development

Make sure you download the latest SDK to your local folder. Currently, the SDK is no longer available through Microsoft, but you can use either NuGet or the following URL where David Yack has simplified the process: `https://xrm.tools/SDK`. Now that we have decided to use Dynamics 365 online and created the instances for development, the next step is to set up Visual Studio for the development work. When it comes to developing solutions for Dynamics 365, Visual Studio itself won't be enough. You need some additional support or extensions. Primarily, two tools are essential for you to be a productive developer: Productivity Tools (see Figure 2-8) and Web Essentials (Figure 2-9). You can easily download and install them through Extensions and Updates of Visual Studio.

Figure 2-8. *Visual Studio Productivity tools plugin*

Figure 2-9. *Visual Studio Web Essentials plugin*

We all know that Dynamics 365 Toolkit and the Dynamics 365 Extensions are available, but still, they are not compatible with Visual Studio 2017 at the time of writing this book. There are workarounds to make them work with Visual Studio 2017, but this is not always successful. It is not essential to have them, and it is out of the scope of this book.

So, let's create the solution for development. Here are the components we will be needing for this project:

- Plugins

- Workflows

- Customizations

- Web resources

You will need Azure and Reporting projects as well, but they will be added to the solution later in the book. Now, you might be thinking about what might be the ideal design pattern to be used. For CRM projects, keeping it simple is best, so you will stick to the basics here. There is no harm in using a fancy design pattern, but for Dynamics 365 projects, keeping it simple is highly important.

So, when creating the Visual Studio solution, give a proper name to the solution. The most important thing is to select the correct project type. You are initially going to create a class library for plugins, so select the Class Library (.NET Framework) project type because .NET Standard and .NET Core are still not ready for CRM development. See Figure 2-10.

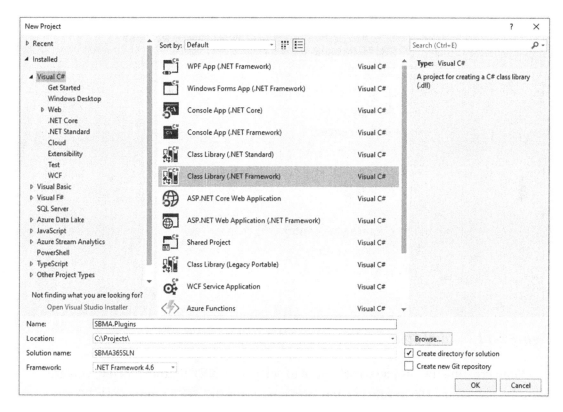

Figure 2-10.   *Creating a Visual Studio project*

Once you click OK, the solution will be created. So, you need to add projects for workflows and web resources. The completed solution looks like Figure 2-11.

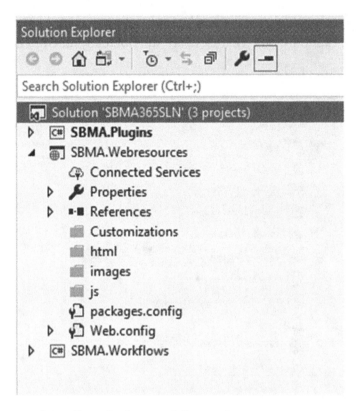

Figure 2-11. *Visual Studio solution and the projects*

When creating the projects, make sure to select the .NET Framework 4.6; you are using the Dynamics 365 online version, and it requires the .NET Framework 4.6. Also, when creating the web resources project, create an empty ASP.NET Web Application (Framework) project. You will not compile this project; it is just a placeholder for the web resources.

As you can see, the Webresources project contains a few folders.

- **Customizations:** This will hold any customizations done against the entities.

- **Html:** This will hold any HTML files.

- **images:** This will contain the icons and other images used in the solutions.

- **js:** All the JavaScript libraries will be stored in this folder. Later we will look at how to extend this to use TypeScript, which is becoming more and more popular among the CRM developers.

To write plugins and workflow activities, you will require the latest Dynamics 365 assemblies. You can easily download them via the NuGet package manager. Enable the Package Manager console and execute the following command:

```
PM> Install-Package Microsoft.CrmSdk.CoreAssemblies -Version 9.0.2.4
```

You can loacte previous versions and the command to execute at https://www. nuget.org/packages/Microsoft.CrmSdk.CoreAssemblies/.

Note   The previous command will install the assemblies to the plugin project only. You will have to install it to the workflow project by just selecting the project from the "Default project" drop-down list.

Source Control

Now that the solution is created, it is time to discuss source control. This is extremely important no matter what solution you are developing. Therefore, you will also check in our example solution to Azure DevOps. You will be using the same project you have created for capturing the requirements.

1. In your Azure DevOps project, create a folder under Code to store the artifacts. See Figure 2-12.

Figure 2-12. *Azure DevOps source code repository*

The solution will be checked into this folder. The purpose of creating this folder is to make it tidier. You can directly push all the solution artifacts to the root without creating any folder structure. See Figure 2-13.

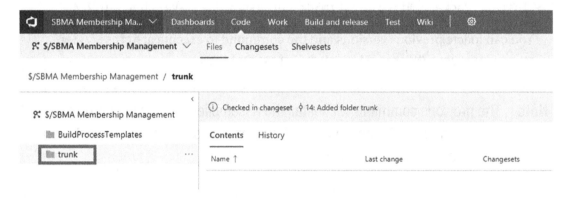

Figure 2-13. *New folder created in Azure DevOps for storing source code*

2. Now you need to connect to the project from Visual Studio. Open Visual Studio and open the Team Explorer. On the Home tab, click Manage Connections to add a new connection to the team project. See Figure 2-14.

Figure 2-14. *Connecting to the team project via Visual Studio*

Note   Follow the link to discover more details on setting up the connection: `https://msdn.microsoft.com/en-us/library/ms181474(v=vs.80).aspx`.

---

3. If you have successfully connected, you can see all the Azure DevOps organizations. Expand the one where your team project was created. Select the team project and click Connect. Now you can see the project from Team Explorer. See Figure 2-15.

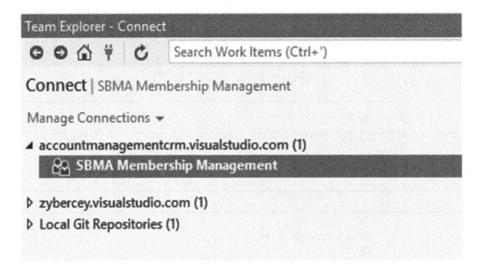

Figure 2-15. *Azure DevOps Team Project connected to Visual Studio*

4. Click the Home button and click Source Control Explorer. See Figure 2-16.

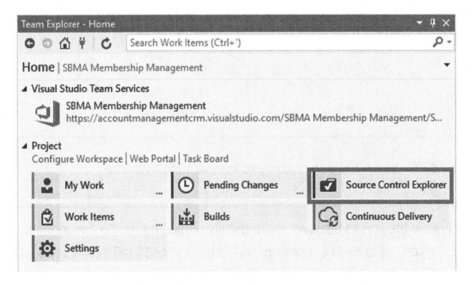

Figure 2-16. *Navigating to Source Control Explorer*

5. Now you can see the Code section of the project. Navigate to the Solution Explorer and right-click the solution. Click Add Solution to Source Control, which will display the dialog shown in Figure 2-17.

Figure 2-17. *Add solution to Azure DevOps Source Safe dialog*

6. Click OK, and your code will be added to TFS. Finally, right-click the solution in Solution Explorer and click Check In. You will have to add check-in comments and click Check In. It is always a best practice to add the some comment with your check-in, which will be extremely useful when you backtrack changes in source control. See Figure 2-18.

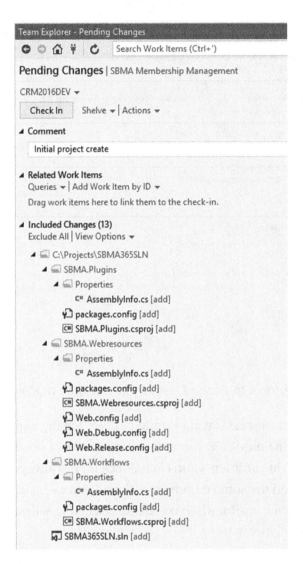

Figure 2-18. *Adding comments to a check-in*

Now you can see a small light blue padlock indicating that your solution has been checked in. See Figure 2-19.

Figure 2-19. *Solution added to the Azure DevOps source control*

Explaining Solutions

Before we start the debate on managed versus unmanaged, it is better to revisit what a solution is in the Dynamics 365 space. Solutions are the mechanism to author and release business solutions to Dynamics 365. They are similar to .NET assemblies. In other words, solutions are used to package the artifacts for an implementation of a given business requirement. The following is a list of potential artifacts that can be included in a solution. Remember, you can create multiple solutions, and each solution may contain different components.

- **Schema:** Entities, attributes, relationships, global option sets

- **Process/code:** Dialogs, actions, workflows, plugins, custom workflow activities

- **User interface:** Site map, forms, entity ribbons, application ribbon, web resources

- **Security:** Field-level security profiles, security roles

- **Templates:** E-mails, contracts, articles

- **Analytics:** Reports, dashboards, views, visualizations

Fundamentally, a solution is a bucket that can be used to carry your customizations from one environment to another. There are three different types of solutions.

Default Solution

All the out-of-the-box customizations are included in the default solution. You can customize components here but cannot export them for distribution. Besides, it is always a best practice to leave the default solution as it is. You can view the default solution by navigating to Settings ➤ Customize the System (see Figure 2-20).

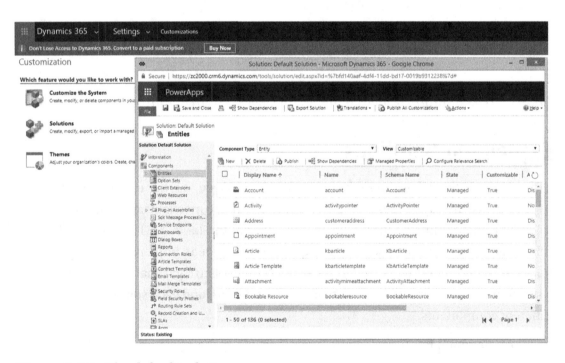

Figure 2-20. *The default solution*

Unmanaged Solution

When you create a new solution, it will be an unmanaged solution. As a best practice, create a separate solution for every project or hotfix. But there are pros and cons to this approach, which we will discuss in the upcoming sections. In this unmanaged state of the solution, you can add, edit, update, remove, and test the customizations done against the components.

Managed Solutions

Once all the customizations to the components are completed, when you export your solution for distribution, you can export it as a managed solution. When a solution is set as managed, then no further customizations can be done. Managed solutions can be layered on top of each other, and you can declare unmanaged customizations on top of them. These solutions are installed on top of the default solution. Managed solutions are ideal for Independant Softare Vendors (also known as ISVs).

Managed vs. Unmanaged Solutions

When you are selecting between managed and unmanaged solutions, it all depends on how you want to release or distribute your customizations to target users.

If you are solving your software requirements in-house, then go for unmanaged solutions. Dynamics 365 solutions will be your baby, and you can create projects and hotfixes as solutions. Since you can create any number of unmanaged solutions, over time your production Dynamics 365 instance will end up in a huge pile of solutions, which will be a maintenance nightmare. Therefore, you should have some control over how you release your work. Your development environment may contain several solutions, but you must always have an integration environment where you can combine all the changes. Recently Microsoft introduced solution patches and solution upgrades, which removes most of the complexities related to solution deployment. We will be discussing this in detail in the next section.

Most of the time, the managed solutions are used by vendors to distribute solutions to their clients, and they do not want clients to modify the solution. It is like a piece of software that you would get from the market and install. Previously, managed solutions were locked for any changes. But now, by declaring managed properties, vendors can allow limited customizations. Also, when a managed solution is removed from your system, all the customizations that were in the managed solution will also be removed. This is similar to uninstalling a software component from your system.

Solution Patches and Upgrades

The solution patches enable you to release only the customizations done against a component, eliminating the risk of releasing unintended customizations to target environments. You can apply solution patches for both managed and unmanaged solutions. When creating patches, it should be based on the existing solutions. What does this mean? As a best practice, in addition to the default solution, you should create a base solution for your project. For instance, you can create a base solution that contains all the entities that are required for the project and both system and custom entities. You also can have the advanced customizations such as plugins and processes in one solution and web resources in another. Then you can create solution patches for the individual parent solutions that you have created when changes are required.

When you decide to use this mechanism, you must start using version numbers consistently. The version of a patch will depend on the version of the parent solution. The format will be same as the solutions, which includes <major>.<minor>.<build>.<release>. See Figure 2-21.

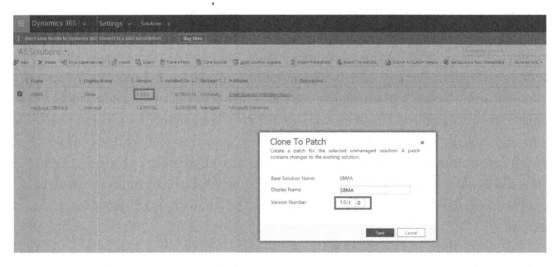

Figure 2-21. *Solution patch versioning*

The beauty of this is that it does not contain any of the noncustomized components or any of the related components. Unlike solutions, patches do not have a dependency on each other, meaning that you can easily remove a patch without impacting another one. Remember, when you uninstall a parent solution from the target environment, then the patches related to that solution will also be removed.

Let's assume you are planning a big roll-out of your project, Phase 2. It should include all the patches that you have released after the last major release. Dynamics 365 provides you with the clone solution to meet this requirement. See Figure 2-22.

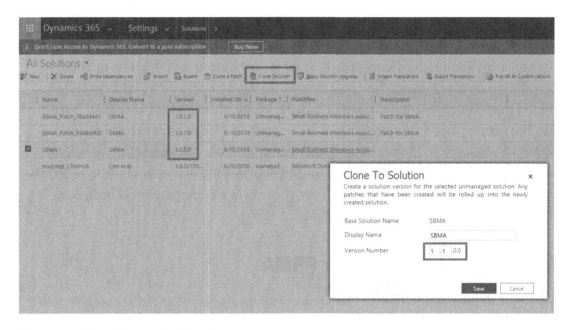

Figure 2-22. *Clone solution for an upgrade*

When you are cloning or upgrading, you must pay special attention to the version number because it only allows you to change the major and minor parts of the version. Once the cloning is completed, you can see that all the patches will be removed, and the parent solution will have the new version number. This indicates that the changes in the patches are combined with the parent solution. At this point, you can do the necessary customizations as well. For demonstration purposes, this book has used unmanaged solutions, but in the real world when cloning, the best practice is that the solution patches should be used only with managed solutions. See Figure 2-23.

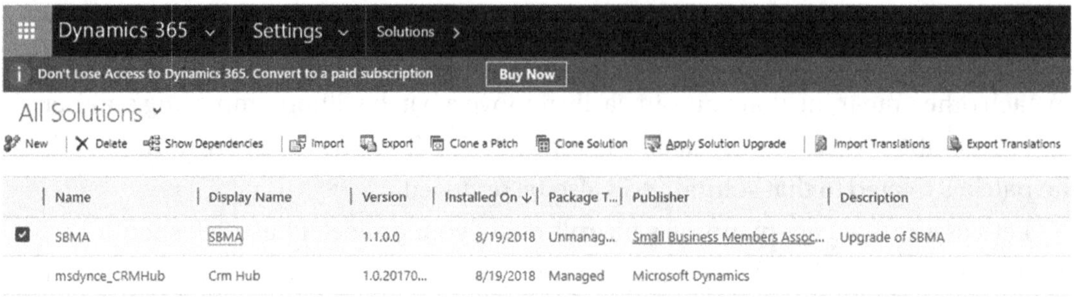

Figure 2-23. *Cloned solution*

The advantage of the solution upgrade is that when you import the solution to the target environment, Dynamics 365 automatically detects that this is an upgrade to an existing solution and notifies you. During the import process, you will be asked to import the solution as a "holding solution." By default, this option is selected if there are patches for the parent solution that you are upgrading. This is extremely useful when removing unwanted customizations. The holding solution will retain customizations until removing the existing customization and applying the new upgrade. Microsoft has simplified this process, and needless to say, it works like a charm. We will be looking at this process in more detail later in this book.

Management Strategy for SBMA

This book demonstrates the Dynamics 365 customization through a real application implementation as an independent software vendor (ISV). All the development work will be done with an unmanaged solution and released to the target environment as a managed solution. There are many debates about whether to use managed or unmanaged solutions, but this is out of the scope of this book.

Before you make any decisions, research the topic. If you are an ISV, then it is always best to use managed solutions. But if you are doing in-house development work, then there are many factors to consider. The following article gives you a wealth of information on this topic: `https://community.dynamics.com/crm/b/razdynamicscrmconsultant/archive/2016/03/04/managed-vs-unmanaged-solutions`.

Source Controlling the Customizations

So far, we have created a Visual Studio 2017 solution to hold all the plugins, custom workflow activities, and web resources. Now we are going to look at how to source control the customizations. For this, we will be using the Solution Packager tool provided by Microsoft, which is distributed as part of the Microsoft.CrmSdk.CoreTools NuGet package.

We need to come up with a proper solution to automate the repetitive work. For instance, we will be developing our solution and need to release it to a target environment. For simplicity, this book will use only two environments: Development and UAT. But you can have multiple environments or instances.

As shown in Figure 2-24, the release will begin in the development environment and go through the Azure DevOps release process. For the process shown, you will also need the Microsoft.Xrm.Data.PowerShell module. You can find more details about it at `https://github.com/seanmcne/Microsoft.Xrm.Data.PowerShell`.

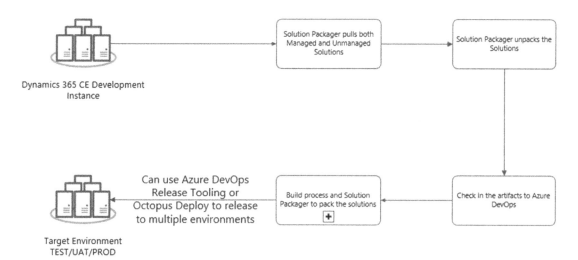

Figure 2-24. *Release process*

The process is briefly explained in the following steps and will be explained in detail when we start the actual development work:

1. The development work is done on the Dev instance. All the base solutions and patches are created as unmanaged solutions.

2. Once the customizations are done, the Solution Packager will be executed to extract the solutions.

3. You can then check in the extracted files to Azure DevOps. As you all know, it is not necessary to check in any DLLs. Besides, you already have the plugins and the workflows.

4. Once that is done, you can start the build process and pack the solutions.

5. As mentioned, we will be releasing the unmanaged version of the solution. You can use Azure DevOps release tooling or a third-party tool like Octopus to automate the releases. In your configuration, if you have multiple environments, you can use these systems to automate the releases.

6. Also, there are other components such as Reports, Azure Logic Apps, and Azure WebJobs that we are planning to use, and the release mechanism will be different for them. We will discuss these when we add these components to the solution later in this book.

Why Is It Important to Automate Releases?

A few years ago, automating a release was a tedious task. At that time, automating Dynamics CRM releases was even more difficult. But now, both Dynamics 365 and release management software have been enhanced to a state where it can be done with minimum effort. The primary reason to automate releases is to eliminate the mistakes that people make when releasing. There is no point in wasting valuable time performing release activities manually over and over again. Besides, in Agile development environments, the releases are more frequent. In such scenarios, deployments must be automated.

Many release automation techniques can be used. SPKL Task Runner is a set of tools that can be used to automate deployment. You can find more details at `https://github.com/scottdurow/SparkleXrm/wiki/spkl`. Also, there is the Nullfactory Generator, which is a framework that is designed especially for Dynamics 365 projects. You can find more details at `www.nullfactory.net/2018/06/generator-nullfactory-xrm-1-7-0-released/`. You also have the option to create your own process from scratch, and there are many resources to guide you.

In this book, we will be using SKPKL Task Runner to implement the build and release process. This was developed by Scott Durow, and it is a robust and well-tested set of tools. To begin with, let's create the base solution.

> **Note**   If you are going to create your own build and release process, then you will have to learn about Solution Packager and Solution Deployer. Needless to say, you will have to use PowerShell extensively to accomplish this. For PowerShell, you will also have to use the Microsoft.Xrm.Data.PowerShell PowerShell module.

Creating the Base Solution

You will be starting the application development process by creating the base solution. For the demonstration prposes of this book base solution will contain only the entities.

Creating the Publisher

Before you start creating the solution, you must create a publisher for the solutions you are going to create. So, who is this publisher? It is a real-world entity that publishes a solution. In other words, people/team/department/organization who possess the ownership and the control over the solution. By default, there will be a default publisher. But for our solutions, we are going to use a new publisher.

1. Navigate to the Settings area and click Customizations. As illustrated in Figure 2-25, click the Publishers link.

Figure 2-25.   *Customization landing page*

2. In the top-left corner of the Publishers grid, click the New button, and the New Publisher window will pop up. Enter the display name, and the Name field will be automatically populated. Next, you can give a prefix of your choice. This value is important, especially for customizations. For instance, when you create a field or an entity in the solution, the prefix defined in the publisher of the entity or field. This is useful for ISVs to identify the solution components added by their solution. Also, the option value prefix will be used for the value of the option sets that you will be creating. You can enter other details such as contact details, but they are optional. After filling the required values, click Save and Close. See Figure 2-26.

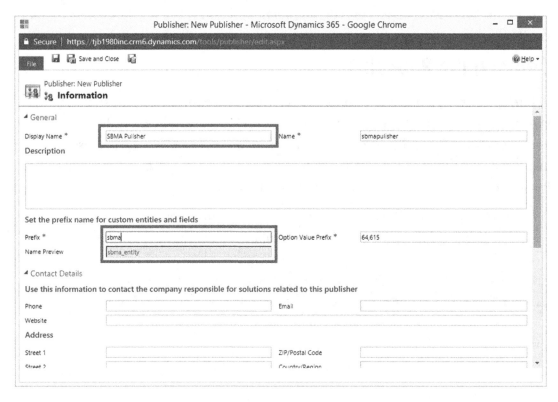

Figure 2-26. *Creating a new solution publisher*

3. To commence, go to Settings and select Solutions, as illustrated in
    Figure 2-27. This is where you create a base solution.

Figure 2-27. *Navigating to solutions*

Creating the New Solution

To create the new solutions, follow these steps:

1. Click the New button to create a new solution, and the new
    solution window will be displayed. After entering the display
    name, the Name field will be automatically populated. Next, click
    the lookup search button of the Publisher field. Click the lookup
    search button and select the new publisher you have created. At
    this point, the version number is set as 1.0.0.0, meaning that it is
    the first version. See Figure 2-28.

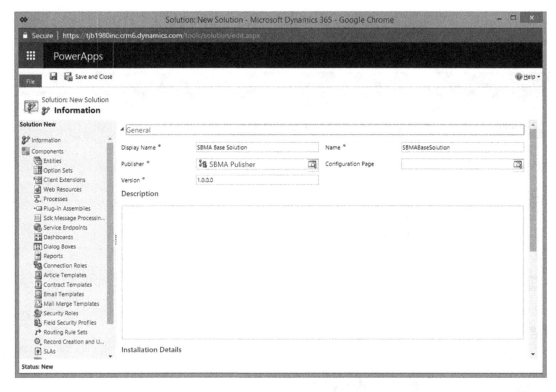

Figure 2-28. *Creating a new solution*

2. After setting these initial values, click the Save button, and the solution will be created. You have not added any entities to the solutions. First, let's add the existing entities identified in Chapter 1 that are required for our solution. You need the Account, Lead, Contact, Users, Knowledge Base Articles, and Incident entities. Click the Add Existing button on the toolbar to access the existing entities from the default solution. See Figure 2-29.

Figure 2-29. *Adding existing entities to the solution*

Adding Entities to the Solution

When you click the "Add existing" button, you will see the prompt to select the entities required for the solution.

1. On this screen, select the entities from the default solution. See Figure 2-30.

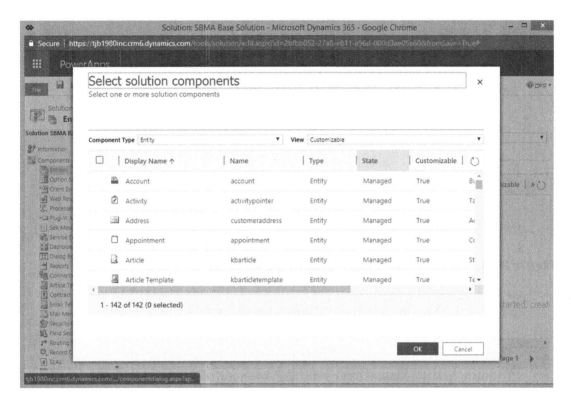

Figure 2-30. *Selecting the existing entities*

2. The next step is to select the entity assets to be included in the solution. You have the option to select only the required components or all the components by just selecting the Add All Assets option. The important thing that you should consider here is when you select this option, it will select components that you may not require. It is always a best practice to select only the components required for the base solution. See Figure 2-31.

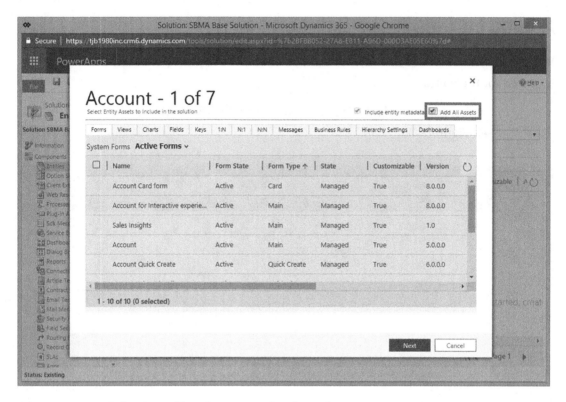

Figure 2-31. *Selecting all entity assets for the solution*

3. Click the Next button. You will have to perform this action against
    all the entities you have selected. In this example, there are seven
    entities selected, so you will have to perform this action seven
    times. Now that your solution is filled with out-of-the-box entities,
    you will create the custom entities required by the solution.
    Similar to creating any database table, you will have to create all
    the required fields for these new entities. To create new entities,
    click the New button on the toolbar, as seen in Figure 2-32.

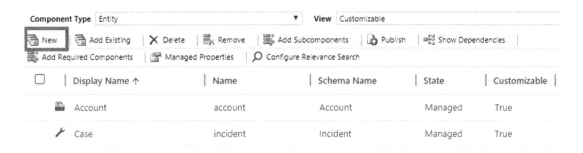

Figure 2-32. *Creating new entities*

4. As shown in Figure 2-33, you must enter the required fields.
    Display Name, Plural Name, and Name will be automatically
    populated as soon as you tab away from the Display Name field.
    As a best practice, make sure you have entered a singular name.
    In addition to these fields, you must select the ownership of the
    entity. If Organization is selected, the entity will be displayed to
    the entire organization, and if User or Team is selected, it will be
    displayed to a specific team or a user in the system.

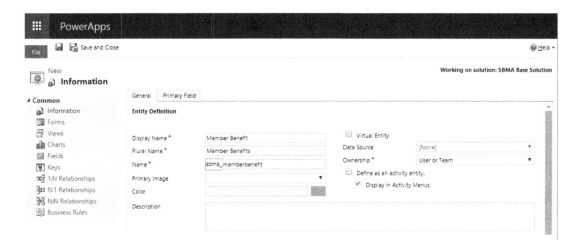

Figure 2-33. *Setting up entity properties*

Other Entity Settings

Also, there are several check boxes that you should consider checking at this point.

1. For instance, "Areas that display this entity" defines in what section of the Dynamics 365 navigation bar the entity should be visible. For this example, sales and service would be enough. This is not mandatory, but if you want the users to discover the entity easily, then you should do it. In fact, one of the key requirements of the SBMA application is that it must be user-friendly. Remember, you can't change these settings for system entities. However, using the site map, you can modify where the entity should be visible. Since Dynamics 365 is moving toward an app model and a unified interface, this can be designed using the App Designer.

2. There are other options available under Communication & Collaboration, Data Services, Auditing, Outlook & Mobile, and Help that are self-explanatory. You can select these options at this stage or after creating the entity. But keep in mind once set, some of these options cannot be disabled or enabled in edit mode of the entity. See Figure 2-34.

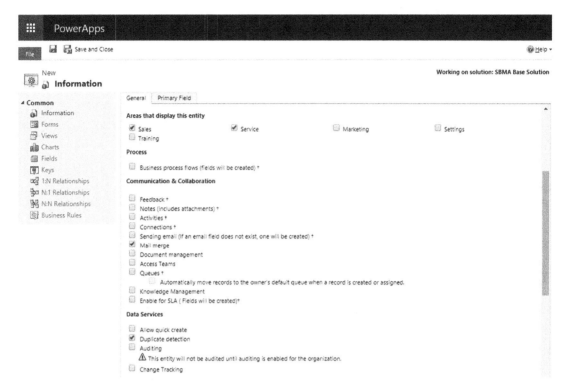

Figure 2-34. *Entity metadata*

3. Each entity defines a primary field, which is typically a link to the
    record that can be found on the Primary Field tab of this window.
    This field must be set to Single Line of Text with the format set to
    Text. See Figure 2-35.

Figure 2-35. *Primary Field properties of a custom entity*

4. After setting all these properties, you can save the entity. You
    can add the other fields after saving, or you can add the fields
    after creating all the entities. Also, to make the solution more
    eye-catching, you could add icons to the entities you have
    created. You must first download the icons to the local machine
    and then navigate to the web resources of the solution. Click
    the New button, and a window will pop up to enter the details
    of the icon and import the icon to Dynamics 365, as illustrated
    in Figure 2-36. With the introduction of the Unified Interface,
    you cannot use traditional image formats such as jpeg. Instead
    you must use Scalable Vector Graphics (SVG). Following url will
    give you more details on how to create and add SVG icons to
    the Unified Interface: https://community.dynamics.com/365/
    projectserviceautomation/b/d365tipsandtricksfunctional/
    archive/2018/11/05/adding-icons-for-the-unified-
    interface.

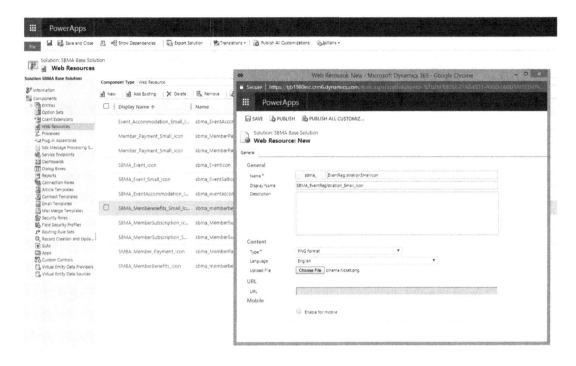

Figure 2-36. *Upload icons for custom entities*

Add Entity Icons

Keep in mind that you need to upload two images in the sizes 16×16 and 32×32 to be used as both the icon for the entity and the icon for the form. After uploading the icons, you can map them to the entity. As mentioned earlier, this is for the web interface, but if you are using the Unified Interface, please follow the steps given in the reference shared in previous section.

1. Navigate to an entity where you want to add the icon and click the Update Icon. As you can see in this window, you can upload two images. One is for the web application, and the other one is for the entity forms. As mentioned earlier, the web application icon must be 16×16, and for the entity forms the icon must be 32×32.

2. When you click the lookup search button next to the field, you will see the topmost resources in the solution. If you cannot find your icon web resource there, then scroll down and click Lookup More Records, which will open the Lookup Search window where you can search and add your icons to the entity. See Figure 2-37.

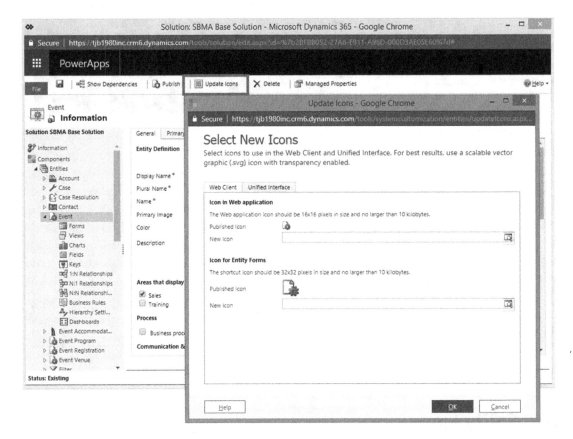

Figure 2-37. *Mapping icons to the entity*

3. Keep in mind that you need to upload two images (a 16×16
    version and a 32×32 version) to be used both for the entity and for
    the form. After uploading the icons, now you can map them to the
    entity. Navigate to an entity where you want to add the icon and
    click the Update Icon button, as shown in Figure 3-37. As you can
    see from this window, you can upload two images.

4. When you click the Lookup Search button next to the field, you
    will see the topmost resources in the solution. If you cannot find
    you icon web resource there, then scroll down and click Lookup
    More Records, which will open the Lookup Search window where
    you can search and add your icons to the entity. See Figure 2-38.

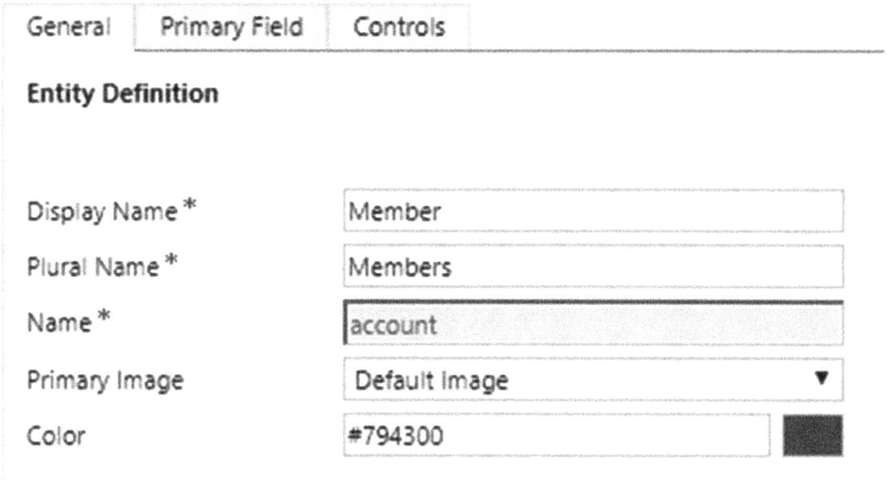

General   Primary Field   Controls

Entity Definition

Display Name *	Member
Plural Name *	Members
Name *	account
Primary Image	Default Image ▼
Color	#794300

Figure 2-38. *Changing the entity display name*

5. The next step is to create the relationships between the entities.
    Open the entity where you want to be set up the relationship and
    select 1:N Relationships. Since Member (Account) is a system
    entity, the relationship with other system entities like Contact is
    already set up. See Figure 2-39.

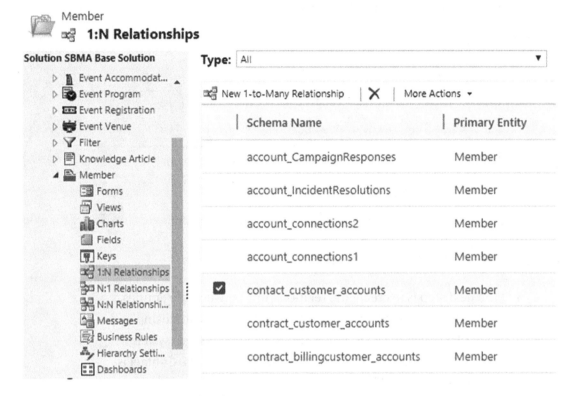

Figure 2-39. *The relationship between system entities*

6. When you click the New 1-to-Many Relationship button on the
    grid toolbar, a window to set up the relationship will be displayed.
    On this form, there are a few mandatory fields that you must enter
    before saving the relationship between the entities such as Related
    Entity, Display Name, Field Requirement, and so on.

These fields are categorized into four sections.

- **Relationship Definition:** This section lists the properties that
  describe the relationship.

- **Lookup Field:** This is the field that is displayed at the related entity.

- **Navigation Pane Item for Primary Entity:** This describes how the
  relationship is presented at the primary entity navigation.

- **Relationship Behavior:** In general terms, these are the settings that
  preserve the data integrity.

Once the fundamental properties are set, then you can set the others as per your requirements. In this example, we will be leaving the default settings as they are. See Figure 2-40.

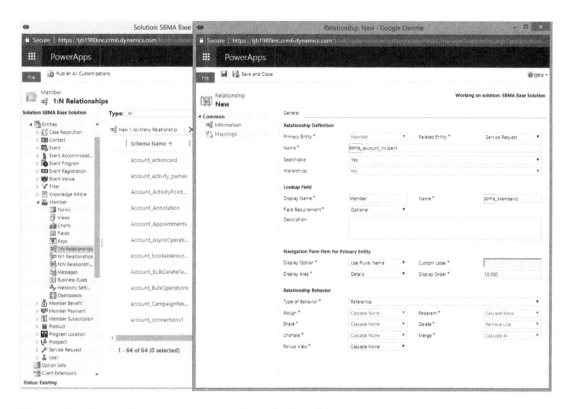

Figure 2-40. *Setting up a new entity relationship.*

Once all the relationships are set up, you can verify whether the relationships are correct. The best way is to compare your high-level ERD with a diagram created with Dynamics 365. Figure 2-41 was extracted from the XrmToolBox plugin Entity Relation Diagram Creator after creating the entities and setting up the required relationships with the newly created entities. You can find out more about the tool from `https://www.xrmtoolbox.com/plugins/JourneyIntoCRM.XrmToolbox.ERDPlugin`.

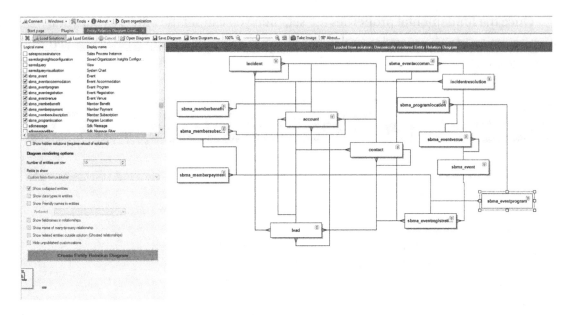

Figure 2-41. *The relationship between system entities*

This is an easy to use tool. You first have to set up the connection to the Dynamics 365 instance via the XrmToolBox. Then on the tool, there is an option to load the entities. This will load all the entities including the custom entities in the system. You can select the entities in your base solution to make sure all the relationships are set up as per the initial design.

Installing SPKL Task Runner

SPKL Task Runner can be installed via the NuGet package manager. Use the following command to install SPKL Task Runner to the SBMA.Solutions project:

```
PM> Install-Package spkl
```

Optionally, you could install a specific version by using -Version <version number> with the previous command. Once it's installed successfully, a few components will be installed to the project, as shown in Figure 2-42.

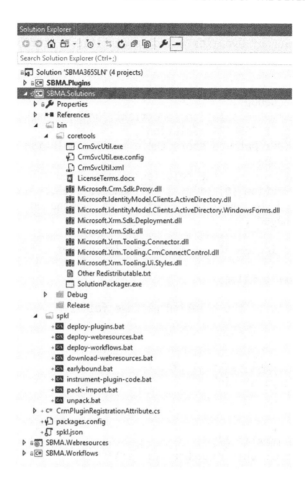

Figure 2-42. *After installing the SPKL Task Runner*

You only have to execute the `.bat` files under the `spkl` folder to export and import your solutions. First, open `spkl.json` and change the `solution_uniquename` and `packagetype` attributes. `solution_uniquename` is the name of the solution, and the package type is set to `managed` since we are going to release a managed version of the package to the target environment.

The `spkl.json` file contains all the folder mappings and settings required to extract and pack the solutions. See Figure 2-43.

```
/*The solutions section defines a solution that can be extracted to individual xml
files to make versioning of Dynamics metadata (entities, attributes etc) easier
*/
 "solutions": [
 {
    "profile": "default,debug",
    /* The unique name of the solution to extract, unpack, pack and import*/
    "solution_uniquename": "SBMABaseSolution",
    /* The relative folder path to store the extracted solution metadata xml files*/
    "packagepath": "package",
    /* The relative path name of the solution to pack into*/
    "solutionpath": "solution_{0}_{1}_{2}_{3}_managed.zip",
    /* Set to 'unmanaged' or 'managed' - default to 'unmanaged' if omitted*/
    "packagetype": "managed",

    /* Set to 'true' to increment the minor version number before importing from
       the xml files*/
    "increment_on_import": false,

    /* Map code artefacts to the solution package folder*/
    "map": [
    {
      "map": "path",
      "from": "PluginAssemblies\\**\\*.*",
      "to": "..\\..\\Plugins\\bin\\**"
    },
    {
      "map": "path",
      "from": "WebResources\\*.*",
      "to": "..\\..\\Webresources\\Webresources\\**"
    },
    {
      "map": "path",
      "from": "WebResources\\**\\*.*",
      "to": "..\\..\\Webresources\\Webresources\\**"
    }
    ]
  }
]
```

Figure 2-43. *SPKL Task Runner configuration*

After setting these values, you can right-click the spkl folder of the SBMA.Solutions project and click the Open Command Line menu item. From the submenu, click Standard Command Prompt to open the command prompt from Visual Studio. From the list of .bat files under the spkl folder, enter the unpack.bat file to the command prompt and hit Enter. You will have to provide the following parameters to make the connection.

The beauty of the SPKL Task Runner tool is that it remembers your credentials, so you do not have to enter them over and over again. In Figure 2-44, we will be selecting option [0] to enter the server details.

```
 Microsoft Windows [Version 10.0.14393]
 (c) 2016 Microsoft Corporation. All rights reserved.

C:\Projects\SBMA365SLN\SBMA.Solutions\spkl>unpack.bat
Using 'C:\Projects\SBMA365SLN\packages\spkl.1.0.227-beta\tools\spkl.exe'
spkl Task Runner v1.0.227.1  Tasks v1.0.227.1

(0) Add New Server Configuration (Maximum number up to 9)
(1) Server: CRM2016dev:80, Org: CRMDEV2016, User: crm2016dev.local\crmadmin

Specify the saved server configuration number (1-1) [1] : 0

Enter a CRM server name and port [crm.dynamics.com]: crm6.dynamics.com
Is this organization provisioned in Microsoft Office 365 (y/n) [y]: y

    Enter Username: xxxx@xxxxxxxx.onmicrosoft.com
    Enter Password: **************

List of organizations that you belongs to:
(1) OrgNameXXXXX (OrgNameXXXXXinc)

Specify an organization number (1-1) [1]: 1
Unpacking solution
Searching for packager config in 'C:\Projects\SBMA365SLN\SBMA.Solutions\spkl\...'
Using Config 'C:\Projects\SBMA365SLN\SBMA.Solutions'
```

Figure 2-44. *Executing unpack.bat and providing credentials to connect to the Dynamics 365 instance*

Once successfully connected with the server, the tool will display the available organizations, and it will ask you to select the organization, as shown in Figure 2-44. Then the tool will locate the solution on the server and download the solution components to the local folder. You can include the folder and check in the customizations. See Figure 2-45.

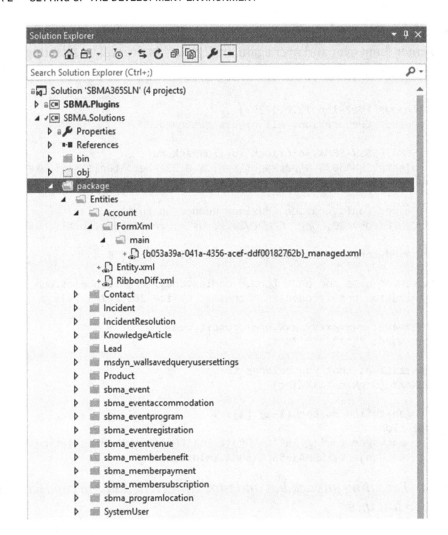

Figure 2-45. *Unpacked solution*

Now let's deploy this to the target environment. For that, you will have to use the
pack+import.bat command file from the spkl folder. Again, if your target environment
is not in the tool's memory, you can add it by selecting this option: [0] Add new server
configuration. The process is the same as executing the unpack command.

When the command executes, you will get to see the progress of packing and
importing, and when successfully imported, the command will also publish the solution
at the target environment. Once successfully executed, you will be able to see your base
solution at the target environment. See Figure 2-46.

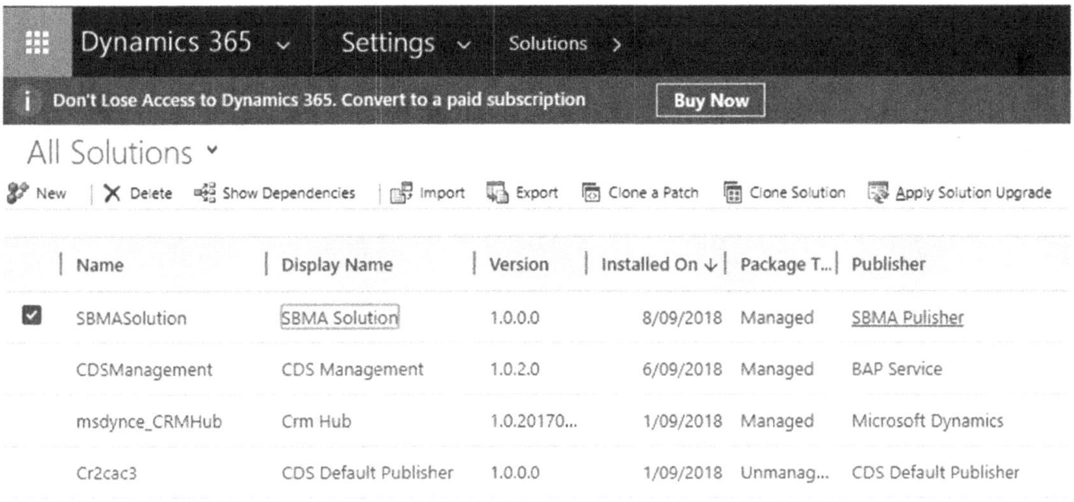

	Name	Display Name	Version	Installed On ↓	Package T...	Publisher
☑	SBMASolution	SBMA Solution	1.0.0.0	8/09/2018	Managed	SBMA Pulisher
	CDSManagement	CDS Management	1.0.2.0	6/09/2018	Managed	BAP Service
	msdynce_CRMHub	Crm Hub	1.0.20170...	1/09/2018	Managed	Microsoft Dynamics
	Cr2cac3	CDS Default Publisher	1.0.0.0	1/09/2018	Unmanag...	CDS Default Publisher

Figure 2-46. *Base solution deployed to target environment*

Summary

With this, we end Chapter 2. In this chapter, you set up a development environment and dug deep into managed and unmanaged solutions. You also looked at the solution patching and upgrading. Lastly, the chapter discussed the release management approach suitable for the project. The book will demonstrate how to extend and improve the release process when the project get matures. From Chapter 3 onward, the book will guide you through how to customize Dynamics 365 with examples from the SBMA project.

CHAPTER 3

Out-of-the-Box Customizations

In this chapter, you will start developing the SBMA membership application. In this initial phase of development, the primary focus will be on out-of-the-box customizations. In Chapter 2, we discussed the details of how to create the base solution, and in this chapter, we will create basic customizations as solution patches and showcase the steps to add the solution to source control and to the target environment.

Form Customizations

To get started with form customizations, you will first create the solution patch that will include the form customizations. By using solution patching, you can include the forms that you are going to modify in the patch without bothering to have all the other components in the solution. This section will cover how to add fields and custom entities to the system and how to arrange the main forms of those entities.

When creating the solution patch, navigate to Settings and select Solutions. In the solutions grid, select the SBMA solution and click Clone a Patch in the grid toolbar, as illustrated in Figure 3-1.

© Sanjaya Yapa 2019
S. Yapa, *Customizing Dynamics 365*, https://doi.org/10.1007/978-1-4842-4379-4_3

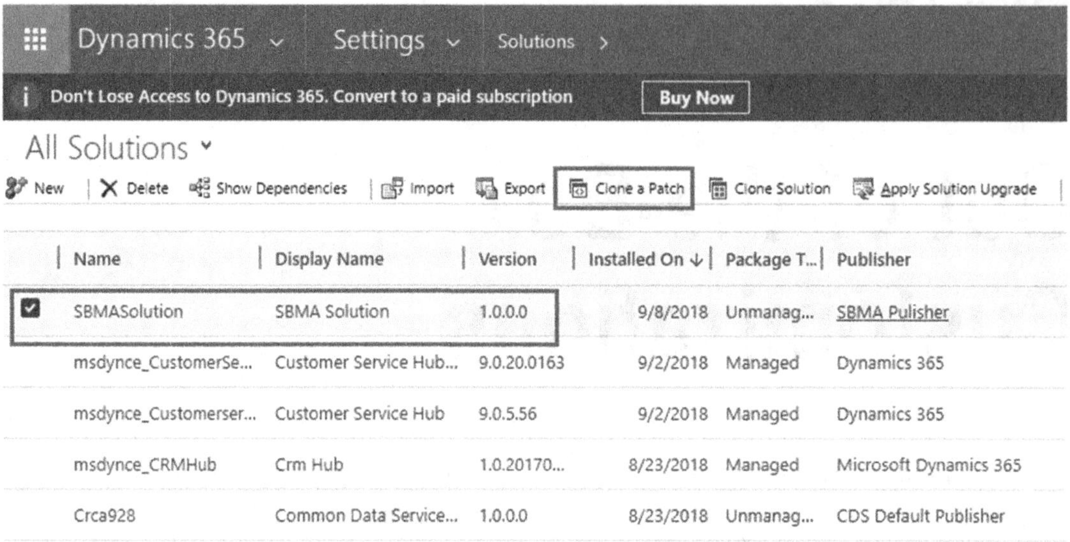

Figure 3-1. *Cloning the base solution*

Note that the version number has increased, and the base solution will not allow any modifications. All modifications should go into solution patches hereafter until you clone the solution. Click the Save button, and the solution patch will be created. See Figure 3-2.

Figure 3-2. *Solution patch versioning*

Now you can add the components. Remember, you will be modifying only the main form and adding new fields as required. So, you have to add the entity and the main form only. This is the same as adding existing items to the base solution. The only difference is that you are selecting the required components only.

After selecting the item in the Missing Required Components window, select "No, do not include the required components." You already did this when you first imported the base solution. As shown in Figure 3-3, the solution patch contains all the required components.

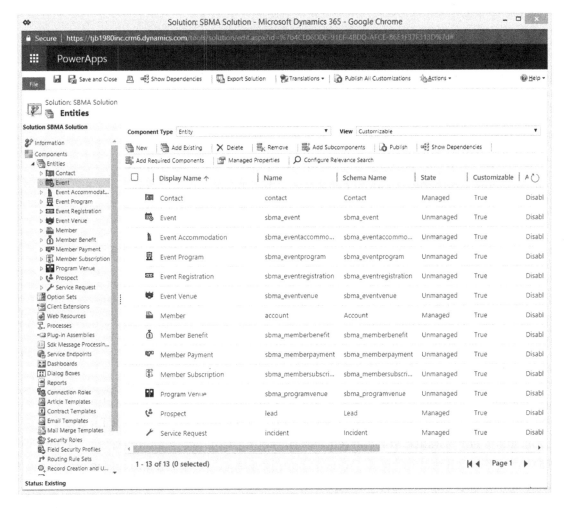

Figure 3-3. *Solution patch with entities*

Expand the entity and the forms; you will see that only the main form is included in the solution patch (see Figure 3-4).

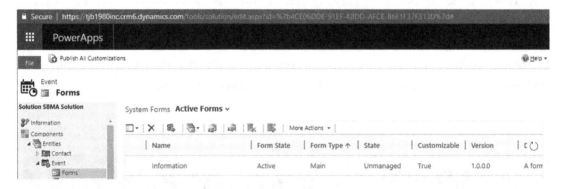

Figure 3-4. *Solution patch containing only the main form*

To begin with the customizations, you will start with the Member form. It is always good to list the changes that you are going to do to the form.

1. Identify the fields that are required. Member is a custom entity, and it already has some fields out of the box. It is always good to use these as much as possible. Since the form is going to be modified to meet SBMA's requirements, it is a best practice to create a new main form so that the default, out-of-the-box form remains as it is.

2. If any additional fields are required for the final application, create those additional fields.

3. Arrange the interface by adding the new fields and removing any unnecessary fields and sections.

The default Member form is a huge form; you do not require all the sections on the form for the application, so you can remove the sections not necessary for the application. For instance, you can remove Marketing, Contact References, etc., as per the SBMA application requirements. You can simply select the section and hit Delete on the keyboard or click the Remove button on the ribbon.

To arrange the form properly, double-click the Summary tab, and on the Properties tab, click the desired layout; then click OK. See Figure 3-5.

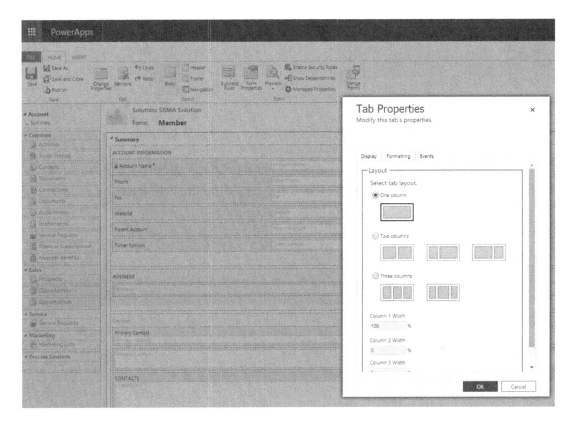

Figure 3-5. *Form tab formatting*

Note   When removing sections, keep in mind that the components in that section will also be removed. If that happens, then you will have to add the items again. For instance, by default on this form there are three columns, and if you change the formatting to have two columns, then you will lose the components in the third column. The trick is that you can move the items in column 3 to column 1 and change the formatting to One Column. You also have Undo and Redo options. The nice thing about the form editing is that while editing the form, you can preview the changes. See Figure 3-6.

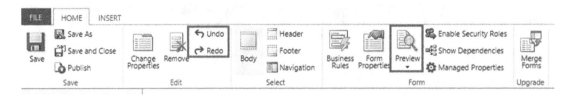

Figure 3-6. *Form editor ribbon: Preview, Undo, and Redo buttons*

To remove an unnecessary field, you can select a field and click the Remove button on the ribbon. To add new fields to the form, drag and drop the field from the Field Explorer to the desired location on the form. See Figure 3-7.

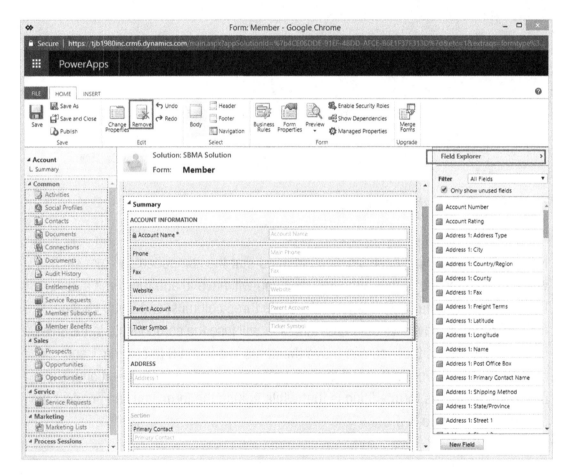

Figure 3-7. *Form customizations: adding and removing fields*

As shown in Figure 3-8, forms can be edited with the new WSYWIG Form Editor, which is in preview at the time of writing the book. You can sign into PowerApps, expand Data in the left pane, and select Entities. Select the entity, and on the Forms tab you can select the form and edit it. You can find more information at `https://powerapps.microsoft.com/en-us/blog/introducing-the-new-wysiwyg-model-driven-form-designer-public-preview/`.

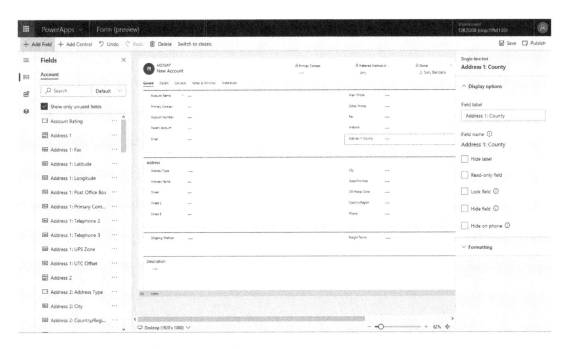

Figure 3-8. *Form Editor(preview)*

To add a new field to the Member entity, just click the New Field button in the Field Explorer pane. This will open the form to add a new field. Or you can go back to the solution and select the fields from the usual left pane under the Fields menu of the Member entity. As shown in Figure 3-9, a new option set field can be added to the entity.

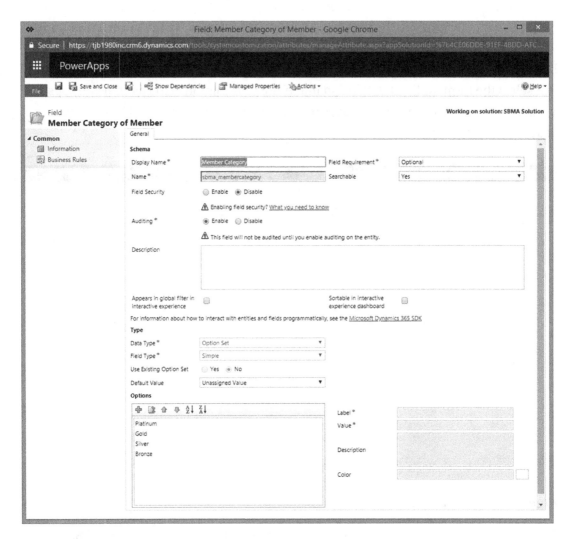

Figure 3-9. *Adding a new option set field to the Member form*

After making all these changes, you can save the form and click Publish Customizations, which will apply the changes to the form, as shown in Figure 3-10.

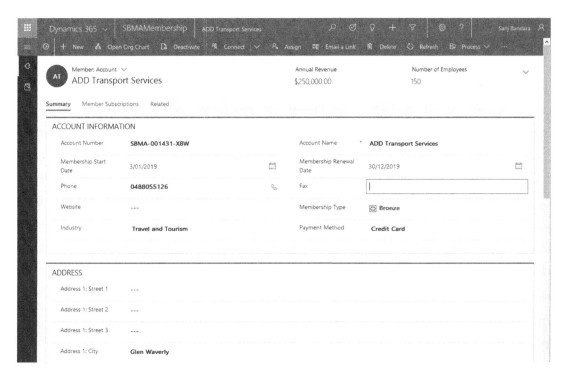

Figure 3-10. *Member form in the Unified Interface*

Like with the Member form, add the fields to the other entities and place them on the forms as required. The event form fields are laid out as shown in Figure 3-11. For instance, the following are the fields that should be used to capture the event-related information:

- **Event Code:** This field is used to identify the events and is a unique code. As you can see, the field is set to Business Required, and the length of the field is 10 characters. All these properties can be set when you create the field.

- **Name:** This is also set to Business Required, and it is an out-of-the-box field.

- **Event Status:** This is an option set that defines the workflow of the event from start to completion or cancellation.

- **Event Budget:** This is a currency type field for allocating the funds for the event.

- **Start Date and End Date:** These are date-time fields that define the event's start date and end dates. When defining date-time fields, you can choose not to show the time field. But in this context, the time part is required. This is set to Business Required because for a given event, there must be a start date and an end date.

- **Registration Start and End Date:** Like with the event start and end dates, you can define the start and end dates for event registrations. Again, these fields also require a time part.

- **Event Capacity:** This defines the number of registrations allowed in the event, which is usually a whole number. This is not always required because there could be events with unlimited registrations such as fundraising events.

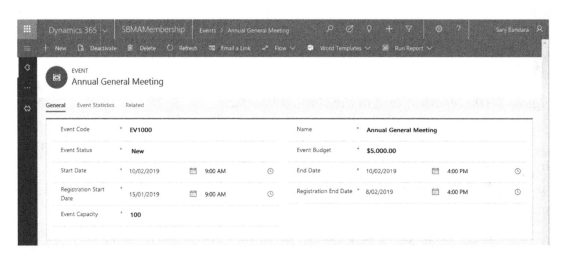

Figure 3-11. *Event form*

After completing all these customizations, it is good to add the changes to source control. So, as explained in Chapter 2, update the solution name in `SPKL.json` with the unique name of the solution patch (`SBMASolution_Patch_4ce06dde`). Then use the SPKL `unpack.bat` file to extract and check in the solution patch to source control, and use the SPKL `pack+import.bat` tool to package it and import it to the target environment.

In the next section, the book will elaborate on how to set autonumbering for the entities.

Autonumbering Option

Autonumbering was one of the biggest pain points until the recent past because not all entities supported autonumbering option. Developers had to invent ways of implementing autonumbering for custom entities. But, ever since the version 9.0 release, you can create autonumbering for any entity. At the time of writing this book, there is no interface to configure the autonumbering, but in XrmToolBox, there is a plugin called Auto Number Manager that can be used to configure the autonumbering for any entity of the solution.

There are several autonumber formats supported by this feature. You can find more details about autonumbering at `https://docs.microsoft.com/en-us/dynamics365/` `customer-engagement/developer/create-auto-number-attributes`.

Since this is going to involve more customizations, you can create another solution patch and include the entities that require autonumbering. Similar to the previous patch you created, include only the entity and the main form, and click "No, do not include required components." For the examples given here, we will be using the Member and Event entities.

First, let's establish a connection from XrmToolBox to the Dynamics 365 instance. Open the toolbox and click the Connect button on the toolbar, as illustrated Figure 3-12. Also, you will have to provide the instance URL and on the next screen the username and the password.

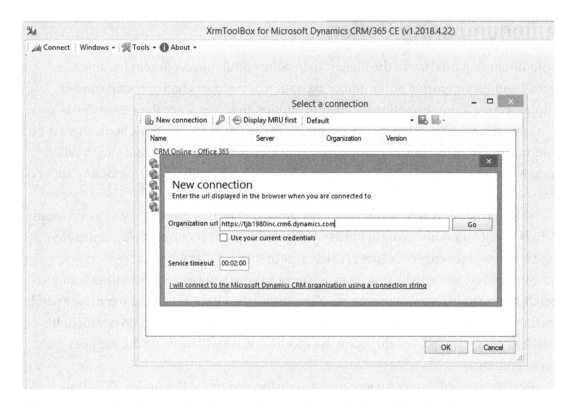

Figure 3-12. *Connect to the Dynamics 365 instance from XrmToolBox.*

Once that is successfully connected, you will be asked to give a name to identify the connection, and then you will see the list of connections available. Select the connection and click OK. This means you are now connected to the Dynamics 365 developer instance. See Figure 3-13.

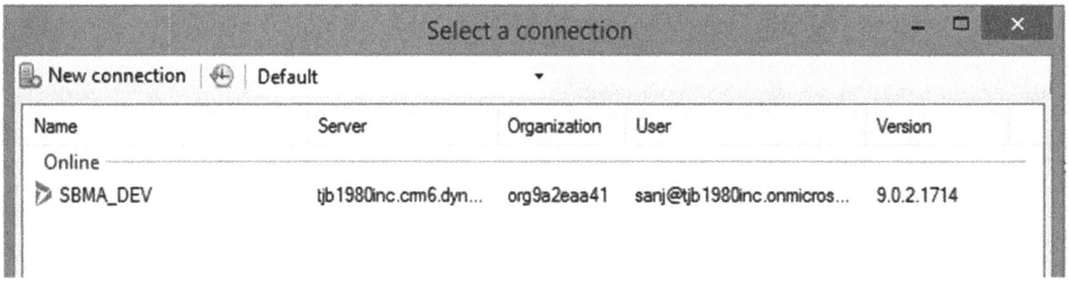

Figure 3-13. *Dynamics 365 connections listed in XrmToolBox*

Now, let's install the plugin to configure the autonumbering. As shown in Figure 3-14, click the Tools menu and select Plugin Store. You will see the Auto Number Manager plugin list.

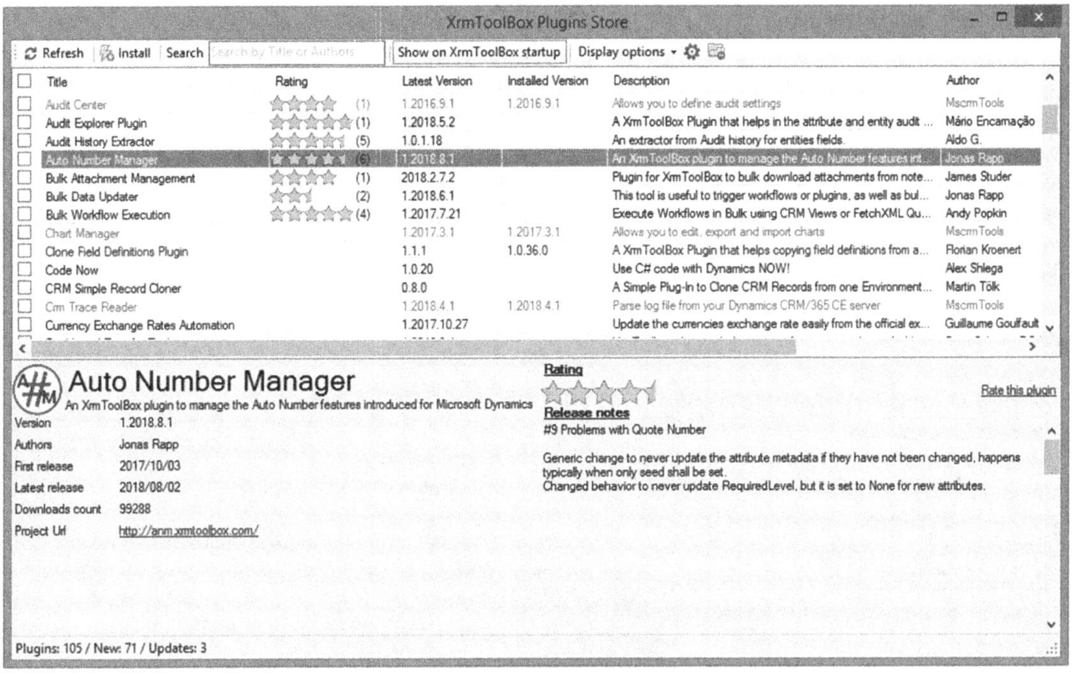

Figure 3-14. *XrmToolBox: Auto Number Manager*

Click the Install button on the toolbar of the plugin window, and the plugin will be installed to your local plugin list. As shown in Figure 3-15, select the plugin, and you will be directed to the configuration page. On this configuration form, you must enter the following information:

- **Solution:** When you are successfully connected to the Dynamics 365 instance, the plugin will list all the solutions in your instance. Select the solution patch you have created to configure the autonumbering.

- **Entity:** Select the entity for which you want to configure the autonumbering field.

  - You have two options: either you can create a new autonumber field by clicking the New Field button or you can select an existing field and update it with the autonumber you require, which is what you will be doing here to the Account Number field of the Member entity.

- Next, define the number format. You can click the snippet, and it will enter the snippet in the field. For this example, enter the prefix **SBMA**, a sequence number with a length of 6 digits, and a random string.

- **Seed:** This is the starting number of the sequence, and you will see the sample number that is generated when the new records are created.

After setting these values, click the Update button, and the settings will be applied to the autonumber field.

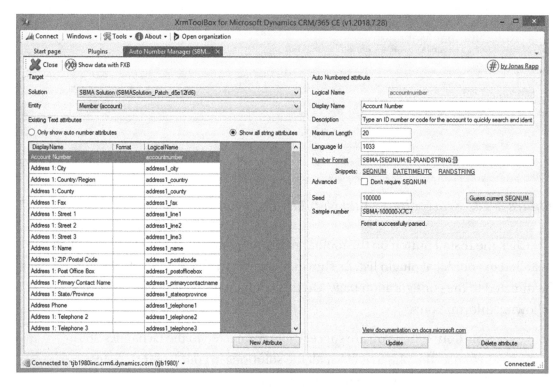

Figure 3-15. *Autonumber configuration window*

When updating, you will be warned that autonumbering will make the field read-only across all the forms; click OK. In this example, you are updating an existing field and entering a seed number; it will also warn you about duplicate data. If you have duplicate data, you should create a new field. Since in this example you are using a fresh instance, it is OK.

So, when you create the new record, the account number will be generated as per the configuration. See Figure 3-16.

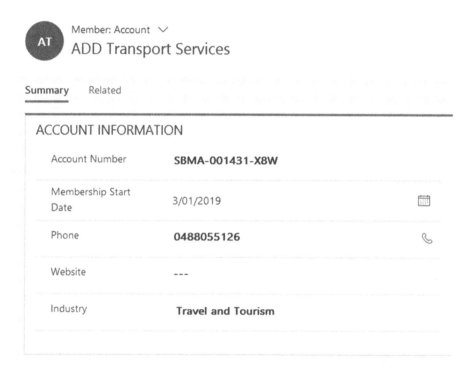

Figure 3-16. *New account number generated based on the configuration*

Similarly, you can create autonumbering for all the required entities. The Member entity is a system entity, so in the next example, let's look at setting an autonumber for the event code in the Event entity, which is a custom entity. First, select the entity from the Entity drop-down in the Auto Number Manager and set the configuration as you did in the previous example. See Figure 3-17.

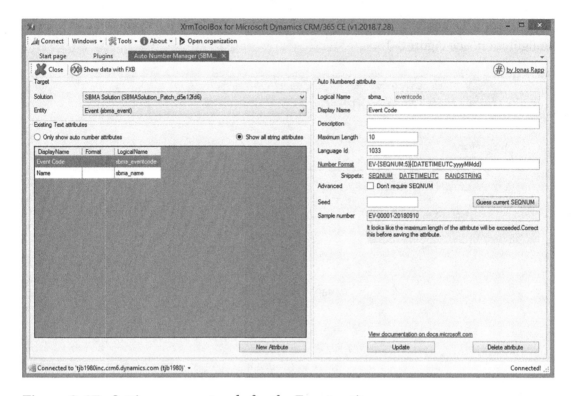

Figure 3-17. *Setting an event code for the Event entity*

It is good to keep the autonumber format unique to each entity, but you should create some standards across the autonumbers that you create. In this example, the last part of the code contains the date and time for the event. As shown in Figure 3-18, the new event record will be created with the event code.

EVENT
Annual General Meeting

General   Event Statistics   Related

Event Code	* EV-0101-20190210			Name	* Annual General Meeting		
Event Status	* New			Event Budget	* $5,000.00		
Start Date	* 10/02/2019	9:00 AM		End Date	* 10/02/2019	4:00 PM	
Registration Start Date	* 15/01/2019	9:00 AM		Registration End Date	* 8/02/2019	4:00 PM	
Event Capacity	* 100						

Figure 3-18. *Event code configured*

Likewise, you can select all the relevant entities and add the autonumber as per the end-user requirements. Finally, check in the solution to Azure DevOps and release it to the target environment. In the next section, you will look into some of the basic validation techniques provided by Dynamics 365.

Basic Validations

When entering data, there is always a possibility of entering invalid or incorrect data into the system, which will cause incorrect transactions and outputs. Therefore, whatever system you develop, data validations are a must. In this section, we will be looking at a few of these techniques.

Setting a Field as Required

This is one of the basic forms of validations that will make sure all the relevant information for the record is submitted. For instance, on the event form, Event Code, Name, Event Status, Start Date, and End Date are defined as required fields, meaning that the user must enter data in those fields to describe the event. As shown in Figure 3-19, if you miss a field, the application will notify you.

Figure 3-19. *Required field validations*

Calculated Fields

These types of fields are ideal for performing simple calculations, and they help the user avoid making simple mistakes at the data entry. For instance, in the SBMA application, when a membership is created, it is required that the Membership Renewal Date field should be populated. When you create the field, you have to set the field as a calculated field by setting Field Type to Calculated, as illustrated in Figure 3-20.

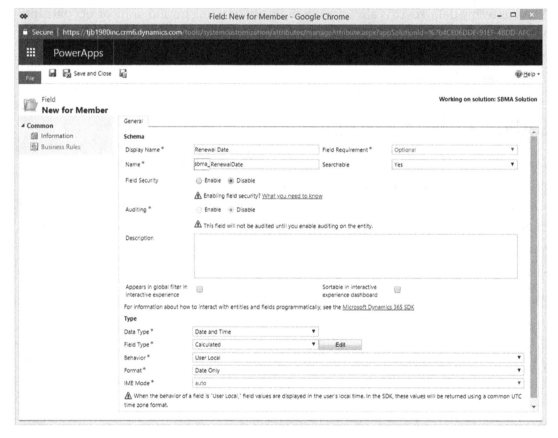

Figure 3-20. *Setting up a Calculated field*

Click the Edit button to configure the settings. In this example, you will be using Membership Start Date as the source field to calculate the renewal date. In Figure 3-21, you are validating whether Membership Start Date has a value and then whether it is greater than or equal to the CreatedOn value. If the conditions are true, then set Renewal Date to be 12 months past the Membership Start Date value. Besides AddMonths, there are several other functions available: AddMonths, AddHours, Concact, DiffNDays, DiffNMonths, SubstractDays, SubstractMonths, etc.

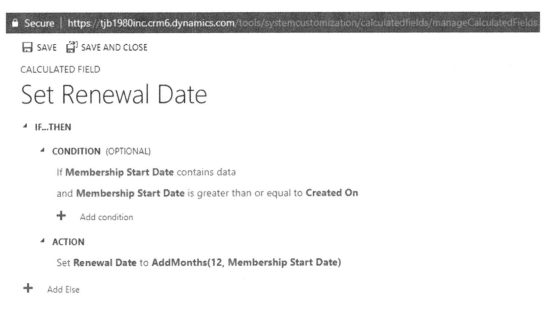

Figure 3-21. *Setting the conditions for the calculated fields*

Once saved and published, these settings will be applied to the renewal date field, and the field become read-only. Figure 3-22 illustrates a record created, and the renewal date is set as expected.

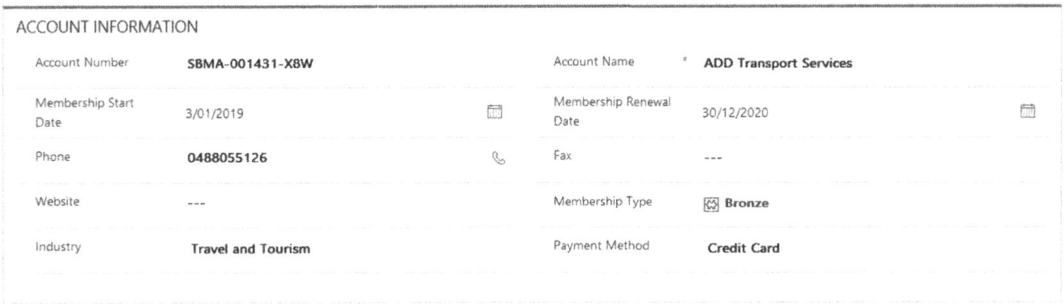

Figure 3-22. *The renewal date is set based on the Membership Start Date field.*

Since the execution occurs on the server side, the users will see the changes only after the save event is triggered, which is when the user clicks Save. Also, the calculated fields are read-only and do not consider the end user's security roles. Note that there are several limitations with calculated fields such as they cannot trigger workflows or plugins on calculated fields, duplicate detection rules are not triggered, etc. You can find out more at https://docs.microsoft.com/en-us/previous-versions/dynamicscrm-2016/administering-dynamics-365/dn832103(v=crm.8)#Considerations.

Rollup Fields

Like calculated fields, rollup fields are an exciting feature introduced recently that have reduced the volume of code required. Rollup fields are accumulated values computed over a set of records in relation to a record such as the total number of registrations for a given event. For example, the event organizers may want to know the number of paid registrations, payment pending registrations, total number of attendance, and cancellations. All these can be considered as event statistics, and recording them with the event provides insight about the event so the planners can make critical decisions. Therefore, calculating these values should be automated and ensure the values are correct. In this example, you will be categorizing these fields into a tab on the form by inserting a tab.

For this example, you will group the Event Statistics fields in a separate section. Remember that when you create these fields, you must set Field Type to Rollup. Once the fields are added to the form, the form will look like something like Figure 3-23, where the fields are grouped into a separate tab.

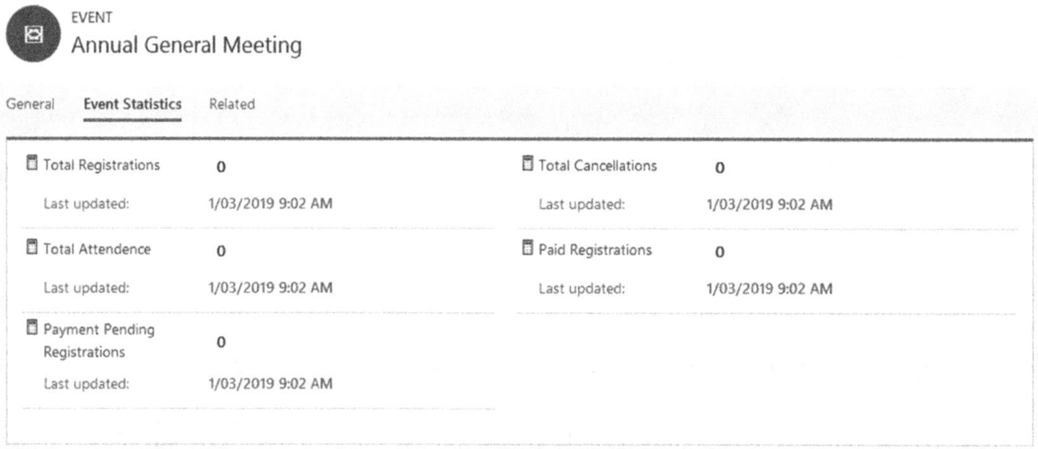

Figure 3-23. *Rollup fields on the Event form*

To configure the rollup fields, you should click the Edit button next to the Field Type property. As shown in Figure 3-24, you will be setting up the total registration for the given event. The source entity is by default selected, and you can select the related entity. In this example, it is the Event Registrations entity. Next, you can add filters, but for the total count of registrations, this is not required because it is the count of all the registrations. Once you're done setting this up, save and close the form.

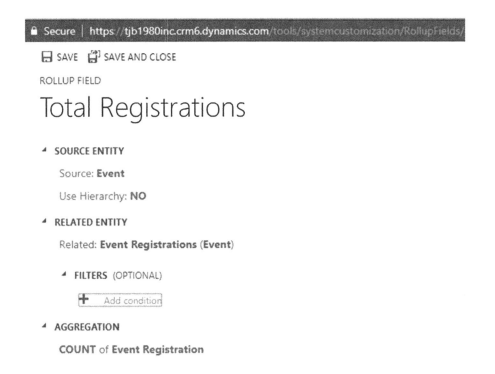

Figure 3-24. *Setting up rollup fields*

As shown in Figure 3-25, you can simply select the required filter to pick up the records and set up the rollup fields with filters.

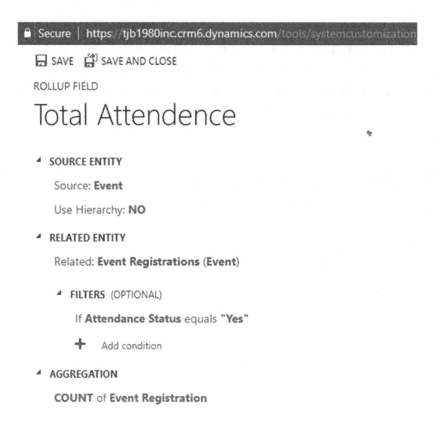

Figure 3-25. *Setting up rollup fields with filters*

After adding a few registrations, you should open a particular event and hover your mouse over each statistic field. You should be able to see a Refresh button, as shown in Figure 3-26. When you click it, the field will be updated with the values based on the rollup settings. Also, you can navigate to Settings ➤ System Jobs and look for the system job with the name "Calculate rollup fields for the <Entity Name> entity." Open the job, and in the Actions menu, select Modify Recurrences. In the pop-up window, you can change the frequency of the field refresh to make sure the end users will see the latest values.

Figure 3-26. *Rollup field updated*

Similar to calculated fields, the rollup fields are read-only, and they will not take the user's security settings. You can define only 100 rollup fields per organization and only 10 per entity. You can find out more about rollup fields at `https://technet.microsoft.com/en-us/library/dn832162.aspx`.

Business Rules

When business rules were first introduced, users, especially power users, greeted them with great pleasure because they reduce the amount of JavaScript and plugin code required. They are effective in setting up fast-changing business rules while avoiding the trouble of writing complex code snippets. This is useful in scenarios where a rule is scoped at the entity level. Business rules are capable of showing or hiding fields, enabling/disabling fields, validating data and showing error messages, setting field values, etc.

To set up the business rules, open the solution patch, and select the entity where you want to apply the rule. Next, click Business Rules in the left pane and click the New Business Rules button in the grid, as shown in Figure 3-27.

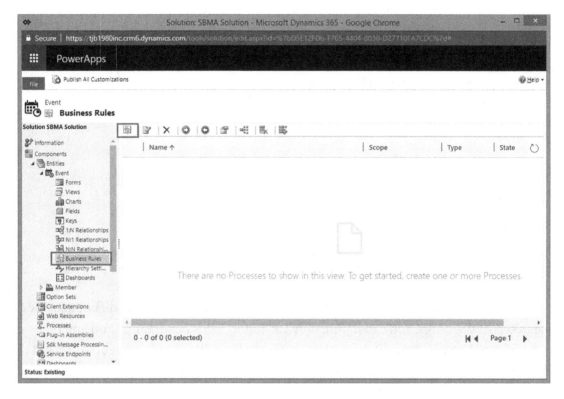

Figure 3-27. *Creating a new business rule*

When click the New Business Rule button, the business rules designer window will be displayed. The design window is used to define the rule as a graphical workflow. In the left corner of the design area, there is a mini-map that enables you to quickly navigate to components in the workflow. You can drag and drop components from the Components tab on the right. The Properties tab next to the Components tab allows you to set the conditions and the properties of each component. For instance, for a condition component, you will have to define the condition on the Properties tab.

One thing to keep in mind is that a business rule always starts with a condition. When you click the component, you can see the properties. For instance, as shown in Figure 3-28, you can check whether the start date is greater than the end date. If it is, then the message will be displayed next to the field.

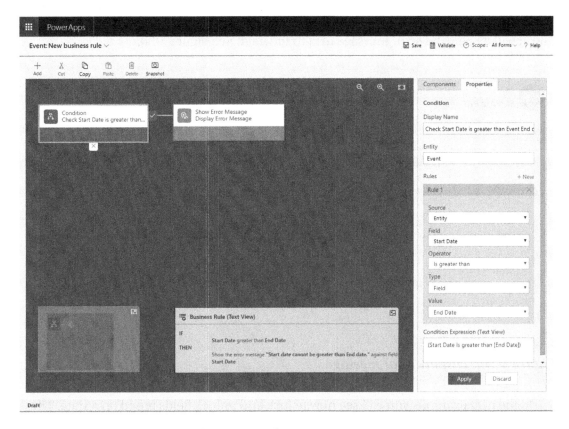

Figure 3-28. *Designing the business rule*

After defining, you have to save and then click the Activate button in the toolbar of the business rules grid, as shown in Figure 3-29. The business rule will not take effect until you do so. Finally, as always, publish the customizations.

Figure 3-29. *Activating a business rule*

When the user enters a start date greater than the end date, then as per the business rule, it will display the error message next to the field. See Figure 3-30.

Figure 3-30. *Display error message*

In the next example, you will see how to lock and unlock fields based on a state. The scenario is that when Event Registration Status is set to Paid only, the Attendance Status field will be enabled. This is to ensure only the paid registrations will be able to attend a given event. As explained previously, open the business rules designer and create the rule, as shown in Figure 3-31.

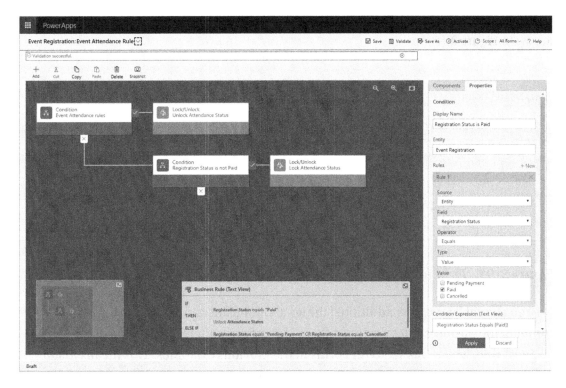

Figure 3-31. *Business rules designer: enabling/disabling fields*

In this design, we have used two condition components. The topmost one will check whether the registration status is Paid and, if so, unlock the field. For the second condition, which is the "else-if" part of the flow, it will check whether the registration status is Pending Payment or Cancelled and lock the field if either is true. Once the rule is configured, you have to save it, activate it, and publish all the customizations. On the designer screen, you can see that when the status is Pending/Cancelled, a lock icon appears next to the Attendance Status field, as shown in Figure 3-32.

EVENT REGISTRATION
ADD Transport Service

General   Related

Name	* ADD Transport Service	Member Contact	Bell James
Event Accommodation	Hotel Mount Villa	Registration Status	Pending Payment
Attendance Status	No		

Figure 3-32. *Field locked*

When the registration status is set to Paid, then the field will be enabled/unlocked, as shown in Figure 3-33.

Figure 3-33. *Field unlocked*

You should know a few additional things about business rules. In the top-right corner of the business rules designer, there is an option to select the scope of the business rule, which was set to All Forms in the previous examples. This means that if there is more than one form, then all the forms will adhere to the business rules defined, and the rules will apply to the client side only. But if you want the rule to be available on the server side, when operating data outside of the form such as in grids, the Web API, the SDK, and bulk data imports, then you will have to set the scope to Entity. In addition to these nice features, there are few limitations.

First, there is a limit of 10 "if-else" conditions per business rule, and the rules cannot be applied to tabs or sections. The rules will be executed only with on-change and on-load events and will not fire with on-save events unless the scope is set as Entity. Finally, conditions cannot contain a mixture of AND and OR; they must be either one or the other. For additional information about business rules, please visit `https://docs.microsoft.com/en-us/dynamics365/customer-engagement/customize/create-business-rules-recommendations-apply-logic-form`.

JavaScript and TypeScript

When it comes to Dynamics 365 customizations, JavaScript is an essential component that is capable of providing that extra layer of customization to the client side. Being a client-side programming language, JavaScript enables you to do complex validations, record manipulation, and validation on the client side. But the catch is that when you continue to write JavaScript library after library, it becomes more and more complex and can easily end up as spaghetti code in no time. To avoid this, you must have a great deal of programming skills. Even though there are other techniques such as business rules, calculated fields, rollup fields, etc., to limit the client-side code, there are situations where you must write JavaScript to meet specific requirements.

With the Dynamics 365 v9.*x* release, Microsoft has made some changes to the client API object model and deprecated some of the existing client APIs. Compared to the changes introduced in CRM 2011, these are not significant changes. Everything that was used before is still there, but things have been moved around to add more consistency. You can find more about these changes at `https://docs.microsoft.com/en-us/dynamics365/customer-engagement/developer/clientapi/understand-clientapi-object-model`.

Let's jump into an example. This book will present two versions of this example: what it is used to be and how it is now. First, let's look at the scenario. There is a requirement to set the membership start date to today's date. The objective is to ensure that the date is always today or in the future and to eliminate past dates being entered. To begin with, create a new solution to hold the JavaScript code and other web resources. See Figure 3-34.

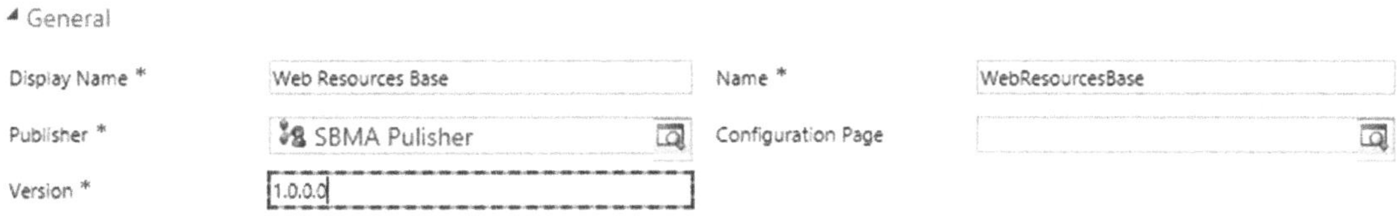

Figure 3-34. *Creating a separate solution to hold the JavaScript and other web resources*

JavaScript Example

You will be writing the JavaScript code in Visual Studio in this example, so let's open the solution. Figure 3-35 illustrates the JavaScript that is in the `SBMA.Common` namespace. As shown in the following code, writing JavaScript in this way is essential because as a best practice, the code needs a good structure, which avoids collisions with other code:

```
SBMA.Common.setCurrentDate = function () {
    //Get the current date

    //set membership start date for today
    var renewalDate = Date.now();
```

```
    Xrm.Page.getAttribute('sbma_membershipstartdate').setValue(renewalDate);
}
```

Now let's see how this can be converted to the new object model. This is a working example, but this book is focused on the new JavaScript object model, and all JavaScript examples are written in the new way.

```
var SBMA = SBMA || {}
SBMA.Common = SBMA.Common || {};

/**
 * This method populates membership renewal date in 1 year from the created date.
 * Executes at page load event.
 * @returns {Void}
 */

SBMA.Common.setCurrentDate = function (executionContext) {
    var formContext = executionContext.getFormContext();

    //set membership start date for today
    var membeshipStartDate = new Date();

    formContext.getAttribute('sbma_membershipstartdate').setValue(membeship
    StartDate);
}
```

The client-side code is triggered with events, which means you should connect the JavaScript code/function to a specific event such as OnSave, OnLoad, etc. Generally, you can use a JavaScript function, which is also known as an *event handler*, and each handler may or may not have parameters. These event handlers can be associated with the events using the GUI, but for those that are not available via the GUI, you should use the client API methods, which provide the mechanisms to call the event handlers. These methods can be used to collaborate with business process flow control, manage form navigation, get/set attribute values, communicate with multiple forms per entity, etc.

As you can see from the previous code snippet, nothing has significantly changed. But when you wire up the JavaScript after deployment, you will have to select the checkbox "Pass execution context as first parameter." Then follow these steps:

1. Upload your JavaScript as a web resource to Dynamics 365 for Customer Engagement. In your new solution, select the web resources in the left pane and click New on the grid toolbar.

2. Provide the name and display name, set Type as Script (Jscript), set Language to English, and browse your code library. Click Save.

3. Close the web resources window, and in the Solution window, click Publish All Customizations.

4. Now, let's wire up the script to the OnLoad event of the form. Open the form via the form editor window. In the ribbon, click the Form Properties button, and in the window that pops up, add your library on the Form Libraries tab.

5. On the Event Handlers tab, select FormLoad as the event and add your function.

6. When adding the function, you must make sure you are passing executionContext as the first parameter. To do this, select the "Pass execution context as first parameter" checkbox.

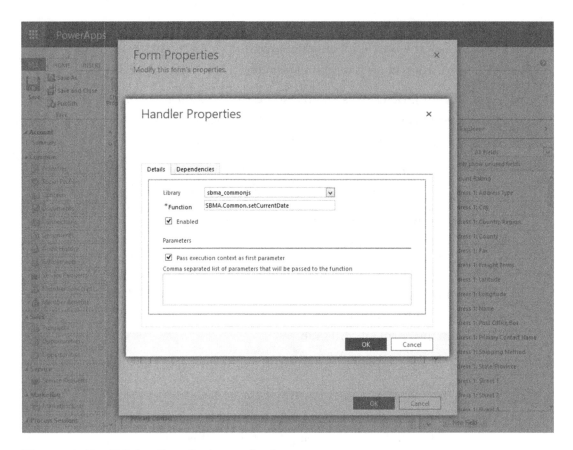

Figure 3-35. *Wiring JavaScript to the form*

After setting up these customizations, save and publish them. When you load the
Membership form, you can see the Membership Start Date field is set to the current date.
See Figure 3-36.

Member: Account ∨
New Member

Annual Revenue

Summary

ACCOUNT INFORMATION

Account Number	---	Account Name *	---
Membership Start Date	3/01/2019	Membership Renewal Date	---
Phone	---	Fax	---
Website	---	Membership Type	---
Industry	---	Payment Method	---

Figure 3-36. *Membership Start Date is set to the current date*

Now, if you look at the function that you wrote, you can use it only with the Membership Start Date field of the Membership form because within the function, you are hard-coding the field name. But there are so many other start date fields where you can use the same logic. To make the function reusable, pass the field name as a parameter to the function, as shown here:

```
var SBMA = SBMA || {}
SBMA.Common = SBMA.Common || {};

/**
 * This method populates membership start date for today.
 * Executes at page load event.
 * @returns {Void}
 */

SBMA.Common.setCurrentDate = function (executionContext, fieldName) {
    var formContext = executionContext.getFormContext();

    //set membership start date for today
    var membeshipStartDate = new Date();

    formContext.getAttribute(fieldName).setValue(membeshipStartDate);
}
```

In this approach, when you wire the function to the event, you must pass the field name as the parameter, as shown in Figure 3-37.

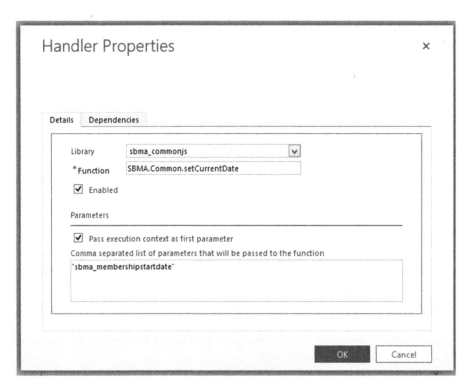

Figure 3-37. *Passing the field name as a parameter*

TypeScript Example

When you have to write more complex JavaScript, the code will become more complex and will be difficult to maintain. The readability of your code will also degrade. In such scenarios, TypeScript is an ideal choice. It is not a new language, but it is the next generation of writing JavaScript code. The coolest thing about TypeScript is that you will be writing ES9 features that will be transpiled to ES6. You can learn more about TypeScript at `https://www.typescriptlang.org/docs/home.html`. Explaining TypeScript in detail is beyond the scope of this book, but you will learn how to write a simple TypeScript and transform it via the Transpiler into JavaScript that can be used with Dynamics 365.

To begin with, you must install NodeJS. You can download NodeJS at `https://nodejs.org/en/`. You also need to install the Open Command Line extension to Visual Studio. You can do this through the NuGet package manager. Next, you can add the TypeScript compiler to the Web Resources project of your solution. See Figure 3-38.

Figure 3-38. *TypeScript compiler*

Now, right-click the Webresources solution, and select Add ➤ Add New Item. From the list of file types, select TypeScript Json Configuration File. Add the `CompileOnSave` option and set it is `true`, as shown here:

```
{
  "compilerOptions": {
    "noImplicitAny": false,
    "noEmitOnError": true,
    "removeComments": false,
    "sourceMap": true,
    "target": "es5"
  },
  "compileOnSave": true
  "exclude": [
    "node_modules",
    "wwwroot"
  ]
}
```

Now, select the Webresources project and press Alt+spacebar to open the command line. This will open the command prompt to your web resources project. Type in the npm init command to generate the package.json file. Accept all the defaults, and the JSON file will be generated.

```
{
  "name": "sbma.webresources",
  "version": "1.0.0",
  "description": "",
  "main": "index.js",
  "dependencies": {
    "npm": "^6.4.1"
  },
  "devDependencies": {},
  "scripts": {
    "test": "echo \"Error: no test specified\" && exit 1"
  },
  "author": "",
  "license": "ISC"
}
```

The next step is to install the TypeScript definitions for the Dynamics 365 client-side SDK. In the same console window, enter the following command: npm install - -save @types/xrm.

This command will install the node_modules folder in your Webresources project, as shown in Figure 3-39.

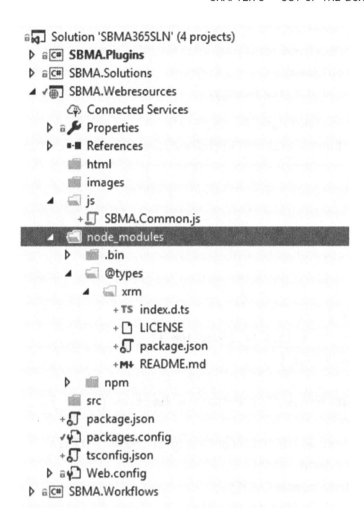

Figure 3-39. *Node modules for XRM installed to the project*

Now, your project is ready, and you can start writing TypeScript. In the `src` folder, add a new item of type TypeScript. You will write the same JavaScript as the previous example to demonstrate how it works.

```
namespace SBMA
{
  export class CommonJs
  {
  public setCurrentDate(executionContext: Xrm.Page.EventContext,
  fieldName: string)
```

```
    {
      var formContext = executionContext.getFormContext();
      //Get Current Date
      var currentDate = new Date();

      //Set the current date to the field
      formContext.getAttribute(fieldName).setValue(currentDate);
    }
  }
}
```

When you save the work, the JavaScript file will be generated, which can be deployed to Dynamics 365.

```
var SBMA;
(function (SBMA) {
  var CommonJs = /** @class */ (function () {
    function CommonJs() {
    }
    CommonJs.prototype.setCurrentDate = function (executionContext,
    fieldName) {
    var formContext = executionContext.getFormContext();
    //Get Current Date
    var currentDate = new Date();
    //Set the current date to the field
    formContext.getAttribute(fieldName).setValue(currentDate);
    };
    return CommonJs;
 }());
SBMA.CommonJs = CommonJs;
})(SBMA || (SBMA = {}));
//# sourceMappingURL=SBMACommon.js.map
```

In the upcoming chapter, the book will use TypeScript instead of JavaScript in the examples.

Summary

In this chapter, you looked at form customizations, autonumbering, calculated fields, rollup fields, business rules, and JavaScript to ensure the validity of data entry. The chapter also discussed the new changes introduced to the JavaScript object model. Finally, the chapter looked at how to use TypeScript to make the client-side scripting more exciting. In the next chapter, you will be looking at automating the business processes.

CHAPTER 4

Automating Business Processes

The main focus of this chapter is to look at automating the key business processes of the proposed application. Every organization has its own unique business operations carried out daily that are a key part of the business. There are automated business processes where no user interaction is required, and there are some processes where user interaction is required. Also, there could be business processes where certain user actions are completed, and then an automated process is triggered to complete the business process.

Dynamics 365 comes with actions, workflows, business process flows, and dialogs that can be used for this purpose. Also, Microsoft Flow is gaining more attention within the community simply because it is a powerful platform that integrates with various Microsoft services and apps, including Dynamics 365 for Customer Engagement. Microsoft Flow is a good option for creating and automating tasks/processes such as workflows. On the other hand, business process flows ensure that users enter data consistently and follow the same process each time they are interacting with their customers. Workflows are used to automate business processes without any user interactions.

Actions are another type of processes that reduce the number of custom workflow activities and plugins. The nice thing about actions is that they can be invoked from workflows, from plugins, from JavaScript, externally via the Web API, and from business process flows. You can learn more about the Dynamics 365 process architecture at `https://docs.microsoft.com/en-us/previous-versions/dynamicscrm-2016/developers-guide/gg309387%28v%3dcrm.8%29`.

© Sanjaya Yapa 2019
S. Yapa, *Customizing Dynamics 365*, https://doi.org/10.1007/978-1-4842-4379-4_4

Business Process Flows

Business process flows define the guidelines for end users to perform their work. These guidelines are defined by the business. For instance, you might use a business process flow for a payment process or a member registration process where there are unique steps to perform the transaction. With business process flows, these user actions can be customized to give a different user experience based on each user's role within the organization.

Business process flows are embodied as a custom entity, and when the user initiates a process, it is stored as a record within that entity. Each of these records is associated with the record it is processing. Business process flows can span more than one entity, and if you want to move the process flow from one entity to another with a related record, then there must be a 1:M relationship between the two entities. If no relationship exists between the entities, you can create a new record but not manipulate an existing record of the related child entity. Figure 4-1 illustrates the membership application process. When a new application comes in, the application details are entered, reviewed, and approved or rejected. In the event of approval, a new membership is created, and if rejected, an e-mail is generated with the reason for the rejection.

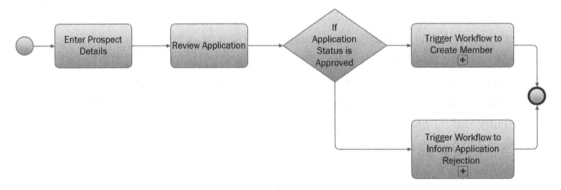

Figure 4-1. *New application review process*

Let's look how you can put this process into a business process flow. First, let's create a new solution patch to hold the business process flows and include all the relevant entities and related components of the solution. In the left navigation pane, click Process, and click the New button of the Actions toolbar. In the Create Process dialog, fill in the required fields and set Category to Business Process Flow. See Figure 4-2.

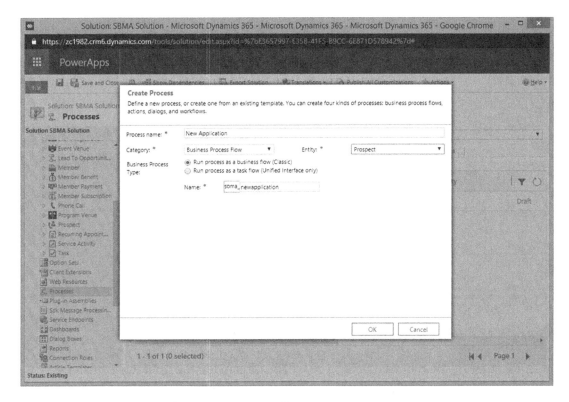

Figure 4-2. *Creating a business process flow*

Note   From the entities list, if you do not see the entity, make sure that the "Business process flows (fields will be created)" option is set in the entity definition. Keep in mind that once you select this option, you cannot revert it (see Figure 4-3).

General   Primary Field   Controls

Entity Definition

Display Name *	Event Registration	☐ Virtual Entity	
Plural Name *	Event Registrations	Data Source	[None] ▼
Name *	sbma_eventregistration	Ownership *	Organization ▼
Primary Image	▼	☐ Define as an activity entity.	
Color		☐ Display in Activity Menus	
Description			

Areas that display this entity

☑ Sales   ☑ Service   ☑ Marketing   ☐ Settings
☐ Training

Process

☑ Business process flows (fields will be created) †

Communication & Collaboration

Figure 4-3. *Enabling an entity business process*

After entering the required fields, you will be directed to the interactive business process flow designer. In the right pane of the design window, you can see the components required for designing the process flow. Simply drag and drop the required components and set the properties as required to configure the flow (see Figure 4-4).

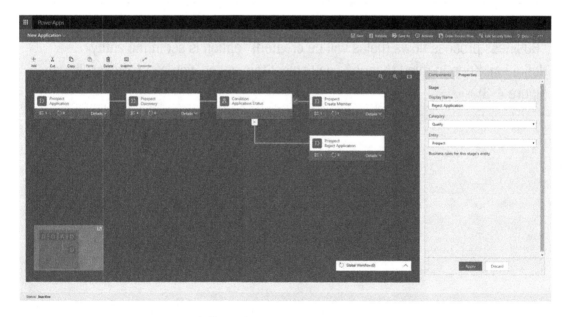

Figure 4-4. *Business process flow designer window*

Generally, when designing process flows, you will have to use stages, and inside each stage, you can define data fields to capture the information, as illustrated in Figure 4-5.

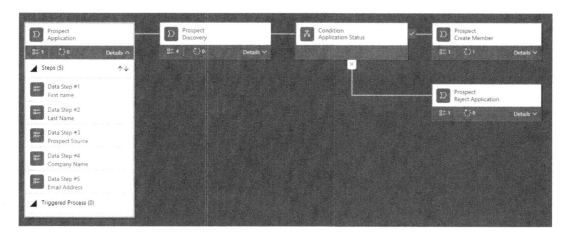

Figure 4-5. *Adding data fields*

Also, you can configure conditions. In Figure 4-6, the condition checks whether the application stage is approved, and if approved, it will move to the next stage, which will create the membership record. On the right, you can enter the condition properties and combine multiple conditions as per the requirements.

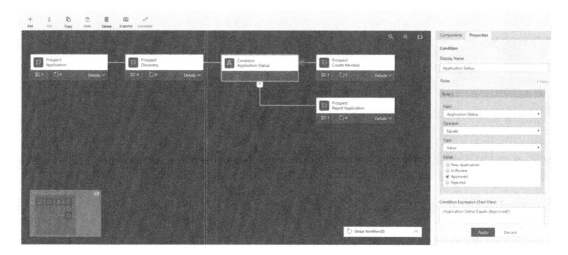

Figure 4-6. *Setting conditions*

As per the design, the membership will be created by triggering a workflow, which we will discuss in the next section. The workflow automatically picks up information from the prospect record and creates the membership record with the primary contact. If the application is rejected, another workflow will be triggered to generate an e-mail to the applicant informing them of the reason for rejection and the next steps (see Figure 4-7).

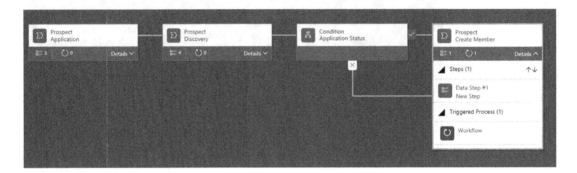

Figure 4-7. *Calling a workflow from the process flow*

When calling a workflow from the stage, you can create the workflow by clicking the +New button in the right pane, or you can select a workflow that is already created. In any case, the workflow must be defined as an on-demand process, which we will be discussing in the next section. See Figure 4-8.

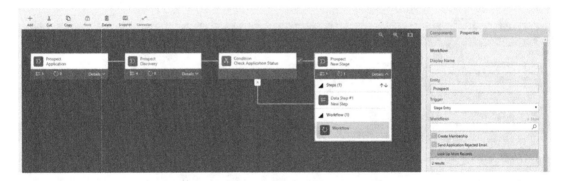

Figure 4-8. *Configuring the workflow step*

As you can see, you must set the Trigger property to either Stage Entry or Stage Exit, meaning that the workflow will be executed either when entering the stage or when exiting from it. Once the process is finalized, you must save and activate it from the toolbar on the top, as highlighted in Figure 4-9.

Figure 4-9. *Activating the business process flow*

Once published, you can see the business process flow on the prospect record. See Figure 4-10.

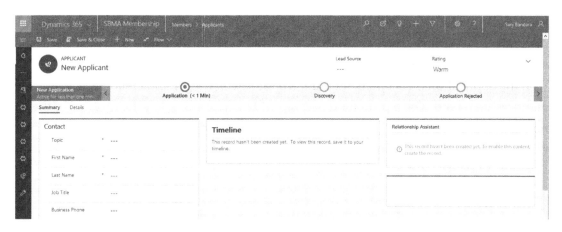

Figure 4-10. *New application process flow the Unified Interface*

Business process flows can be combined with other customizations, saving tons of user time and providing an end-to-end user experience. When the user is navigating through each stage of the flow, the data changes are applied to the fields so that any business logic or scripts wired up with fields can be triggered instantly. In your business process flows, there could be fields that are not presented in the entity forms, and these fields are added to the client object model to be used with scripts. If any of the fields is triggering a workflow, the changes will be visible as soon as the form is refreshed after a save. You can find out more about these at https://docs.microsoft.com/en-us/dynamics365/customer-engagement/customize/business-process-flows-overview.

Workflows

Workflows are useful in automating business processes that do not require any user interaction. When you create a workflow, it is associated with an entity. You can trigger the workflow when a record is created, a record status is changed, a record is assigned, a record field is changed, and a record is deleted. There are three options that can be used to determine how to execute the workflow: "Run as a background process (recommended)" will execute the workflow in the background, "As an on-demand process" is where the user can select one or more records and execute the workflow manually, and finally "Execute as a child process" means that it can be triggered from another workflow/parent workflow.

Let's look at an example from the SBMA solution. In the SBMA solution, when a member applies for membership, the application will be created as a prospect, and the membership officer will review the information provided and accept or reject the application. This part of the process was implemented earlier in this Chapter as a business process flow. The workflow to create the membership and determine the membership category is done through the workflow.

If the application is accepted, then the workflow will trigger and create the membership record. The type of membership will be determined by the revenue of the member. At the end of the process, the workflow will trigger an e-mail to the member with the membership details. See Figure 4-11.

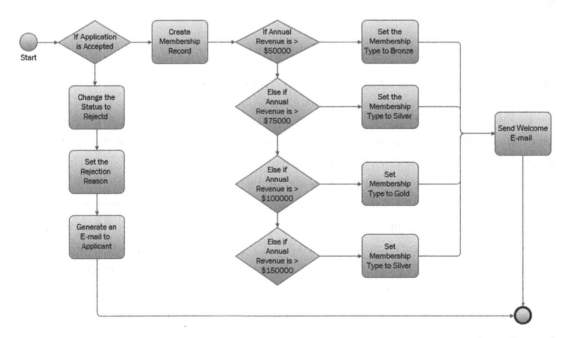

Figure 4-11. *Membership registration flow*

Let's look at how to implement the workflow. In the solution, in the left navigation pane, click Process and click the New button in the Actions toolbar. The Create Process dialog will be displayed, and in this dialog, enter the process name, set the Process category to Workflow, and set the entity as Prospect. This is because the workflow will be triggered when the application status is set to Approved on the Prospect entity.

You must have this information before starting the implementation. For this example, you should know when the workflow should be executed, against which entity it should be triggered, and what the end result will be. If you can determine this information before starting any workflow implementation, then the implementation cycle will be extremely easy. See Figure 4-12.

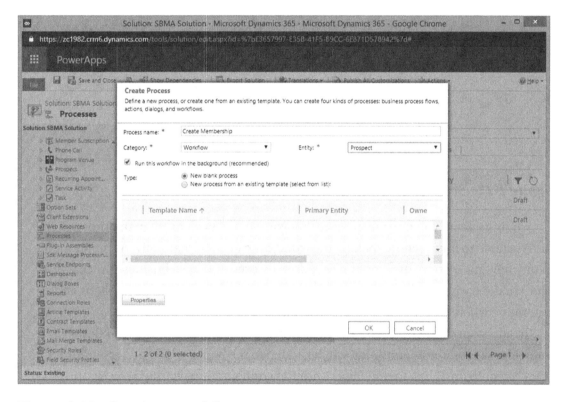

Figure 4-12. *Creating a workflow*

After filling in the primary information in the Create Process dialog, click OK. Next you will see the pop-up to enter workflow properties. See Figure 4-13.

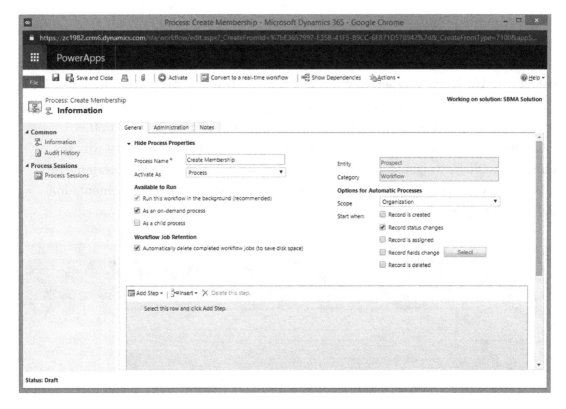

Figure 4-13. *Setting the workflow properties*

On this screen, you must make sure that you select "As an on-demand process" in the Available to Run section, making the workflow executed manually. As mentioned in the previous section, the workflow needs to be executed via a business process flow. The workflow will be implemented on this form, and you can add various steps and determine whether it is a before step or an after step.

To add steps to the workflow, click the Add Step drop-down in the workflow implementation area. A condition will be added to the panel. Click the "<condition> (click to configure)" link to open the condition configuration window. See Figure 4-14.

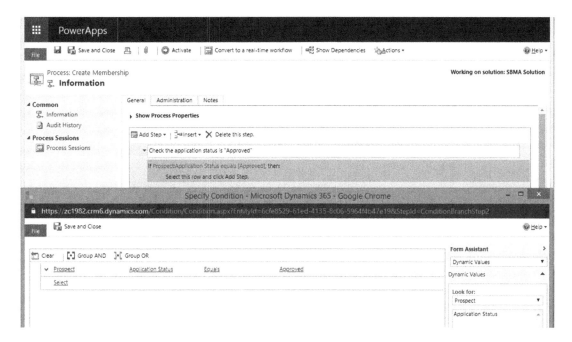

Figure 4-14. *Checking the condition configuration*

In the same way, you can add other steps, and there are many options available for you, as shown in Figure 4-15. You can create steps, update them, assign them, change their status, etc., with workflows. You can even call custom workflow activities, which we will be discussing in the next chapter.

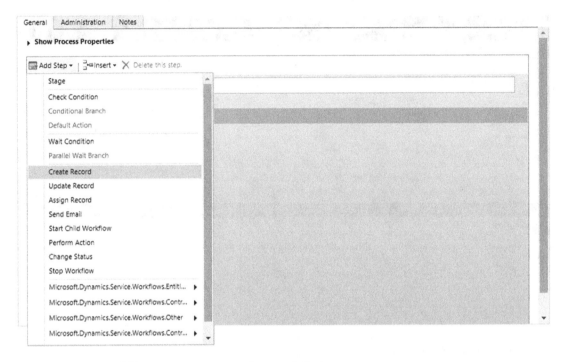

Figure 4-15. *Adding more steps to the workflow*

One thing to keep in mind is that different types of steps will have different type of settings. For instance, the next step is to create the membership record, so you need to set the properties (i.e., set the fields of the membership record). See Figure 4-16.

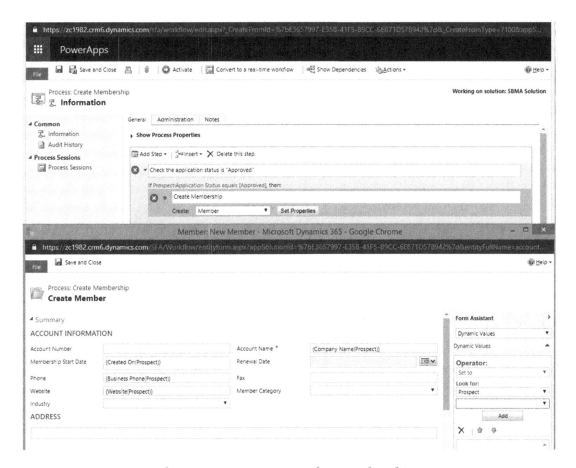

Figure 4-16. *Setting the properties to create the membership*

Just as you did earlier, add the other steps. As shown in Figure 4-17, there are several steps added with check conditions. To add the "else-if" part of a condition, you simply click the check condition, click Add Step, and select the Conditional Branch option from the list.

Note   Until you complete the configuration of each step, an error icon will be displayed next to the each step and in the main step.

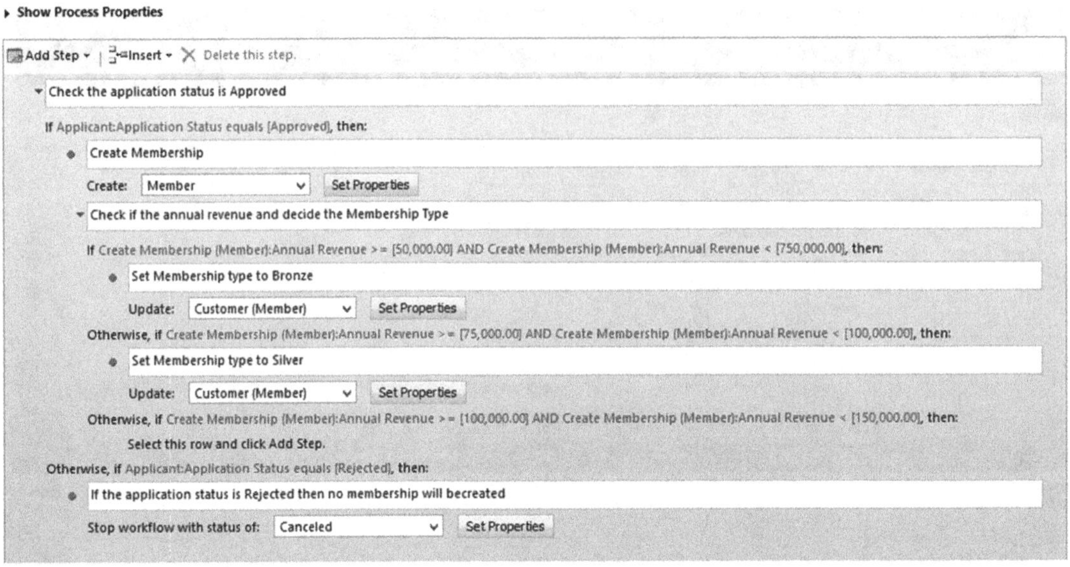

▶ Show Process Properties

Figure 4-17. *Adding other steps*

Also, you can combine the condition of each check condition with AND and OR gates, as shown in Figure 4-18. Just click the drop-drop arrow next to the condition and click the Select Row option. Continue this process for the other conditions as well. Click the Group AND or Group OR option to combine the conditions.

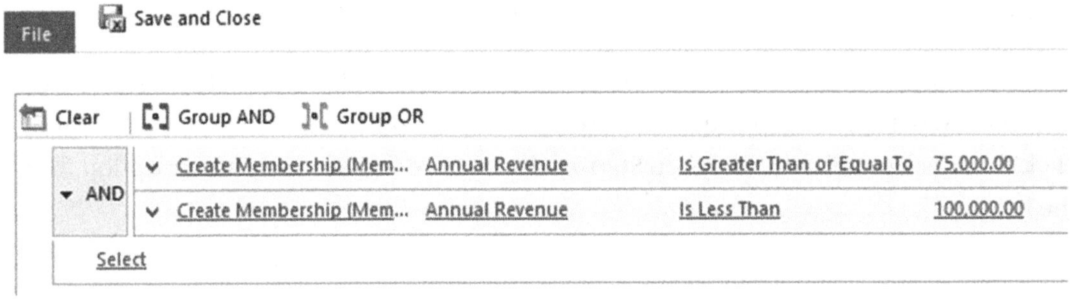

Figure 4-18. *Combining conditions*

Actions

Actions are another way of implementing business processes. Prior to actions, the most popular way of implementing custom business logic was using plugins or custom workflow activities. But with the introduction of actions, you can reduce the amount of code in the implementation significantly. Even power users can configure actions to implement business logic. Actions can be configured to accomplish create, update, delete, and perform action operations. When configured, internally actions create messages that are based on the actions performed against the entity record.

The nice thing about actions is that unlike workflows or plugins, an action does not have to be associated with an entity. That is, actions can be defined as global to be called on their own. When compared to workflows, another distinct fact about actions is that they do not trigger when a record is created or updated, a field is changed, etc. They can be called by workflows, plugins, or JavaScript web API calls. Also, you can call an action from an action step in business process flows. To do this, you should define the action as a business process flow action step.

Let's look at creating an action coupled with the SMBA requirements. In their system, the event management module has a requirement to define event programs while creating the event. There are events that consist of one program, and there could be events where there is more than one program. Here you will be implementing an action that can be called through JavaScript when creating the event.

To begin with, in the left navigation pane of your solution, select Process and click New in the Actions toolbar. On this screen, provide the name and select Action as the category. For Entity, select Event Program. As mentioned earlier, you can define the action as a global action by setting the Entity drop-down to None (global). See Figure 4-19.

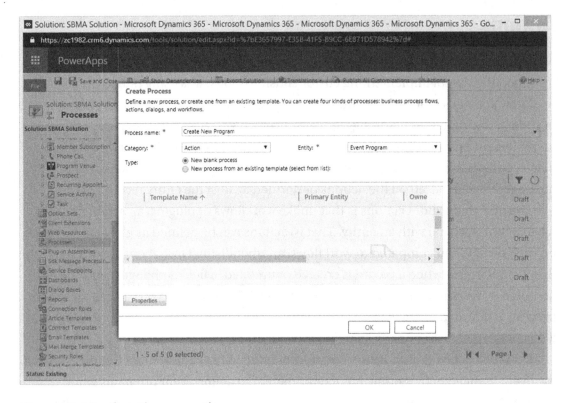

Figure 4-19.   *Creating an action*

Next, you will be directed to a form that is similar to the workflow properties form that you looked at in the previous section. In this form, under Available to Run, check the "As a Business Process Flow action step" option to make it available for business process flows. The significant difference that you can see on this form is that you can define in and out arguments, as shown in Figure 4-20. To add new arguments, click the + sign in the Hide Process Arguments section. As per Figure 4-20, there are five input arguments and one output parameter. The output argument will return the event program created.

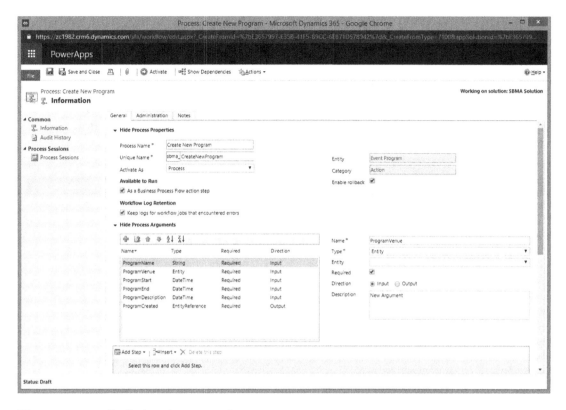

Figure 4-20. *Defining input and output arguments*

Next, you will learn how to define the steps. Similar to defining steps in workflows, you can easily define steps for the actions. The objective here is to create a new program and add the relevant step to create a new action step. See Figure 4-21.

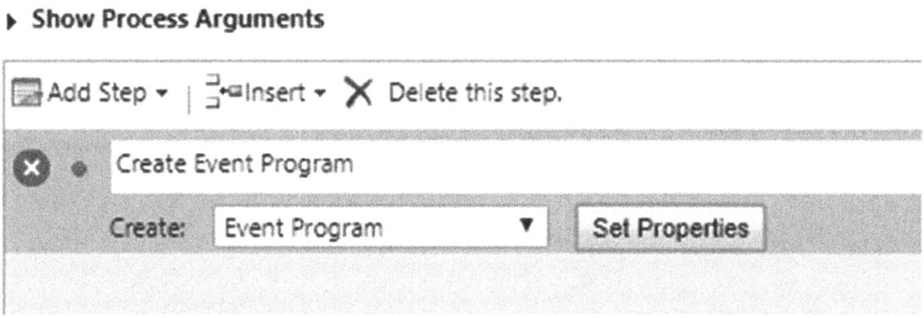

▶ **Show Process Arguments**

📇 Add Step ▾ | ⅔◁Insert ▾ ✕ Delete this step.

❌ • Create Event Program

   Create: Event Program ▾   **Set Properties**

Figure 4-21. *Adding steps*

For the Event Program entity, you have to map the input arguments to the fields of the Event Program entity. Click the Set Properties button, and the window shown in Figure 4-22 will display so you can set the properties. When mapping the arguments, you can find all the arguments defined from the Form Assistant in the Look For drop-down box. In this drop-down, scroll down to the Argument option, and the next drop-down will list all the arguments defined. Hit Save and Close to exit to the main window.

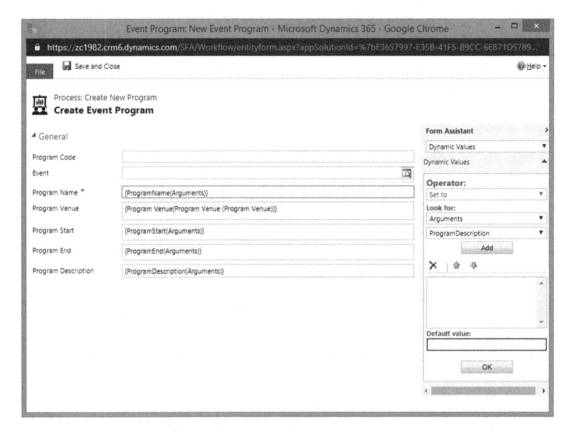

Figure 4-22. *Setting the mapping arguments*

There is one more step, which is to return to the created program. Click Add Step and select the Assign Value option. See Figure 4-23.

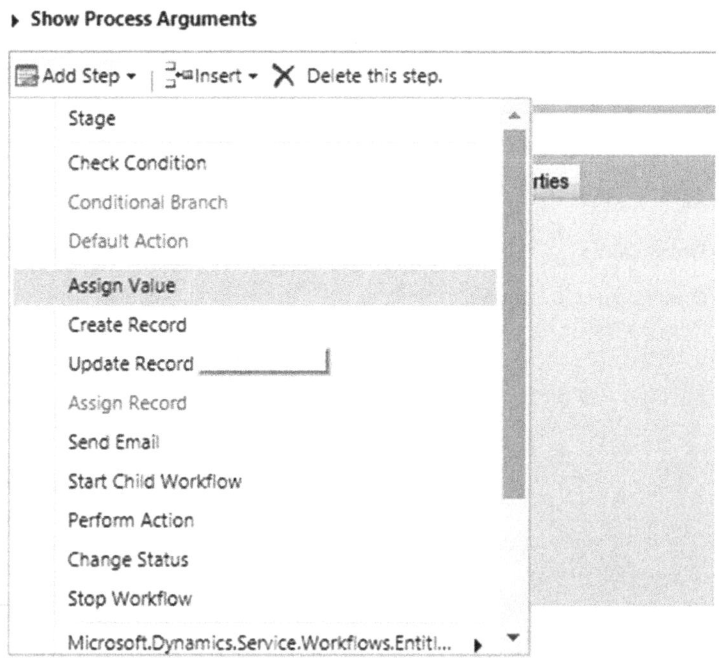

Figure 4-23. *Selecting to assign a value to set up a return argument*

Like setting the in arguments, click the Set Properties button to set the properties, as shown in Figure 4-24. Basically, you will have to select Event Program in the Form Editor.

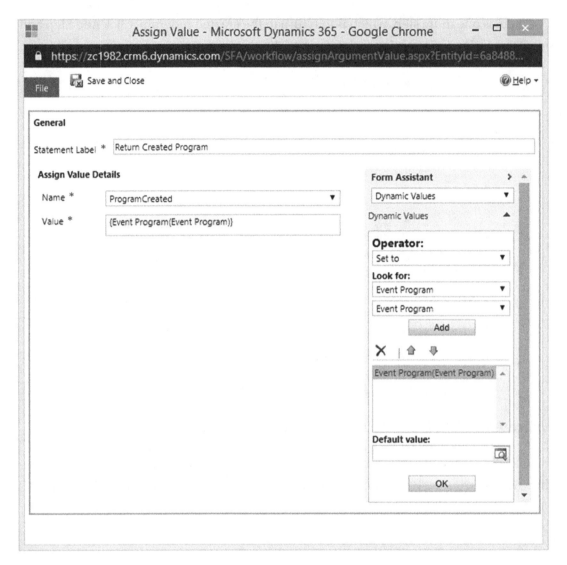

Figure 4-24. *Mapping the output argument*

Now that the action is completed, the next step is to consume the action created. Save the action, and you must activate it like the other process types discussed in this chapter. As mentioned earlier in this chapter, these actions can be consumed by workflows, JavaScript, and plugins, or by using Dynamics 365 web services. We will discuss how the actions can be consumed by JavaScript in Chapter 5.

Microsoft Flow

Microsoft Flow is a powerful and a robust platform that can be used to automate business processes across a variety of web-based services. You can develop flows that collaborate with SharePoint, OneDrive, Twitter, Google Drive, Dropbox, Salesforce, and many more. Similar to Dynamics 365 workflows, Microsoft Flow can be triggered from almost any Dynamics 365 event.

So, the million-dollar question is when should you use Microsoft Flow? Dynamics 365 workflows are internal by design, meaning they can work within Dynamics 365. But Microsoft Flow is an external service and can talk to external web services. Basically, there are many scenarios where you can use Flow over workflows.

- To collaborate with other applications and web services.

- To develop scheduled system jobs such as sending monthly newsletters or creating bulk delete operations that execute x number of times per day/week/month.

- To monitor the validity of data and remind the responsible parties to complete data.

- To send SMS notifications when integrated with the Twilio service and to send e-mail notifications.

- To approve transactions via push notifications, e-mails, or from the Flow app. This does not require the user to log into Dynamics 365. The approval propagates to Dynamics 365 through the Microsoft Flow and updates the record status.

The flow designer can be accessed from Settings, as shown in Figure 4-25.

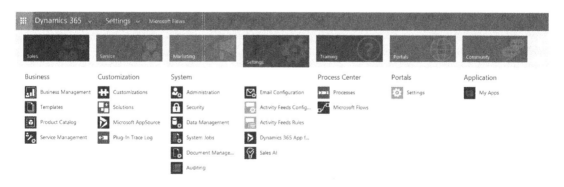

Figure 4-25. *Microsoft Flow under Dynamics 365 Settings*

To create a flow, you could either use a template or start from scratch. When you open the flow designer and click +New, you will be directed to the screen to select the triggers and connectors. As shown in Figure 4-26, click "Search hundreds of connectors and triggers" at the bottom of the page.

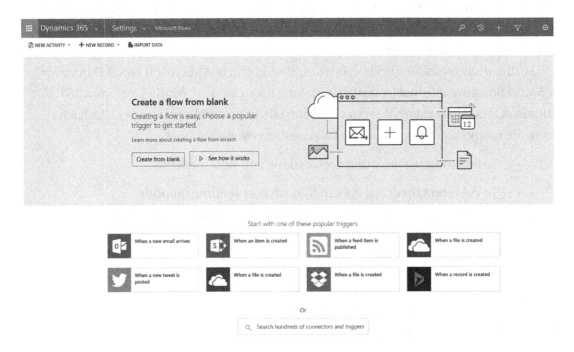

Figure 4-26. *New flow creation*

You can now see the list of triggers and connectors, which opens a whole new domain of automating business processes. See Figure 4-27.

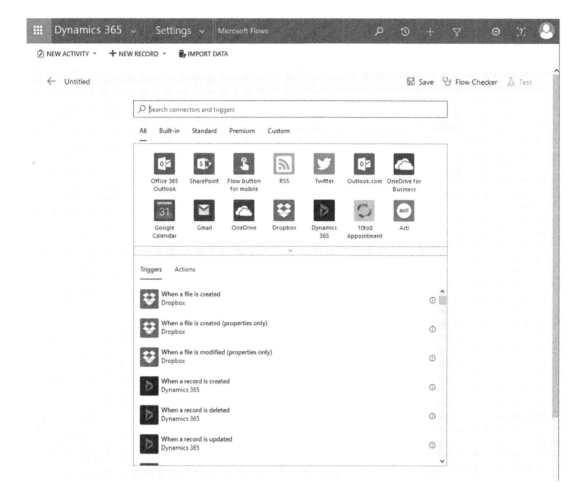

Figure 4-27. *Flow triggers and connectors*

On the canvas, you can start adding components. The flow is triggered when an applicant record is created, and if you want to send an SMS to notify the membership officer, you can simply connect to the Twilio service and send the SMS. See Figure 4-28.

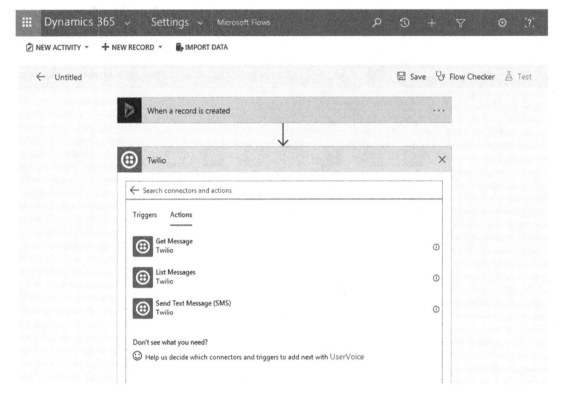

Figure 4-28. *Twilio connection*

Please note that Twilio connectivity is associated with a cost. The standard pricing per SMS is $0.0075. Another scenario would be if a record is deleted and you want to archive the deleted records for later references, then you could use a flow, as shown in Figure 4-29.

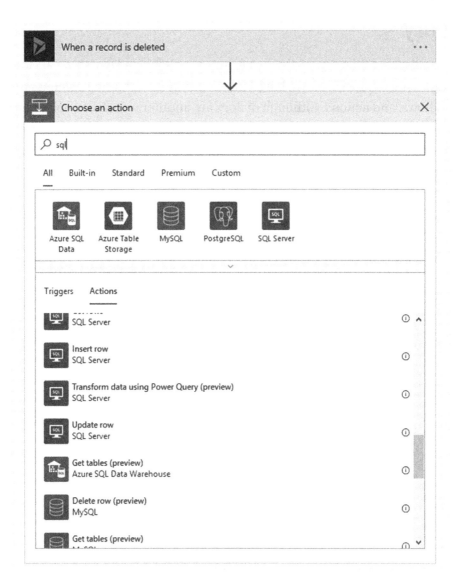

Figure 4-29. *Inserting an external database*

As you can see, these types of tasks cannot be performed with Dynamics 365 classical workflows. The examples given are just two simple scenarios. You can extend them and add complexity based on the requirements. For further reading, please refer to https:// docs.microsoft.com/en-us/flow/connection-dynamics365.

Summary

This chapter discussed the out-of-the-box features available in Dynamics 365 for automating business processes. We have looked mainly into creating business process flows, workflows, and actions. Although dialogs are another means of implementing business processes, they were not covered in this chapter because they have been deprecated. In the next chapter, you will learn about writing plugins, custom workflows, and consuming actions.

CHAPTER 5

Advanced Customizations

The objective of this chapter is to explore the advanced customizations that can be applied to Dynamics 365. This includes implementing complex business processes with plugins and custom workflow activities. Also, you will learn how you can deploy these using the SPKL Task Runner, which was discussed in Chapter 2. Finally, you will also look at querying data using the Web API endpoints.

Getting Ready

To start with advanced customizations, you must first create the early bound types and include them in the Visual Studio project. You can create a separate Dynamics 365 solution to anchor the advanced customizations but you could also include them in the base solution. Having a single solution makes it simple to eliminate any complexities down the line. When it comes to plugin and custom workflow development, you can either use early-bound types or late-bound methods. The primary benefit of using early-bound types is that this eliminates typos when it comes to using attributes, making your code less prone to errors. Plus, this allows you to use LINQ queries, speeding up the development process. Additionally, this allows you to keep your code simple. There are several ways to generate early-bound types.

- You can use the `CrmSvcUtil.exe` tool to generate early-bound types. You can find more details about this tool at `https://docs.microsoft.com/en-us/dynamics365/customer-engagement/developer/org-service/create-early-bound-entity-classes-code-generation-tool`.

- You also have the option to generate early-bound classes using the SPKL Task Runner. To use this option, you must update your `spkl.json` file. You can find more information at `https://github.com/scottdurow/SparkleXrm/wiki/spkl#early-bound-types`.

© Sanjaya Yapa 2019
S. Yapa, *Customizing Dynamics 365*, https://doi.org/10.1007/978-1-4842-4379-4_5

- For this book, we will be using the Early Bound Generator plugin of the XrmToolBox. You can simply install it from the plugin store of the toolbox. See Figure 5-1.

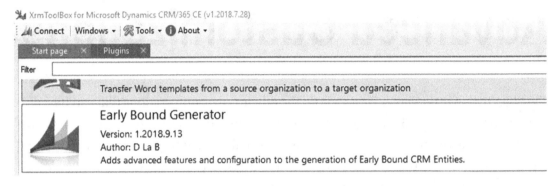

Figure 5-1. *Early Bound Generator plugin*

Creating the Plugin

Let's look at how this plugin can be used to generate the early-bound entity types. First, establish the connection with the Dynamics 365 instance. Once you're connected successfully and open the Early Bound Generator plugin, you will be directed to the screen shown in Figure 5-2.

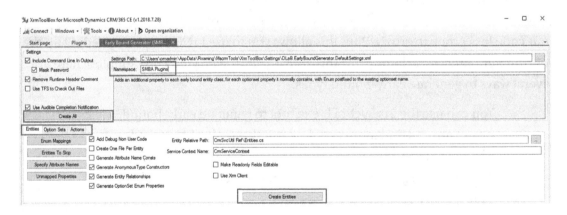

Figure 5-2. *Early Bound Generator plugin after opening it*

You must make sure you enter the correct namespace name for the project in which you are going to use the entity classes. If you click the Create All button, you can create all the entities, option sets, and actions at one time. Or you can create them individually by going into each tab (Entities, Option Sets, and Actions) and clicking the Create Entities/Option Sets/Actions button on each tab, which will generate the relevant class files. The generated files will be located in the folder shown in Figure 5-3.

Figure 5-3. *Generated early-bound classes*

Now you can add these files to the project, as illustrated in Figure 5-4. As you can see, all the namespaces are set as `SBMA.Plugins`.

Figure 5-4. *Adding early-bound generated classes to the project*

So, let's look at the requirements for SBMA. When a new member is created, a subscription must be created based on the membership type (Platinum, Gold, Silver, and Bronze). This action should be automated so the subscription record and relevant payment record are created behind the scenes swiftly so that when the user goes in for the verification, the records are there. Figure 5-5 shows the high-level business process.

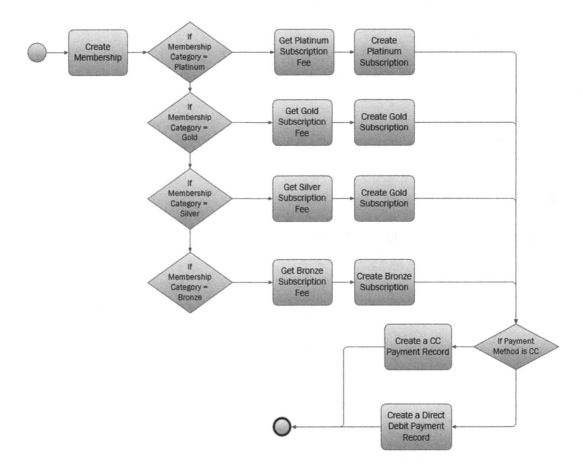

Figure 5-5. *Member subscription and payment creation process*

We will show you a quick trick to make the plugin development easier. If you have Visual Studio 2015 installed, install the Dynamics CRM Developer Toolkit and create a Dynamics 365 plugin project. Navigate to the plugins folder, and you will see the PluginBase.cs class. As part of Microsoft best practices, this particular class will give you a wealth of resources to improve your plugin development. Include it in your project and make sure you change the namespace. Then, when you write the plugin, you can extend your plugin from the `PluginBase` class. Remember, you do not have to use fancy patterns when writing plugins; just stick to the basic code principles and always try to keep it simple.

The plugin code will create only the Member Subscription record. Creating the payment record will be done through a Dynamics 365 action. You can code the payment record creation in the plugin, but actions, as explained earlier, reduce the amount of coding you have to do. You will learn how to create an action to automatically create the Member Payment record through the plugin later in the chapter. See Figure 5-6, the PluginBase.cs class is added to the Plugin Project.

Figure 5-6. *PluginBase class added to the solution*

Let's kick off the development by creating the `MemberPlugn.cs` file, which will extend the `PluginBase.cs` file, as shown here:

```
using System;
using System.Collections.Generic;
```

```csharp
using System.Linq;
using System.Text;
using ThreadTask = System.Threading.Tasks;
using Microsoft.Xrm.Sdk;
using Microsoft.Crm.Sdk;

namespace SBMA.Plugins
{
  public class MembershipPlugin : PluginBase
  {
      private readonly string postImageAlias = "PostImage";
      public MembershipPlugin() : base(typeof(MembershipPlugin)){}

      protected override void ExecuteCrmPlugin(LocalPluginContext
      localPluginContext) {}
  }
}
```

As per the requirements, you will first need to retrieve the member subscription type the user has selected. The following code segment retrieves it by passing the GUID of the new membership record created:

```csharp
/// <summary>
/// Get membership type details of the new member
/// </summary>
/// <param name="crmServiceContext"></param>
/// <param name="memberid"></param>
/// <returns></returns>
private sbma_membershiptype GetMembershipTypeOfMember
                          (CrmServiceContext crmServiceContext, Guid
                          membershipTypeId)
{
    var membershiptype = (from mt in crmServiceContext.sbma_
membershiptypeSet.Where
                          (m => m.sbma_membershiptypeId == membershipTypeId)
                          select mt).FirstOrDefault();
    return (sbma_membershiptype)membershiptype;
}
```

To get the newly created ID of the membership record, you will have to get the post-image of the record. The post-image and pre-image of a record are useful in updates. A *pre-image* can be described as a snapshot of the attributes of a record before the core operations. Similarly, a *post-image* can be described as a snapshot of the entity attributes after the core operations. As shown in Table 5-1, the availability of the pre- and post-images differs within the execution pipeline.

Table 5-1. *Plugin Event Pipeline and Image Availability*

Message	Stage	Pre-Image	Post-Image
Create	PRE	No	No
Create	POST	No	Yes
Update	PRE	Yes	No
Update	POST	Yes	Yes
Delete	PRE	Yes	No
Delete	POST	Yes	No

In this case, the plugin is fired after creating the membership record, which will get you the record after creating it. So, you will update the code file, as shown here:

```
protected override void ExecuteCrmPlugin(LocalPluginContext
localPluginContext)
{
  if (localPluginContext == null)
                throw new ArgumentNullException("Local Plugin Context");
  IPluginExecutionContext executionContext
                        = localPluginContext.PluginExecutionContext;
  ITracingService trace = localPluginContext.TracingService;
  //Get the post image
  Account newMembershipEntity = (executionContext.PostEntityImages != null &&
      executionContext.PostEntityImages.Contains(this.postImageAlias)) ?
      executionContext.PostEntityImages[postImageAlias].ToEntity<Account>() :
          new Account();
}
```

After obtaining all the required data, you are now in a position to create the related subscription record. The following code creates the Subscription record:

```
/// <summary>
/// Creating the member subscription
/// </summary>
/// <param name="organizationService"></param>
/// <param name="member"></param>
private void CreateMemberSubscription(IOrganizationService
organizationService, Account member)
{
  CrmServiceContext crmServiceContext =new CrmServiceContext(organization
  Service);
  //Get Membership Type of the member
  sbma_membershiptype membershipType = GetMembershipTypeOfMember(crmService
                                         Context,
                                         member.sbma_MembershipTypeId.Id);

  //Set the Membershipcription Properties
  sbma_membersubscription membersubscription = new sbma_membersubscription
  {
    //Se the entity reference with Member record
    sbma_MemberId = new EntityReference(member.LogicalName,
    member.AccountId.Value),
    //Set the entity reference with Membership Type record
    sbma_MembershipTypeId = new EntityReference(
        membershipType.LogicalName, membershipType.sbma_
        membershiptypeId.Value),
    //Set the subscription due date
    sbma_SubscriptionDueDate = DateTime.Now.AddDays(7.0),
    //Set the Subscription status to pending
    sbma_SubscriptionStatus = new OptionSetValue(
                (int)sbma_membersubscription_sbma_SubscriptionStatus.
                Pending)
  };
```

```
//Calling the organization service to create the new member subscription
organizationService.Create(membersubscription);

}
```

You can see that you call GetMembershipTypeOfMember in this method. This creates
the member subscription. You need to define the membership type as well. Finally, you
need to call this method in the main execution method, as shown here:

```
protected override void ExecuteCrmPlugin(LocalPluginContext localPluginContext)
{
  if (localPluginContext == null)
    throw new ArgumentNullException("Local Plugin Context");

  IPluginExecutionContext executionContext =
                      localPluginContext.PluginExecutionContext;
  ITracingService trace = localPluginContext.TracingService;

  //Get the post image
  Account newMembershipEntity = (executionContext.PostEntityImages != null &&
    executionContext.PostEntityImages.Contains(this.postImageAlias)) ?
    executionContext.PostEntityImages[postImageAlias].ToEntity<Account>() :
    new Account();
  //Create the membersusbscription
  CreateMemberSubscription(localPluginContext.OrganizationService,
                                    newMembershipEntity);

}
```

Now that you have completed coding the plugin, you must deploy it. You will
be using the SPKL Task Runner for the deployment. Install it in your project, as
demonstrated in an earlier chapter. To deploy the plugin via SPKL, you must add a few
attributes to your code, as shown here:

```
namespace SBMA.Plugins
{
  [CrmPluginRegistration(MessageNameEnum.Create,
      "account", StageEnum.PostOperation,
      ExecutionModeEnum.Synchronous, "name", "Post-Create Account",
```

```
    1000, IsolationModeEnum.Sandbox, Image1Name = "PostImage",
    Image1Type = ImageTypeEnum.PostImage,
    Image1Attributes = "accountid,name,accountnumber,sbma_membershiptypeid")]
public class MembershipPlugin : PluginBase
{
```

As you can see, we have set these attributes to deploy our plugin as a synchronous plugin, and the plugin message is Create. Since this is executed after the Membership record is created, it is set as a Post Create plugin. As discussed earlier, you need a post-image, which is the record that is created and that defines the attributes for the post-image, which will be returned to your code. After setting up these attributes, connect to the Dynamics 365 instance with the SPKL Task Runner by executing the `deploy-plugins.bat` command. To learn more about plugin deployment with the SPKL Task Runner, refer to `https://www.develop1.net/public/post/2017/05/12/Deploying-Plugins-using-spkl-Task-Runner`.

Figure 5-7 shows the membership being created. When the membership record is created, the relevant subscription will be created as well, as shown in Figure 5-8.

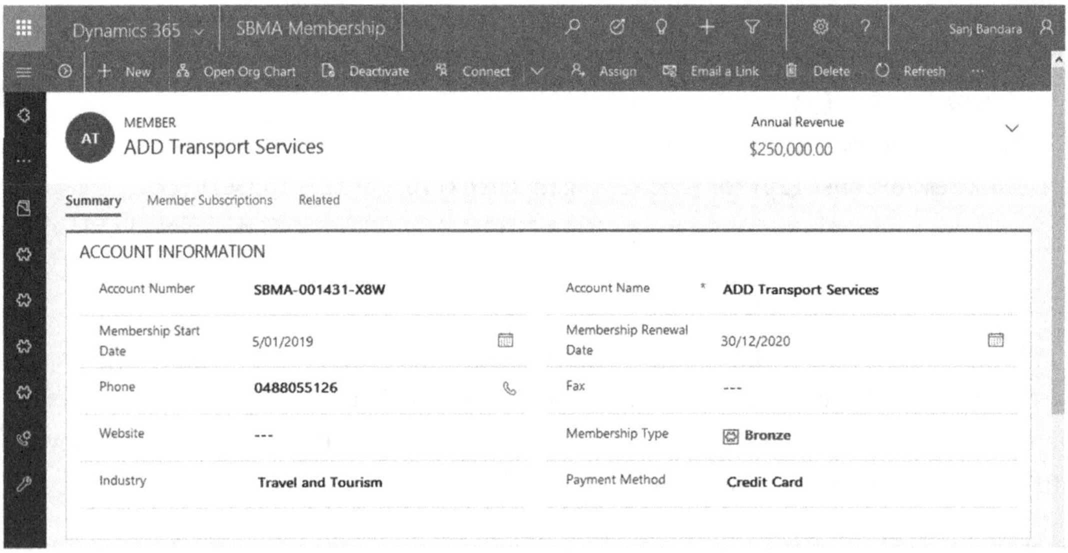

Figure 5-7. *Creating a membership record*

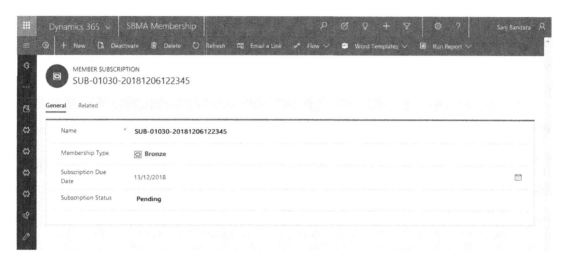

Figure 5-8. *Created membership subscription*

You can do many things with this process. For instance, when the subscription is created, until it is paid, you could trigger a workflow that waits until the due date and sends an e-mail to the member saying the subscription is not paid. The workflow will stop if the subscription status is set to Paid. Another scenario would be to set the subscription status to Paid if the related payment is completed. The takeaway from this is that no matter how complex the scenario is, you can implement it using these advanced customizations of Dynamics 365.

You will need to investigate the other side of this on your own. If you do not map your processes correctly, it will be maintenance nightmare and will have a big impact on the performance. Even though you have a lot of flexibility to extend the application, you need to use that flexibility with care.

Creating Custom Workflow Activities

In this section, you will learn how to write a custom workflow activity to implement complex business processes. As part of the scenario discussed in the previous section, now you must create the payment records to track the payments. To complete the process, a workflow should be triggered behind the scenes to create the payment record as soon as the subscription record is created. This workflow should then wait for seven days from the date the payment record is created and send an e-mail reminder to the primary contact of the business to pay the membership fee.

This workflow will be triggered when the member subscription record is created, and the custom workflow activity will be triggered to create the payment record. You need a custom workflow activity here, because you have to determine the payment method defined on the membership record. Remember, only one level of entity relationship is available to access from a standard workflow. Similarly, when sending the e-mail, you need the e-mail address of the primary contact of the member.

To begin creating the workflow, let's first create the parent workflow. We discussed the details of how to create a workflow in the previous chapter. In this example, we will also demonstrate the use of input and output variables.

To begin writing the workflow activity, you will be using early-bound classes. Follow the steps to generate the early-bound classes described earlier. You need to generate it again, because the assembly for the workflow activity is different, in this case, SBMA.Workflow. In the XrmToolBox, change the assembly name as required, generate the entity reference classes, and add them to the project. See Figure 5-9.

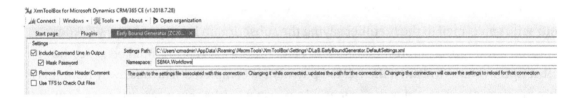

Figure 5-9. *Generating entity references for the workflow activity*

As shown next, after setting this up, add the workflow activity class to your project:

```
using System;
using System.Collections.Generic;
using System.Linq;
using System.Text;
using System.Threading.Tasks;
using System.Activities;
using Microsoft.Xrm.Sdk;
using Microsoft.Xrm.Sdk.Workflow;

namespace SBMA.Workflows
{
  public class CreateMemberPayment : CodeActivity
```

146

```
    {
        public override void ExecuteCRMWorkFlowActivity
            (CodeActivityContext context, LocalWorkflowContext
            crmWorkflowContext)
        {
            base.ExecuteCRMWorkFlowActivity(context, crmWorkflowContext);
        }
    }
}
```

Important   To use the Microsoft.Xrm.Sdk.Workflow library, you must install it from NuGet. Get the latest version from `https://www.nuget.org/packages/ Microsoft.CrmSdk.Workflow/`. Also, as we did with plugins, we will be using the `WorkflowActivityBase` class that was generated and the `CodeActivity` class, which is the parent class of the custom activity and which is a child class of `System.Activities.CodeActivity`.

One of the cool things about workflow activities is that you can pass parameters to the activity and return values from it using out arguments. For this activity, you must pass the Member reference, which is the owner of the subscription created. With this reference, you can determine the preferred payment method of the member. Let's code.

For this workflow activity, you must pass the member reference and subscription reference. You can see from the following code that the two input variables are declared:

```
[Input("Member")]
[ReferenceTarget("account")]
public InArgument<EntityReference> InMember { get; set; }

[Input("MemberSubscription")]
[ReferenceTarget("sbma_membersubscription")]
public InArgument<EntityReference> InMemberSubscription { get; set; }

public override void ExecuteCRMWorkFlowActivity
    (CodeActivityContext context, LocalWorkflowContext
    crmWorkflowContext)
```

```
{
  var accountId = this.InMember.Get(context).Id;
  var memberSubscriptionId = this.InMemberSubscription.Get(context).Id;

  CreateMemberPaymentRecord(crmWorkflowContext.OrganizationService,
              12, memberSubscriptionId, accountId);
}
```

To create the member payment record, you will require the payment due amount, payment due date, payment method, and member subscription reference. The following code illustrates the methods required to get this information:

```
/// <summary>
/// Get Subscription fee
/// </summary>
/// <param name="crmServiceContext"></param>
/// <param name="membersubscription"></param>
/// <returns></returns>
private decimal GetDuePayment(CrmServiceContext crmServiceContext,
                            sbma_membersubscription membersubscription)
{
  var membershipType = (from mt in crmServiceContext.sbma_membershiptypeSet
                      where mt.sbma_membershiptypeId ==
                      membersubscription.sbma_MembershipTypeId.Id
                      select mt).FirstOrDefault();

  return membershipType.sbma_SubscriptionFee.Value;
}
/// <summary>
/// Get member details
/// </summary>
/// <param name="crmServiceContext"></param>
/// <param name="member"></param>
/// <returns></returns>
private Account GetMember(CrmServiceContext crmServiceContext, Guid memberId)
{
  var membership = (from m in crmServiceContext.AccountSet.Where
```

```
                          (a => a.AccountId == memberId) select m).
                          FirstOrDefault();
    return membership;
}

/// <summary>
/// Get Subscription Details
/// </summary>
/// <param name="serviceContext"></param>
/// <param name="memberSubscriptionId"></param>
/// <returns></returns>
private sbma_membersubscription GetSubscription(CrmServiceContext
serviceContext, Guid memberSubscriptionId)
{
  var memberSubscription = (from sm in serviceContext.sbma_
  membersubscriptionSet

                              where sm.sbma_membersubscriptionId ==
                                                    memberSubscriptionId
                              select sm).FirstOrDefault();
  return memberSubscription;
}
```

Then call these methods and create the member payment, as illustrated here:

```
/// <summary>
/// Create member payment record
/// </summary>
/// <param name="organizationService"></param>
/// <param name="memberSubscriptionId"></param>
/// <param name="accountId"></param>
private void CreateMemberPaymentRecord(IOrganizationService
organizationService, Guid memberSubscriptionId, Guid accountId)
{
  CrmServiceContext = new CrmServiceContext(organizationService);
  sbma_membersubscription membersubscriptionlocal =
                      GetSubscription(crmServiceContext,
                      memberSubscriptionId);
```

```
Account membershipLocal = GetMember(crmServiceContext, accountId);

sbma_memberpayment memberpayment = new sbma_memberpayment()
{
    sbma_AmountDue = new Money(GetDuePayment(crmServiceContext,
                                            membersubscriptionlocal)),
    sbma_PaymentDue = membersubscriptionlocal.sbma_SubscriptionDueDate,
    sbma_PaymentMethod = new OptionSetValue(
                            (membershipLocal.sbma_PaymentMethod.Value ==
                            (int)Account_sbma_PaymentMethod.CreditCard) ?
                            (int)Account_sbma_PaymentMethod.CreditCard :
                            (int)Account_sbma_PaymentMethod.DirectDebit),
    sbma_MemberSubscriptionId = new EntityReference
                (membersubscriptionlocal.LogicalName, membersubscriptionl
                ocal.Id)
};
organizationService.Create(memberpayment);

}
```

We will be using the SPKL Task Runner to deploy the custom workflow activity; therefore, we have installed the SPKL Task Runner to the workflow project and set the attributes for the workflow activity as we did for the plugins. The completed code should look something like this:

```
using System;
using System.Collections.Generic;
using System.Linq;
using System.Text;
using System.Threading.Tasks;
using System.Activities;
using Microsoft.Xrm.Sdk;
using Microsoft.Xrm.Sdk.Workflow;

namespace SBMA.Workflows
{
  [CrmPluginRegistration("CreateMemberPayment", "CreateMemberPayment",
                            "","",IsolationModeEnum.Sandbox)]
```

```csharp
public class CreateMemberPayment : CodeActivity
{
  [Input("Member")]
  [ReferenceTarget("account")]
  public InArgument<EntityReference> InMember { get; set; }

  [Input("MemberSubscription")]
  [ReferenceTarget("sbma_membersubscription")]
  public InArgument<EntityReference> InMemberSubscription { get; set; }

  public override void ExecuteCRMWorkFlowActivity(CodeActivityContext
  context, LocalWorkflowContext crmWorkflowContext)
  {
    // Retrieve the account number from the input paramenter
    var accountId = this.InMember.Get(context).Id;

    // Retrieve the membersubscription form the input parameter
    var memberSubscriptionId = this.InMemberSubscription.Get(context).Id;

     CreateMemberPaymentRecord(crmWorkflowContext.OrganizationService,
                              memberSubscriptionId, accountId);
  }

  /// <summary>
  /// Create member payment record
  /// </summary>
  /// <param name="organizationService"></param>
  /// <param name="memberSubscriptionId"></param>
  /// <param name="accountId"></param>
  private void CreateMemberPaymentRecord(IOrganizationService
  organizationService, Guid memberSubscriptionId, Guid accountId){}

  /// <summary>
  /// Get Subscription fee
  /// </summary>
  /// <param name="crmServiceContext"></param>
  /// <param name="membersubscription"></param>
```

```
    /// <returns></returns>
    private decimal GetDuePayment(CrmServiceContext crmServiceContext,
                        sbma_membersubscription membersubscription){}

        /// <summary>
        /// Get member details
        /// </summary>
        /// <param name="crmServiceContext"></param>
        /// <param name="member"></param>
        /// <returns></returns>
        private Account GetMember(CrmServiceContext crmServiceContext,
                                                Guid memberId) {}

        /// <summary>
        /// Get Subscription Details
        /// </summary>
        /// <param name="serviceContext"></param>
        /// <param name="memberSubscriptionId"></param>
        /// <returns></returns>
        private sbma_membersubscription GetSubscription(CrmServiceContext
                        serviceContext, Guid memberSubscriptionId){}
    }
}
```

The next step is to run the `deploy-workflows.bat` command of the SPKL Task Runner to install the workflow activity. Once it's installed, you can see the custom workflow activity when the Add Step drop-down is expanded. See Figure 5-10.

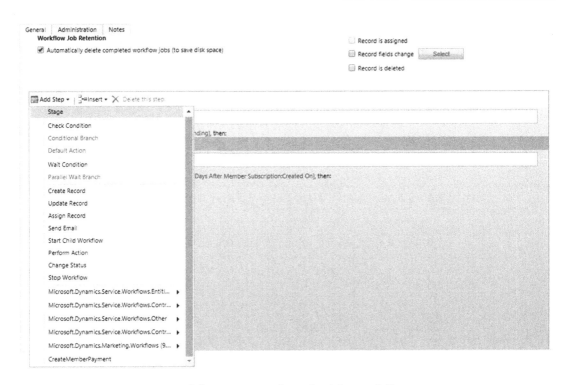

Figure 5-10. *Custom workflow activity listed with workflow steps*

When adding the step to the workflow, you must set the two parameters as illustrated in Figure 5-11.

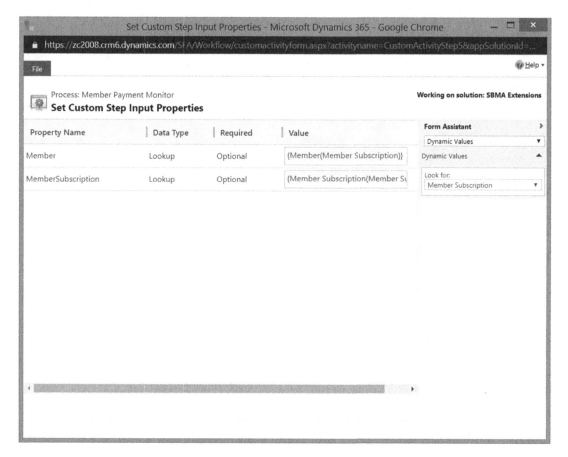

Figure 5-11. *Passing the input arguments to the workflow*

When the workflow is executed, the payment record will be created based on the membership and the member subscription information.

Calling Custom Actions from JavaScript

In this section, let's look at how you can call an action using JavaScript and the Web API. The following code can be used externally to create records in Dynamics 365. This approach is extremely useful in scenarios where you allow external programs to interact with the application. In this example, you will look at applying for membership with the organization. First let's create the action shown in Figure 5-12. This action has a set of parameters that could include the fields of the external application, and once the data is submitted, an applicant record in Dynamics 365 will be created.

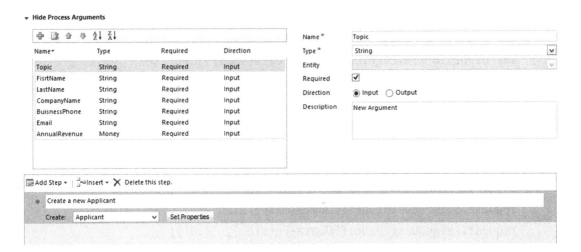

Figure 5-12. *Submitting the application*

The following is the JavaScript code that calls the action. The function `callCustomAction` is a common function that can be used to call any action in Dynamics 365.

```javascript
function submitApplication()
{
    var actionName = "sbma_SubmitApplication";

    // Define the input parameters
    var inParams = {
        "Topic" : ("#Topic"),
        "FisrtName" : ("#FisrtName"),
        "LastName" : ("#LastName"),
        "CompanyName" : ("#CompanyName"),
        "BuisnessPhone" : ("#BuisnessPhone"),
        "Email" : ("#Email"),
        "AnnualRevenue" : ("#AnnualRevenue")
    };

    var actionResponse = callCustomAction(actionName, inpParams);
}

//Call the custom action
callCustomAction = function(actionName, inputParameters)
```

```
{
    var results = null;
    var orgUrl = Xrm.Page.context.getClientUrl();
    // Web request
    var request = new XMLHttpRequest();
    request.open("POST", orgUrl + actionName,false);
    request.setRequestHeader("Accept", "application/json");
    request.setRequestHeader("Content-Type","application/json; charset-
    utf-8");
    request.setRequestHeader("OData-MaxVersion", "4.0");
    request.setRequestHeader("OData-Version", "4.0");

    request.onreadystatechange = function () {
    if (this.readyState == 4) {
        request.onreadystatechange = null;
        if (this.status == 200) {
            alert("Application submitted successfully.");

        } else {
            var error = JSON.parse(this.response).error;
            alert(error.message);
        }
    };

    request.send(window.JSON.stringify(inputParameters);
    return results;
}
```

Again, this is a simple example. Most importantly, there are many other ways to achieve the same functionality within the Dynamics 365 ecosystem, and choosing the one best suited to achieving the project objectives must done with great care.

Summary

This chapter covered the implementation of complex business logic with plugins and custom workflow activities. In the next chapter, you will be taking the implementation a little bit further by integrating Dynamics 365 with Azure.

CHAPTER 6

Azure Integration

In this chapter, we will discuss the Azure integrations that can be leveraged to implement fast and scalable solutions. We will be focusing on three types of Azure technologies that are useful in Dynamics 365 implementations. They are Azure WebJobs, Functions, and Logic Apps. Azure WebJobs is ideal for batch processing, which will run behind the scenes. Since we are talking about Azure technologies in this chapter, we will also take a quick look at some security aspects. Microsoft Dynamics 365 for Customer Engagement leverages the cloud services infrastructure and the built-in security features to safeguard the data. To safeguard access, it depends heavily on Azure Active Directory (AAD) to authenticate the users and prevent unauthorized access to sensitive data. Also, when it comes to licensing, you can buy the license for Dynamics 365, or you can provision the required infrastructure with Azure, and your cost is determined by the usage. When leveraging the power of these technologies, you must take extra precautions to plan and design your solution. There is a huge pile of information provided at `https://docs.microsoft.com/en-us/dynamics365/customer-engagement/admin/manage-subscriptions-licenses-user-accounts`.

Logic Apps can be used to design more advanced workflows, and Azure Functions enables you to write functionality that processes data in a serverless architecture. Especially with Logic Apps, you can connect with many external applications, which we will look at in detail later this chapter.

Azure WebJobs

First let's look at Azure WebJobs, which is a feature of Azure App Service. You can use the WebJobs feature to run processes behind the scenes, and the best thing about WebJobs is that you can schedule when to execute the process. Web jobs can be categorized as continuous or triggered. Continuous web jobs start immediately when the job is created.

© Sanjaya Yapa 2019
S. Yapa, *Customizing Dynamics 365*, https://doi.org/10.1007/978-1-4842-4379-4_6

To execute the app continuously, the application executes within an infinite loop. If the application stops, you can restart it. Triggered web jobs start only on a certain schedule or when manually triggered.

The following are the supported file types with Azure WebJobs:

- PowerShell (`.ps1`)

- Windows CMD (`.cmd`, `.exe`, `.bat`)

- Bash (`.sh`)

- Python (`.py`)

- Node.js (`.js`)

- Java (`.jar`)

- PHP (`.php`)

Keep in mind that a web app can time out after 20 minutes of inactivity, which can be reset with a request to the actual web app. If your application is set up as continuous or scheduled, then enable Always On to make sure the application executes without any interruption.

Writing Code for a Web Job

Let's look at the example with the SBMA membership management solution. The stakeholders want the application to raise the yearly subscription automatically and on time. For instance, if the membership of a member is expiring a month from today, then a subscription and a payment record should be created behind the scenes. One of the options is to create a Windows service, but to deploy it you would need a server, either physical or virtual. Either way, creating a server requires an additional fee for the maintenance, which SBMA is not willing to pay. So, the option available is to create a console application that executes behind the scenes and create the necessary subscription records. When compared to Windows services, the best thing about the WebJobs feature is the ability to create console applications. Creating a console application means that debugging and troubleshooting can be done before deploying to the cloud, whereas Windows services require much more complex debugging scenarios.

This section will list the code used to create the application. Listing 6-1 illustrates the Main program that connects to the Dynamics 365 instance and calls the logic to create the subscription. Remember, you should create only the subscription here; the relevant payment record will be created by the custom workflow activity created in Chapter 5.

Listing 6-1. Main Program That Calls the Process to Create the Subscriptions

```
using System;
using System.Configuration;
using System.Net;
using System.Reflection;
using System.ServiceModel.Description;
using log4net;
using Microsoft.Crm.Sdk.Messages;
using Microsoft.Xrm.Tooling.Connector;
using Microsoft.Xrm.Sdk;
using Microsoft.Xrm.Sdk.Client;
using SBMA.ServiceProcessor.BusinessProcessLayer;

namespace SBMA.ServiceProcessor
{
  public class Program
  {
    public static readonly ILog log = LogManager.GetLogger(MethodBase.Get
                                Current Method().DeclaringType);

    public static void Main(string[] arcs)
    {
      ExecuteLogic();
      Console.ReadLine();
    }

    /// <summary>
    /// Connecting to Dynamics 365 instance
    /// </summary>
```

```csharp
public static void ExecuteLogic()
{
  try
  {
    log.Info("Connecting to Dynamics 365 instance...");
    using (CrmServiceClient crmConnection = new CrmServiceClient
            (ConfigurationManager.ConnectionStrings["Xrm"].Connection
            String))
    {
    log.Info(crmConnection.IsReady);
    if (crmConnection.IsReady)
    {
      log.Info("Application connected to server successfully.");
    }

    IOrganizationService service = (IOrganizationService)crmConnection;
    CrmServiceContext context = new CrmServiceContext(service);

     if (service != null)
    {
      Guid orgId = ((WhoAmIResponse)service.Execute
                        (new WhoAmIRequest())).OrganizationId;
      if (orgId != Guid.Empty)
      {
        log.Info("Connection established successfully.");
       }

      // Call the process to create the
      SubscriptionProcessor subscriptionProcessor = new
      SubscriptionProcessor();
      subscriptionProcessor.CreateRenewalSubscriptionProcess(service);
    }
    else
    {
      Console.WriteLine("Connection failed...");
    }
```

```
        }
      }
      catch (Exception ex)
      {
            log.Error("EXCEPTION: ", ex);
      }
    }
  }
}
```

Note   As you can see, there is a reference to log4net, which is handy when testing code. Also, when you publish the application with web jobs, you can view the details of execution in the logs. This information is really valuable. This link will guide you to set up log4net: `https://stackify.com/log4net-guide-dotnet-logging/`.

The recommended approach for connecting to a Dynamics 365 instance from an external application like this is to use Microsoft.Xrm.Tooling.Connector library, which you can download from NuGet. As shown in Listing 6-1, to establish the connection, you pass the connection string read from the configuration file to the `CrmServiceClient` constructor, which is then used to instantiate the organization service. When you create the connection string, you must make sure that you set the `SkipDiscovery` property to false, as shown in Listing 6-2. If not, the application will throw the exception "Microsoft.Xrm.Entity cannot be converted to type<ex: SBMA.ServiceProcessor.Account>." This is because the service does not know how to deserialize the results into a proper object. You can find more information at `https://community.dynamics.com/crm/b/bettercrm/archive/2018/11/28/dynamics-365-tooling-object-of-type-microsoft-xrm-sdk-entity-cannot-be-converted-to-type-type`.

Listing 6-2. Dynamics 365 Connection String

```
<connectionStrings>
    <add name="Xrm"
        connectionString="AuthType=Office365;
                        Username=XXX@orgname.onmicrosoft.com;
                            Password=***************;
                            Url=https://orgname.crm6.dynamics.com;
                            SkipDiscovery=false;" />
</connectionStrings>
```

Note   For demonstration purposes, we have hard-coded the credentials to connect to the Dynamics 365 instance, but the best practice is to use the Azure Key Vault. Please refer to the following URL for more information: `https://docs.microsoft.com/en-us/azure/key-vault/key-vault-use-from-web-application`.

You have created a separate layer to hold all the data access. Listing 6-3 lists the code that reads and writes to Dynamics 365.

Listing 6-3. Data Access Layer

```csharp
using Microsoft.Xrm.Sdk;
using System;
using System.Collections.Generic;
using System.Linq;

namespace SBMA.ServiceProcessor.DataAccessLayer
{
  public class SubscriptionDataAccess
  {
    /// <summary>
    /// Get members renewing in 30 days from today
    /// </summary>
    /// <param name="crmServiceContext"></param>
    /// <returns></returns>
```

```csharp
public List<Account> GetMembersExpiringIn30Days
                              (CrmServiceContext crmServiceContext)
{
    var accountList = from a in crmServiceContext.AccountSet
            where a.sbma_MembershipRenewalDate.Value ==
                                    DateTime.Today.AddDays(30.0)
            select new Account
            {
                AccountId = a.AccountId,
                AccountNumber = a.AccountNumber,
                sbma_MembershipTypeId = a.sbma_MembershipTypeId
            };
    return accountList.ToList();
}

/// <summary>
/// Check for unpaid subscriptions
/// </summary>
/// <param name="crmServiceContext"></param>
/// <param name="accountNumber"></param>
/// <returns></returns>
public List<sbma_membersubscription>
  GetUnpaidSubscriptions(CrmServiceContext crmServiceContext,
  Guid accountNumber)
{
  var subscriptionList = from s in
                      crmServiceContext.sbma_membersubscriptionSet
                  where s.sbma_MemberId.Id == accountNumber &&
                      s.sbma_SubscriptionStatus.Value ==
              (int)sbma_membersubscription_sbma_
              SubscriptionStatus.Pending
                  select new sbma_membersubscription
                  {
                      sbma_membersubscriptionId = s.sbma_member
                                          subscriptionId,
                      sbma_MemberId = s.sbma_MemberId
                  };
```

```csharp
        return subscriptionList.ToList();
    }

    /// <summary>
    /// Create the member subscription
    /// </summary>
    /// <param name="organizationService"></param>
    /// <param name="membersubscription"></param>
    public void CreateRenewalMemberSubscription(IOrganizationService
        organizationService, sbma_membersubscription membersubscription)
    {
        organizationService.Create(membersubscription);
    }

    /// <summary>
    /// Get membership type details of the new member
    /// </summary>
    /// <param name="crmServiceContext"></param>
    /// <param name="memberid"></param>
    /// <returns></returns>
    public sbma_membershiptype GetMembershipTypeOfMember(CrmServiceContext
                                                crmServiceContext,
                                                Guid membership
                                                TypeId)
    {
        var membershiptype = (from mt in
                            crmServiceContext.sbma_membershiptype
                            Set.Where
                            (m => m.sbma_membershiptypeId == membership
                            TypeId)
                             select mt).FirstOrDefault();
        return (sbma_membershiptype)membershiptype;
    }
  }
}
```

Listing 6-4 shows the logic that is called at the main program. It will manipulate the data access methods and create the member subscription record.

Listing 6-4. Business Logic Implementation

```csharp
using Microsoft.Xrm.Sdk;
using SBMA.ServiceProcessor.DataAccessLayer;
using System;
using System.Collections.Generic;

namespace SBMA.ServiceProcessor.BusinessProcessLayer
{
  public class SubscriptionProcessor
  {
    public void CreateRenewalSubscriptionProcess
                        (IOrganizationService organizationService)
    {
      using (CrmServiceContext crmServiceContext =
                        new CrmServiceContext(organizationService))
      {
        SubscriptionDataAccess subscriptionDataAccess = new
                                            SubscriptionDataAccess();
        // Get the list of accounts that subscription is expiring in 30 days
        log.Info("Get members renewing in 30 days...");
        List<Account> accountsList =
              subscriptionDataAccess.GetMembersExpiringIn30Days(crmService
              Context);

        // Execute only if there are any reocrds, else do nothing
        if(accountsList.Count > 0)
        {
          log.Info("Processing "+accountsList.Count+" members...");
          for (int i = 0; i < accountsList.Count; i++)
          {
            // For each account check whether there are any unpaid
              subscriptions for the period.Create only if there are
              no unpaid subscriptions
```

```csharp
            List<sbma_membersubscription> membersubscriptions =
                        subscriptionDataAccess.GetUnpaidSubscriptions
                        (crmServiceContext,
                                accountsList[i].AccountId.Value);
    if (membersubscriptions.Count == 0)
    {
     log.Info("Creating member subscription for member: " +
                        accountsList[i].AccountId.Value);
     sbma_membershiptype membershiptype =
                subscriptionDataAccess.GetMembershipTypeOfMember
                (crmServiceContext,
                        accountsList[i].sbma_MembershipTypeId.Id);
     //Set the Membershipcription Properties
     sbma_membersubscription membersubscription = new
                                                sbma_membersubscription
    {
       //Se the entity reference with Member record
       sbma_MemberId = new EntityReference
            (accountsList[i].LogicalName,
                                accountsList[i].AccountId.Value),

       //Set the entity reference with Membership Type record
       sbma_MembershipTypeId = new EntityReference
                                (membershiptype.LogicalName,
                        membershiptype.sbma_membershiptypeId.
                        Value),

       //Set the subscription due date
       sbma_SubscriptionDueDate = DateTime.Now.AddDays(7.0),

//Set the Subscription status to pending
sbma_SubscriptionStatus = new OptionSetValue(
    (int)sbma_membersubscription_sbma_SubscriptionStatus.
    Pending)
};
```

```
    // Create the subscription
    subscriptionDataAccess.CreateRenewalMemberSubscription
            (organizationService, membersubscription);
    log.Info("Subscription created successfully.");
      }
     }
    }
   }
  }
 }
}
```

When all the coding is completed, you can build the application. Navigate to the `bin` folder and zip the content of the folder. You will need to upload the content to Azure WebJobs. The zip file must contain all the reference `.dlls` and config files. Now let's start creating the Azure web job.

Creating a Web Job

To create a web job, you must first create a web app under Azure App Service. Provide the relevant details and click Create. See Figure 6-1.

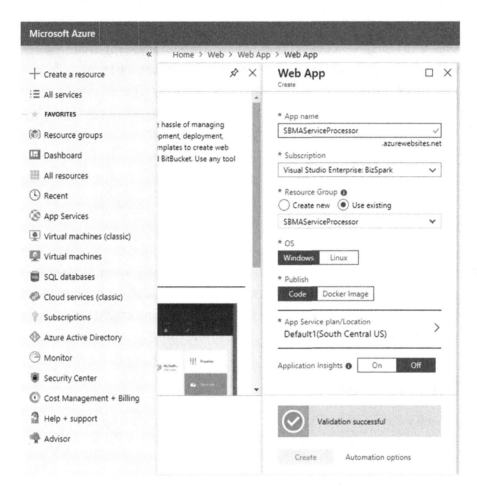

Figure 6-1. *Creating a web app*

Once the web app is created successfully, you will see it listed as an app service. See Figure 6-2.

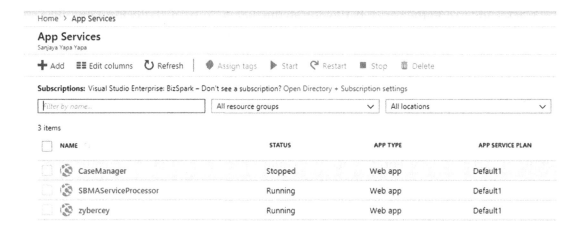

Figure 6-2. *App service created*

Navigate inside the web app created and select WebJobs in the left pane, as illustrated in Figure 6-3.

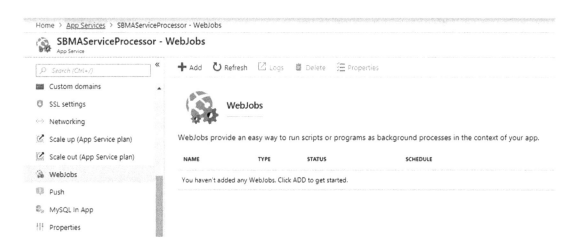

Figure 6-3. *WebJobs in left pane*

Click +Add to add the web job. Provide all the details. You must provide a unique name and upload the zip file you created. Set the type as Triggered and the type of trigger as Scheduled. The unique thing about the scheduled triggers is the interval must be provided as a CRON expression. You can learn about cron expressions at `https://docs.microsoft.com/en-us/azure/azure-functions/functions-bindings-timer#cron-expressions`. Figure 6-4 shows the settings for the web job. For the demonstration purposes, the cron expression is set to every two minutes. Ideally, this type of batch job should be executed daily. For instance, you could enter it as **0 30 23 * * ***, meaning the process will be executed at 11:30 p.m. every night.

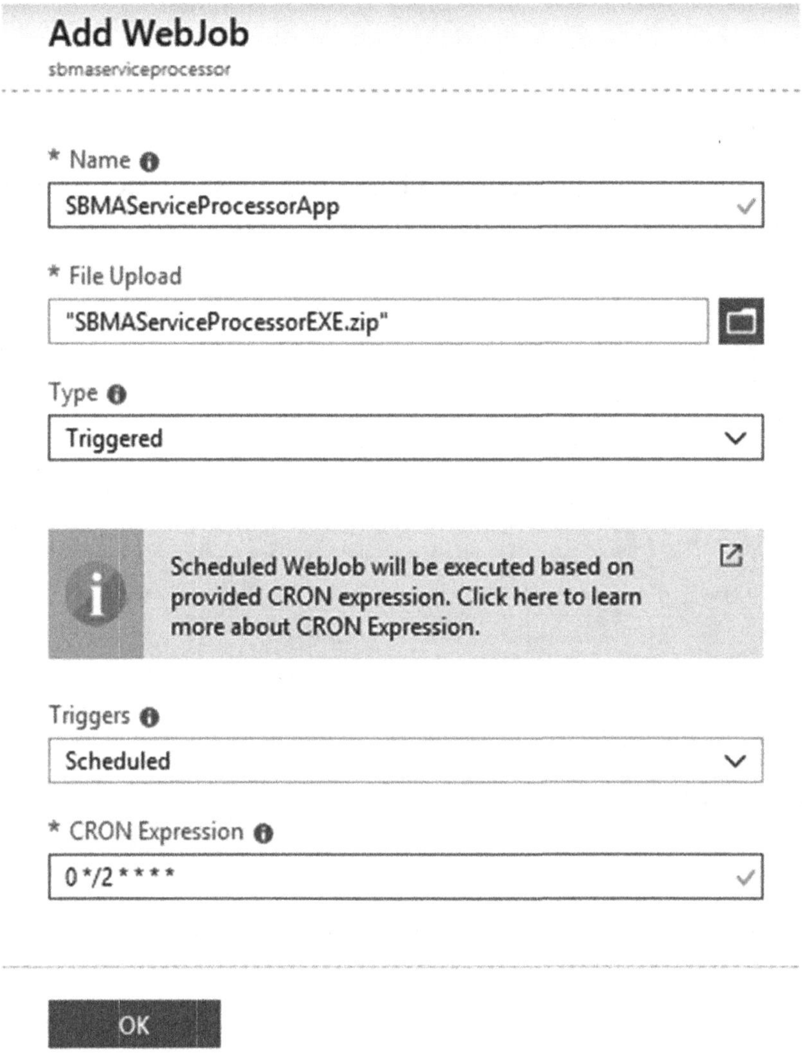

Figure 6-4. *Web job settings*

After configuring these settings, you can click OK, which will create the web job, as shown in Figure 6-5. You can see that Status is set to Ready.

Figure 6-5. *Web job created and ready to execute*

Select the web job and click Run to start the job, and the status will change to Running. See Figure 6-6.

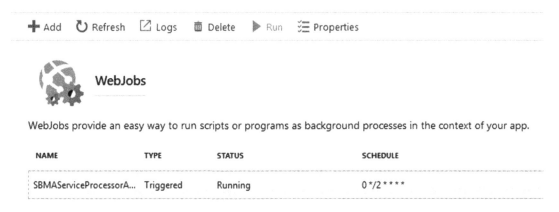

Figure 6-6. *Web job running*

To view the progress of the web job and troubleshoot any issues, click Logs in the toolbar to see the progress. Also, all the messages entered through log4net will be shown on the console. See Figure 6-7.

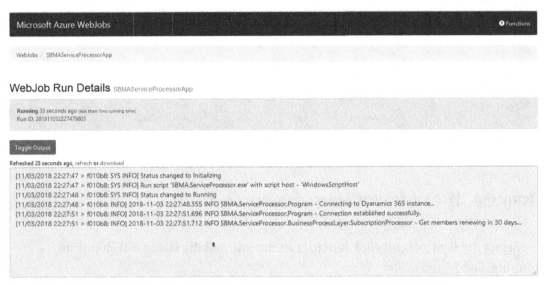

Figure 6-7. Web job execution status

As mentioned earlier in this section, to make the application execute without any interruption, you must enable the Always On option in the "General settings" section of the web job. Keep in mind that this action involves an additional cost. See Figure 6-8.

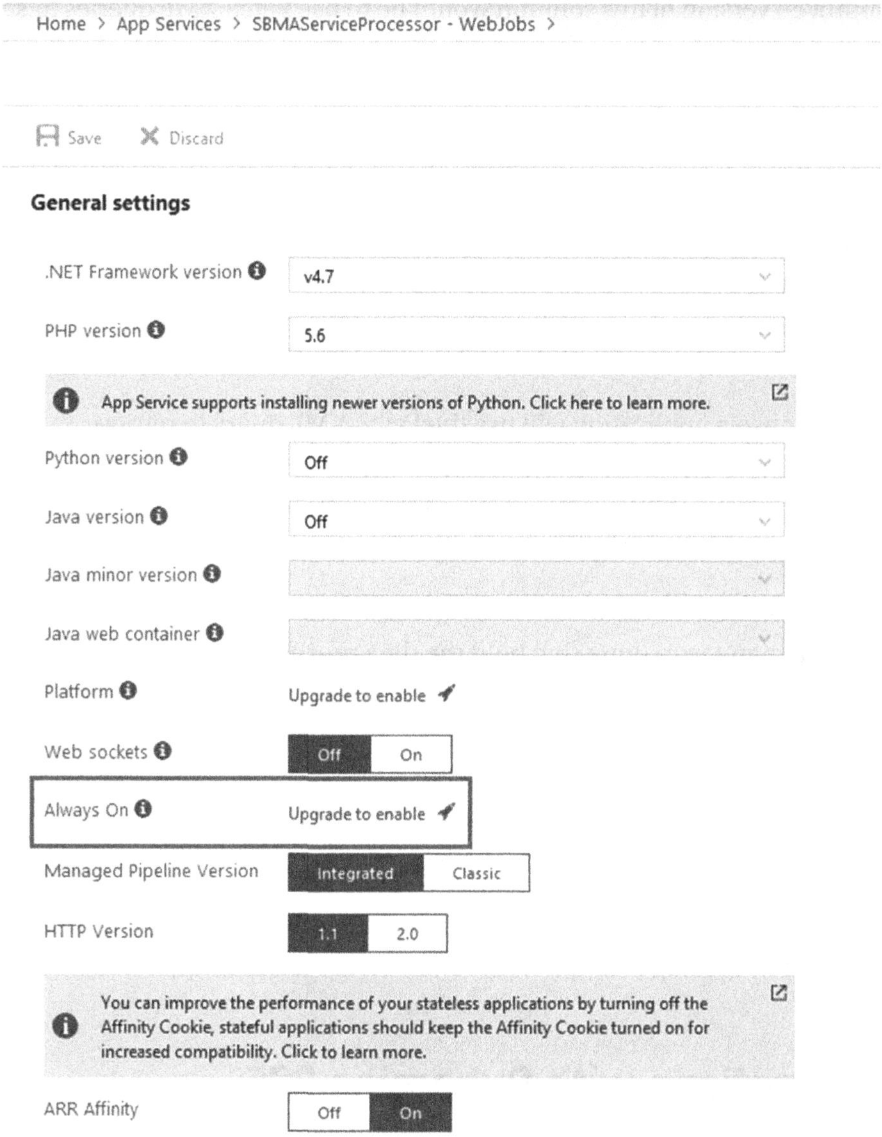

Figure 6-8. *Enabling Always On for the web job*

An improved version of this solution would be to use Fetch XML queries to select the data required for processing. The benefit of using Fetch XML queries is that when the business wants simple changes to the query, you can easily alter the Fetch XML code without any development work and releases. The following are the high-level steps to create such a solution:

1. Create an entity that holds the Fetch XML query in Dynamics 365. You must have a couple of unique fields to identify the query such as which method will use the query, which process will use the query, etc.

2. The console application will use the Fetch XML query to retrieve the batch of records to process on the Dynamics 365 end. You could write .NET classes as you did in the previous example to process the data.

3. A further improvement would be to use workflows. You can create on-demand workflows that hold the data processing logic, which will be invoked by the console application. Using workflows gives you a rich set of execution logs within Dynamics 365. This is similar to creating an Advanced Find view and executing the on-demand workflow against all the records in the results view.

As you can see, if the business requires any batch processing, you can easily do it with Azure WebJobs by creating a console application that processes data. In the next section, you will be looking at another serverless Azure technology, Azure Functions.

Azure Functions with Dynamics 365

Dynamics 365 and Azure Functions integration in v9.0 enables various integration scenarios for your applications. As mentioned earlier in this chapter, Azure Functions is serverless, and the pay-per-use pricing makes it cost effective. Azure Functions comes with built-in capabilities to integrate with PowerApps, Logic Apps, and Microsoft Flow, providing a new set of building blocks to power users to design and develop state-of-the-art solutions. You can do many amazing things in the context of Dynamics 365 integrations.

- Export and import data from external applications or web services.

- Get notifications from third-party services.

- When there are heavy processes that should performed, you can pass them to Azure Functions without disrupting the user.

- You can connect to third-party endpoints such as payment gateways, making it easy to change the endpoint at any time without changing the internal logic.

The primary reason for using Azure Functions is to minimize the necessity to write plugins and custom workflows, which are difficult to debug. Also, using third-party libraries with plugins in Dynamics 365 online is not possible, unless you have the source code of the third-party library and compile it into the plugin DLL. Therefore, you can easily write an Azure function that references third-party libraries. In this section, we will look at processing credit card payments via Azure Functions. In the future, if the client wants to change the payment gateway, they can easily change the endpoint from the function rather than having to alter plugins or custom workflows.

Creating an Azure Function

First let's create an Azure function. Click +Create Resource and in the Compute section you will find Function App. Provide all the necessary information and click Create. See Figure 6-9.

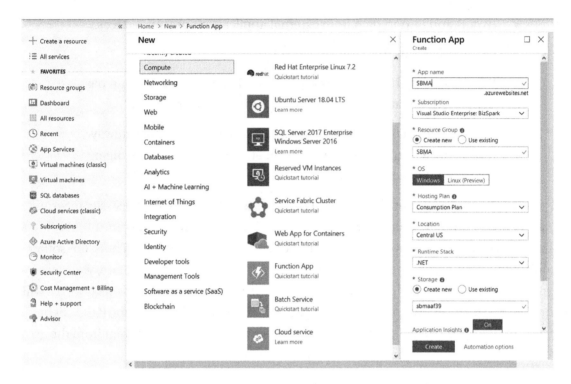

Figure 6-9. *Creating an Azure Functions app*

It will take few seconds to create the app. Once the app is created, you will see the details of the app. See Figure 6-10.

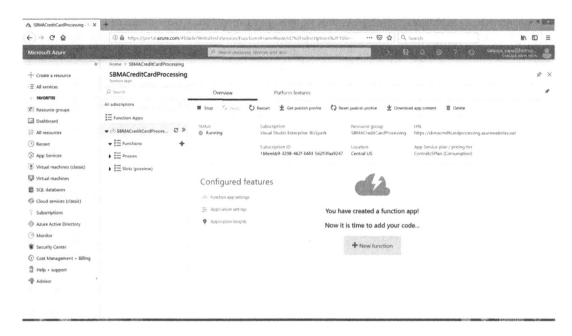

Figure 6-10. *Azure Functions app details*

Next, let's create the function that processes the payment. Click the + sign next to Functions in the left pane. Then you will be asked to select the template. For this example, you will trigger the function with HTTP triggers. Select API & Webhooks from the Scenario drop-down box. From the options available, select HTTP Trigger. See Figure 6-11.

Figure 6-11. *Selecting the function template*

When you select the trigger, you will be prompted to enter the name of the function and the authorization level. See Figure 6-12.

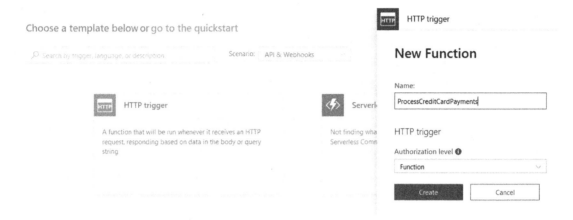

Figure 6-12. *Function properties*

The script editor window will open, as shown in Figure 6-13. This is where you write the function. Please note that the example given here is a simple one, and we will not go into the details of implementing the payment gateway because that is out of the scope of this book. This example will demonstrate when the state is changed on the Dynamics 365 end; then it will trigger the function via JavaScript.

Figure 6-13. *Function editor window*

Replace the default code with the following code. Please note that you can create this function using Visual Studio and publish it directly to your Azure subscription. For more information, visit https://docs.microsoft.com/en-us/azure/azure-functions/functions-develop-vs and https://docs.microsoft.com/en-us/azure/azure-functions/functions-create-your-first-function-visual-studio. To keep things simple, this example will be created using the default browser-based editor.

```
#r "Newtonsoft.Json"

using System.Net;
using Microsoft.AspNetCore.Mvc;
using Microsoft.Extensions.Primitives;
using Newtonsoft.Json;

public static async Task<IActionResult> Run(HttpRequest req, ILogger log)
{
  log.LogInformation("Credit Card Payment request recieved...");
  string cardHoldersName, expiryDate, cardNumber, amount;

  cardHoldersName = req.Query["cardHoldersName"];
  expiryDate = req.Query["expiryDate"];
  cardNumber = req.Query["cardNumber"];
  amount = req.Query["amount"];

  string requestBody = await new StreamReader(req.Body).ReadToEndAsync();
  dynamic data = JsonConvert.DeserializeObject(requestBody);
  cardHoldersName = cardHoldersName ?? data?.cardHoldersName;
  expiryDate = expiryDate ?? data?.expiryDate;
  cardNumber = cardNumber ?? data?.cardNumber;
  amount = amount ?? data?.amount;

  // Payment Gateway Implementation

  if(cardHoldersName == null)
  {
      return new BadRequestObjectResult
      ("Please pass a name on the query string or in the request body");
  }
```

```
return (ActionResult)new OkObjectResult
($"Payment processed successfully: {cardHoldersName} - {cardNumber}");
}
```

You can test the function by navigating to the Test tab in the right pane. After entering the JSON, click the Run button. Figure 6-14 shows the output. You can see the test result in the output window and the logs in the Logs window on the bottom of the screen. This will help you to ensure your function is working and accept the data as JSON.

Figure 6-14. *Testing the function*

Consuming the Azure Function

As the next step, you will have to create the JavaScript file, which will be used to call the function. But before that, you need to click the </> Get Function URL link next to the Run button and copy the URL with the key. See Figure 6-15.

```
run.csx                    Save              ▶ Run.        </> Get function URL

1  #r "Newtonsoft.Json"
2
3  using System.Net;
4  using Microsoft.AspNetCore.Mvc;
5  using Microsoft.Extensions.Primitives;
6  using Newtonsoft.Json;
7
8  public static async Task<IActionResult>
9  {
10     log.LogInformation("C# HTTP trigger function processed a request.");
11
12     string cardholdername = req.Query["cardholdername"];
13     string expirydate = req.Query["expirydate"];
14
15     string requestBody = await new StreamReader(req.Body).ReadToEndAsync();
16     dynamic data = JsonConvert.DeserializeObject(requestBody);
17     cardholdername = cardholdername ?? data?.cardholdername;
18     expirydate = expirydate ?? data?.expirydate;
19
20     return cardholdername != null
21         ? (ActionResult)new OkObjectResult($"Hello, {cardholdername} \nCard Expiry: {expirydate}")
22         : new BadRequestObjectResult("Please pass a name on the query string or in the request body");
23  }
24
```

Get function URL   ✕

Key   URL
default (Function key) ▾   https://sbmacreditcardprocessing.azurewebsites.ne   ⧉ Copy
                                  t/api/ProcessCreditCardPayment?code=ISCPrJwBXdpk8
                                  bbTI8Y8YIbawj9cNPo8Cg/DotanIAnrb9XEepoQ==

Figure 6-15. *Copy function URL and the key*

Before leaving, you must configure cross-origin resource sharing (CORS) so that you can consume your function from Dynamics 365. Navigate back to the Functions app and select the Platform Features tab. As shown in Figure 6-16, click the CORS icon, and you will be prompted to enter the URL. Enter the instance URL and click Save.

Figure 6-16. *Configuring CORS*

Now it is time to enter the JavaScript that calls the function. The following JavaScript code invokes the function:

```javascript
(function (SBMA)
{
 //constants
  Constants = function () {
      this.CALLING_MODULE = "sbma_MemberPayments.js";
      this.AZURE_BASE_ENDPOINT = "https://sbmacreditcardprocessing.azure
                                  websites.net/api/";
      this.AZURE_FUNCTION_ENDPOINT = "ProcessCreditCardPayment?code=
      ISCPrJwBXdpk8bbTI8Y8yBYIbawj9cNPo8Cg/DotanIAnrb9XEepoQ==";
      this.FORM_TYPE_UPDATE = 2;
      this.SUCESS_MESSAGE = "Payment processed successfully.";
      this.FAILURE_MESSAGE = "Payment failed.";

      return this;
  }();

  var formContext = null;

  SBMA.processCCPayment = function (executionContext) {
      formContext = executionContext.getFormContext();

      var formType = formContext.ui.getFormType();
      var fieldValue = formContext.getAttribute("sbma_paymentstatus").
      getValue();
      alert(fieldValue);

      if (formType === Constants.FORM_TYPE_UPDATE) {
        if (fieldValue === 646150001) {
          var ccPayment = {
              cardHoldersName:
                formContext.getAttribute("sbma_nameoncard").getValue(),
              expiryDate:
                formContext.getAttribute("sbma_cardexpirydate").getValue(),
```

```
                cardNumber:
                  formContext.getAttribute("sbma_ccnumber").getValue(),
                amount: formContext.getAttribute("sbma_amountdue").getValue()
         };
         executeAzureFunction(ccPayment, paymentSuccessHandler,
         paymentFailureHandler);
        }
      }
  };

  paymentSuccessHandler = function (response) {
      formContext.ui.setFormNotification(SUCESS_MESSAGE, "INFO", null);
  };

  paymentFailureHandler = function (response) {
      formContext.ui.setFormNotification(FAILURE_MESSAGE, "ERROR", null);
  };

  executeAzureFunction = function (payment, successHandler, failureHandler)
{
      var endpoint = Constants.AZURE_BASE_ENDPOINT + Constants.AZURE_
      FUNCTION_ENDPOINT;
      var req = new XMLHttpRequest();
      req.open("POST", endpoint, true);
      req.setRequestHeader("Accept", "application/json");
      req.setRequestHeader("Content-Type", "application/json; charset=utf-8");
      req.setRequestHeader("OData-MaxVersion", "4.0");
      req.setRequestHeader("OData-Version", "4.0");
      req.onreadystatechange = function () {
          if (this.readyState === 4) {
              req.onreadystatechange = null;

              if (this.status === 200) {
                  successHandler(JSON.parse(this.response));
              }
```

```
        else {
                failureHandler(JSON.parse(this.response).error);
        }
      }
  };
  req.send(window.JSON.stringify(payment));
};
})(window.AzureServicesLib = window.AzureServicesLib || {});
```

Now you need to combine the JavaScript code with the OnChange event of the Payment Status field of the Member Payment form. So, when you change the status to Paid, you will see that the form notification appears, meaning that the request has been successfully sent to the function and the function returned a success message. See Figure 6-17.

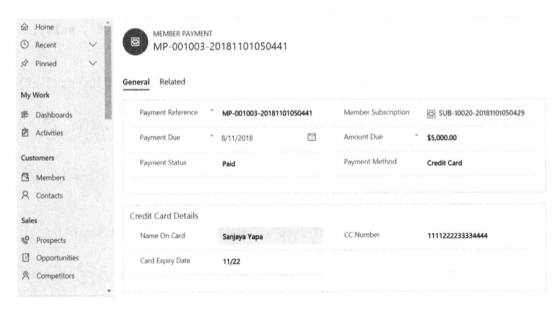

Figure 6-17. *OnChange event triggered the function and the success message*

In terms of best practices, one other option to consume an Azure function is to register it as a webhook using the plugin registration tool. Open the plugin registration tool and connect to your Dynamics 365 instance. In the Register menu, click the Register New Web Hook option, as shown in Figure 6-18.

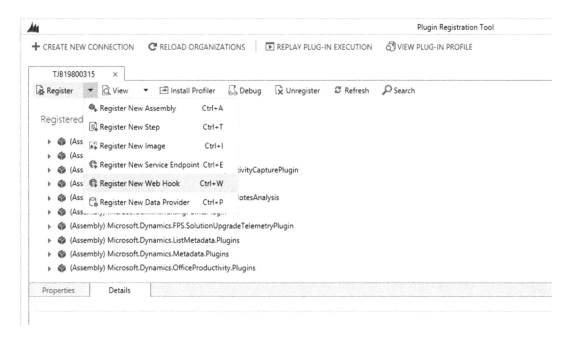

Figure 6-18. *Registering a new webhook with the plugin registration tool*

Specify the name of the webhook. In the Endpoint URL field, paste the URL copied from without the code/key. For the authentication, select WebhookKey and paste in the key, as shown in Figure 6-19.

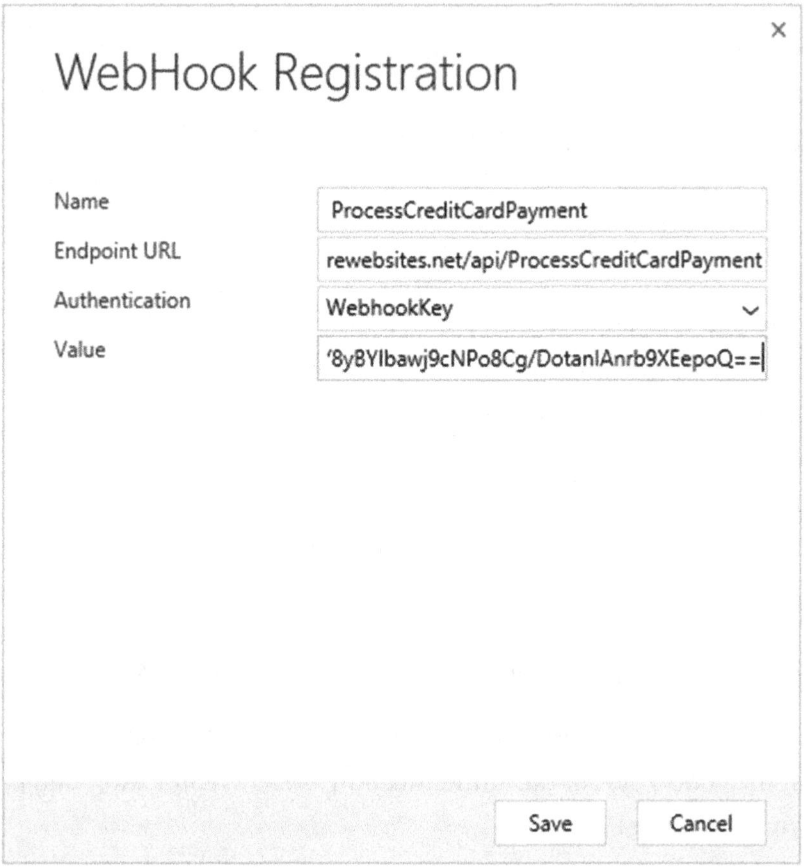

Figure 6-19. *Webhook settings*

There's one important thing to remember with the key here. For demonstration purposes, we have used the default key. From the Manage option in the Azure portal, you can have more than one key. Best of all, you can revoke or renew any key if you found out that the key has been compromised. Just click the "Add new function key" button. See Figure 6-20.

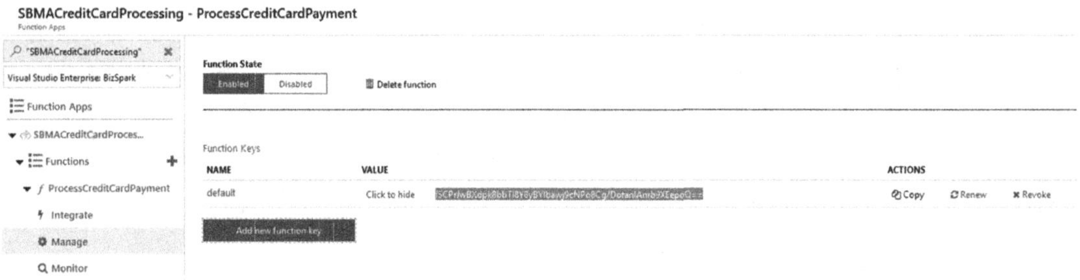

Figure 6-20. *Adding a new function key option*

Then the screen will display the settings for the configuring the key. As instructed, leave the Key field blank to generate it automatically. See Figure 6-21.

Figure 6-21. *New function key settings*

Click the Save button, and your new key will be generated, which you can use with the webhook registration. See Figure 6-22.

Figure 6-22. *New function key generated*

As shown in Figure 6-22, you can renew and revoke the function keys. Moving back to the plugin registration tool step, when you click Save after entering the key, the webhook gets registered, and now you can register the steps on it.

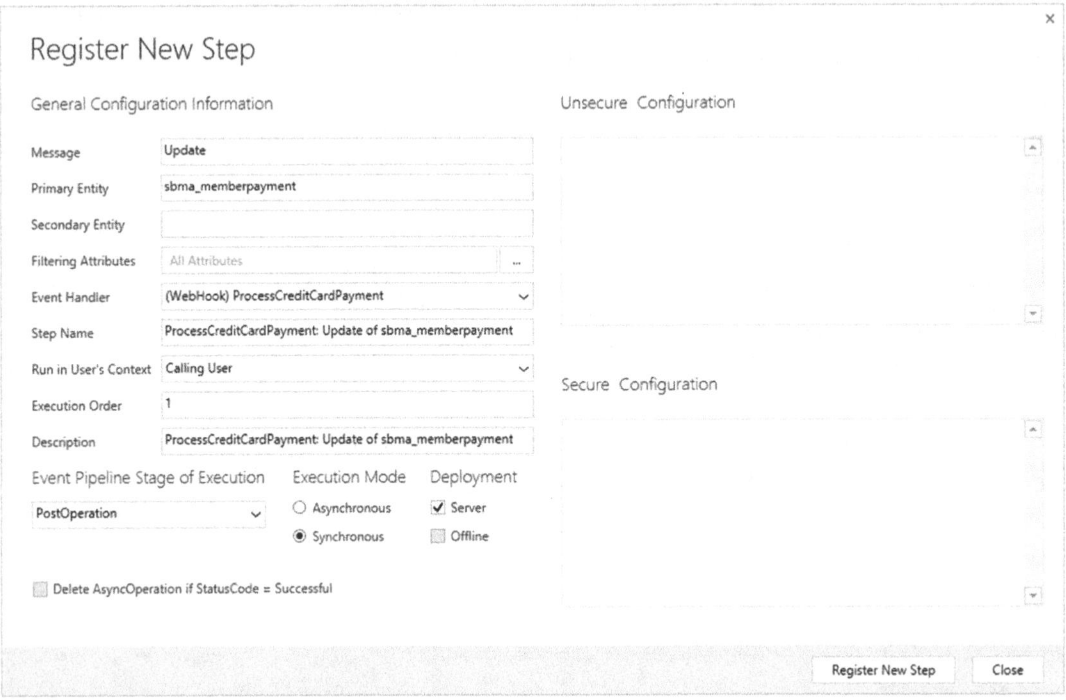

Figure 6-23. *Registering the new step for a webhook*

This is a simple example of how you can communicate with the functions provided by the Azure Functions feature. You can use the concept to implement more complex scenarios. In the next section, we will look at another popular Azure integration, Azure Logic Apps.

Integrating Azure Logic Apps with Dynamics 365

Azure Logic Apps is considered Microsoft's offering for enterprise-scale integration and workflow in the cloud. With it you can off-load heavy integrations easily and quickly with a low cost. This service is part of the platform as a service (PaaS) offering from Microsoft. Even though you can develop custom workflow applications to meet your integration needs, you should consider Logic Apps because it provides an out-of-the-box retry policy that eliminates extra coding. Also, the true power comes with its automatic scalability, eradicating the requirements of additional VMs.

Azure Logic Apps provides a vast diversity of integration points including Dynamics 365. You can learn more about these integration points at `https://docs.microsoft.com/en-us/azure/connectors/apis-list`. Also, Logic Apps has built-in triggers that kick off the workflow. For instance, an event could be receiving an e-mail or detecting a change in an Azure Storage account that triggers the Logic Apps engine and creates a new logic instance that runs the workflow. Next, the execution moves to the actions, which are all the steps or tasks that should happen after the trigger. These actions could be managed connections, custom API calls via Azure Functions, or custom connections. Logic Apps also include enterprise capabilities with BizTalk Server.

You can create apps in Logic Apps with Visual Studio, Visual Studio Code, and Azure Portal.

- Visual Studio: `https://docs.microsoft.com/en-us/azure/logic-apps/quickstart-create-logic-apps-with-visual-studio`

- Visual Studio Code: `https://docs.microsoft.com/en-us/azure/logic-apps/quickstart-create-logic-apps-visual-studio-code`

- Azure Portal: `https://docs.microsoft.com/en-us/azure/logic-apps/quickstart-create-first-logic-app-workflow`

Similar to Logic Apps, Microsoft Flow is becoming popular as the go-to workflow engine for Dynamics 365. We discussed this in Chapter 4. The following is a high-level comparison between Logic Apps and Microsoft Flow:

- Logic Apps is more suitable for advanced developer integration scenarios, whereas Microsoft Flow is for self-service workflows that power users can create and use.

- Unlike Microsoft Flow, Logic Apps involves a running cost. It incorporates the pay-per-usage costing model. Microsoft Flow, on the other hand, has a free tier with 750 flow executions per month. Flow plan 1, which is a paid plan, increases the executions to 4,500. Flow plan 2, which is known as the premium plan, increases the executions to 15,000 flows per month.

- You can use the browser and Visual Studio to design Logic Apps workflows, but Microsoft Flow workflows can be designed in the browser only.

- Microsoft Flow workflows can be easily designed and tested in a nonproduction environment and then promoted to the production environment. Logic Apps workflows can be source controlled, tested, and automated and managed via Azure Resource Management.

- Since Logic Apps uses the Azure Portal as its backbone, Logic Apps workflows have more management and monitoring options for administrators; troubleshooting is much easier as well.

Since both options have their own pros and cons, you must wonder when to use these technologies. When you do not have an Azure subscription but you must implement a workflow, then the Microsoft Flow free tier is the go-to workflow engine. Microsoft Flow is part of the Power Platform, so you can easily manipulate data with the Common Data Service using the workflows created by Microsoft Flow. Azure Logic Apps comes into action when you need more control over your development in more complex integration scenarios on an enterprise scale. As mentioned, if you want automation and source control, then you should go for Logic Apps.

Among various integration points, Azure Logic Apps comes with Dynamics 365 connectors, and in this section you will look at a scenario where connectors are used in relation to the SBMA membership application.

The Azure Logic Apps Solution

This scenario is again related to membership payments. In this application, there are two different types of payments, credit card and direct debit payments. For direct debit payments, a list of payments must be sent to the bank on a given day to process the payments. So, for all the direct debit payments, the payment details including the account number, bank code, amount, and account name must be sent to the bank or the direct debit processing services. The bank will process the payments and send a file that contains the successful and failed payments. The process should pick up this file and update the Dynamics 365 solution accordingly.

You could write a custom workflow, but this is cumbersome and time-consuming, and you might end up spending more money just for the implementation. Let's look at how you can implement this scenario in Azure Logic Apps. We will be using Visual Studio to create and publish the apps. Let's open the SBMA solution and add a new project. See Figure 6-24.

Figure 6-24. *Selecting the project type*

Select the Logic App template from the template list, and click OK, as shown in Figure 6-25.

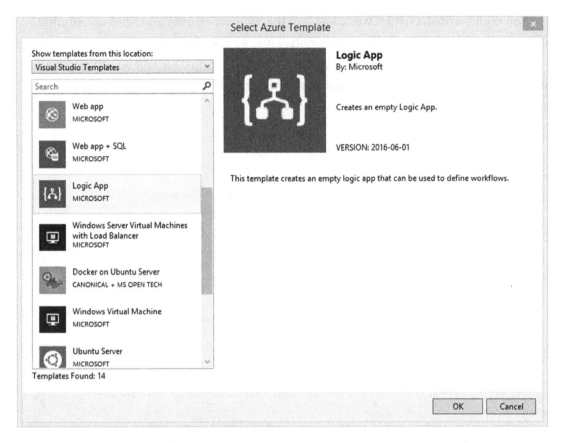

Figure 6-25. *Selecting the Logic App template*

Visual Studio will create the project; you can see that there are three files created under the project. Right-click the `LogicApp.json` file, and click Open with the Logic App Designer (Ctrl+L). You will have to log into your Azure subscription at this point. Once you're logged in successfully, Visual Studio will open the Logic App properties window; now click Create New from the Resource Group drop-down, provide the details of the resource group, and click OK. See Figure 6-26.

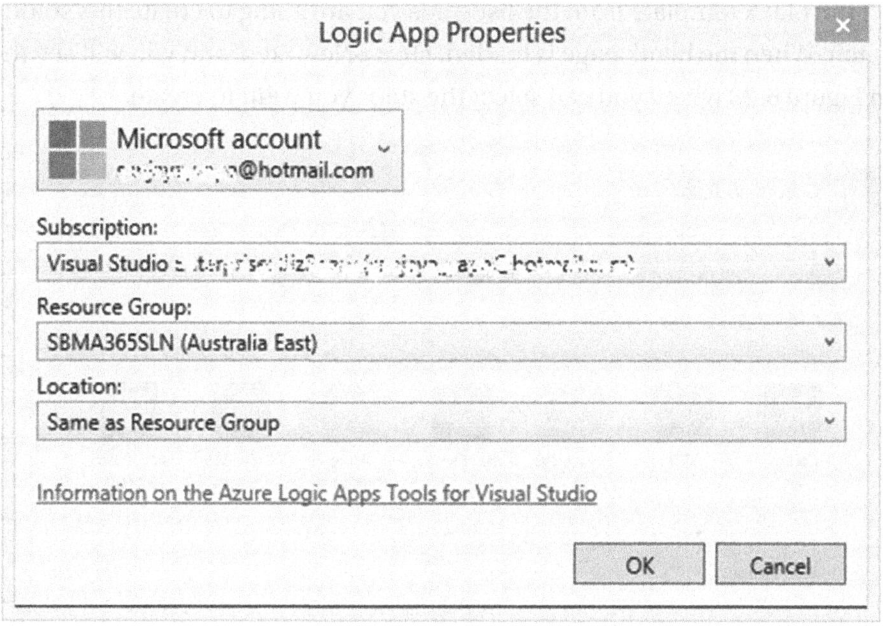

Figure 6-26. *Logic App Properties window*

Visual Studio will load the `LogicApp.json` file, as shown in Figure 6-27. You can see that there are many built-in templates that you can use if they match up with your requirements.

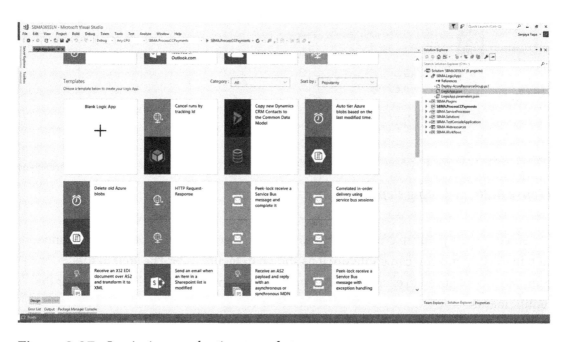

Figure 6-27. *Logic Apps, selecting templates*

Select the blank template from the list since you are going to create this solution from scratch. When the blank page is loaded, click +New Step, and you will see the dialog shown in Figure 6-28 where you can select the steps you want to create.

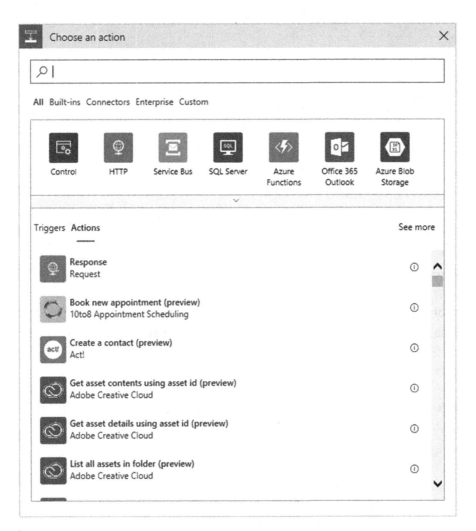

Figure 6-28. *Selecting steps*

Since you are going to create a process that is recurring, search for the Recurrence step in the list, and you can configure it as shown in Figure 6-29. The step in the example is configured to execute every three minutes, but it can be changed as per the requirements.

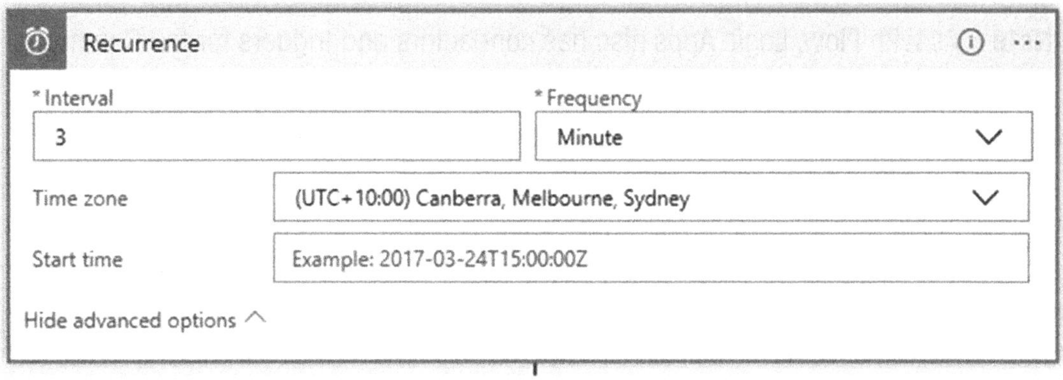

Figure 6-29. *Configuring the recurring step*

The next step is to get the pending direct debit payment records from the Dynamics 365. There are a few Dynamics 365 endpoints that you can choose. For this instance, you need to list all the records filtered by Payment Status and Payment Method. Therefore, you select the "List records" steps. When you add the Dynamics 365 endpoints, you will have to connect your step to the Dynamics 365 instance. Once you enter the credentials and have successfully connected to the instance, you will see the organization name and all the entities. We will be using the Member Payments entity. See Figure 6-30.

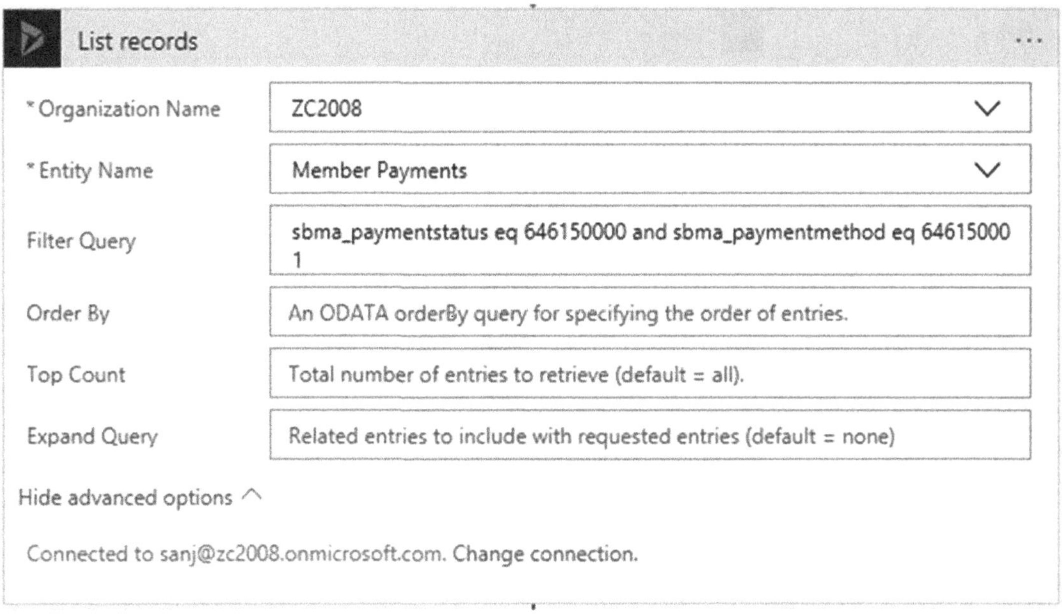

Figure 6-30. *Configuring Dynamics 365 list step*

Note   As with Flow, Logic Apps also has connectors and triggers for the Common Data Service. You can find more information about Common Data Services at `https://docs.microsoft.com/en-us/powerapps/maker/common-data-service/data-platform-intro`.

As shown in Figure 6-31, the filter query has been configured using an OData query. You can learn more about OData queries at `https://docs.microsoft.com/en-us/rest/api/searchservice/odata-expression-syntax-for-azure-search`. For simplicity, this example will leave the other settings as the defaults. Now that you have retrieved data, the next step is to format it as a form accepted by the direct debit service of the client. Again, for simplicity, you will be creating a CSV-formatted file, but you can create any file type. To create a CSV-formatted file, you will be using the Create CSV table step. The output from the previous step, which is the value, will be used in the From field. In the Columns drop-down, if you select the Automatic option, then all the columns will be added to the CSV table. To avoid that, select the Custom option, enter the column names, and pick the value in the Add Dynamic Content window.

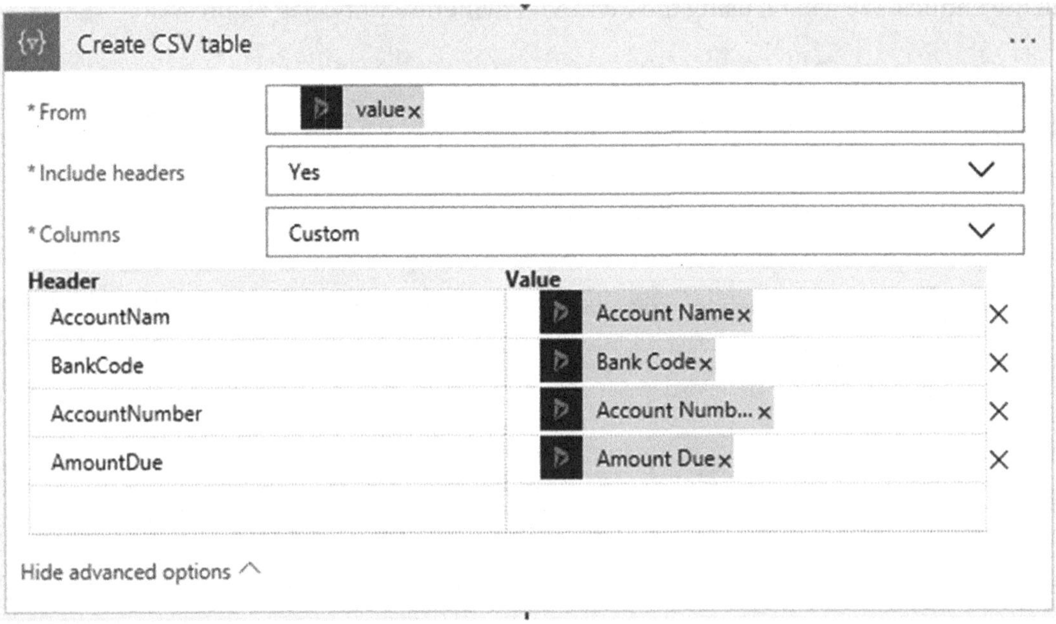

Figure 6-31. *Creating a CSV table*

When you click the Value column, the Add Dynamic Content window will be displayed on the side, as shown in Figure 6-32. You can see that all the columns are listed here, and you can pick only the columns you required.

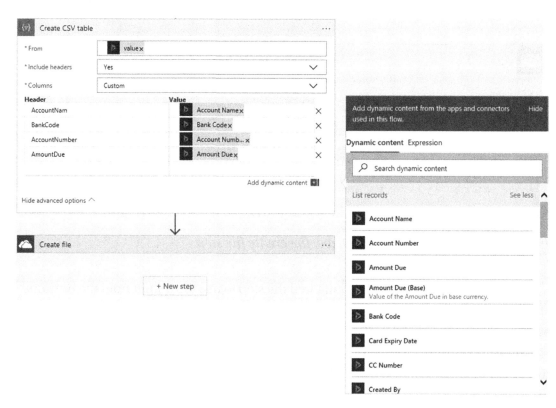

Figure 6-32. *"Dynamic content" window*

Finally, you must save the result set to a location. Here, we will be saving the file to a common location in OneDrive. Add the Create File step and configure it as shown in Figure 6-33. Pay close attention to the File Name field where it adds a date and time to avoid duplicates.

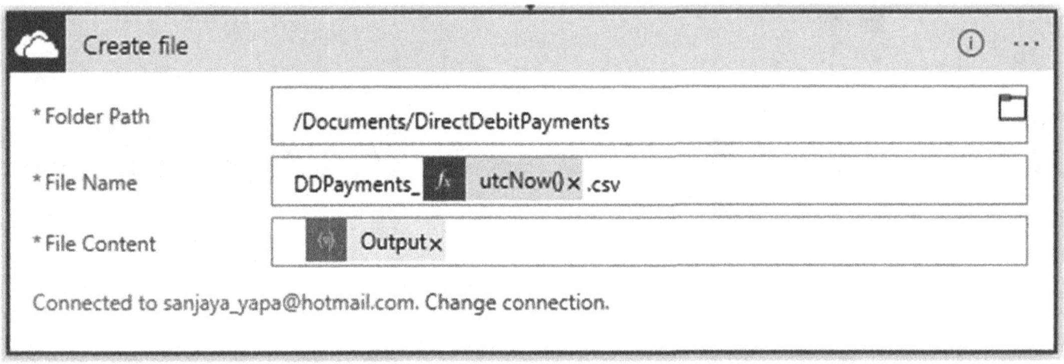

Figure 6-33. *Configuring OneDrive, the create file step*

For the file content, we have configured the step to use the output from the previous step. To add a unique file name, we have used a function to capture the date and time. When you click the File Name field, the Add Dynamic Content window will pop up. Go to the Expression tab, which has a whole plethora of various functions nicely categorized that will be displayed so you can build any expression. See Figure 6-34.

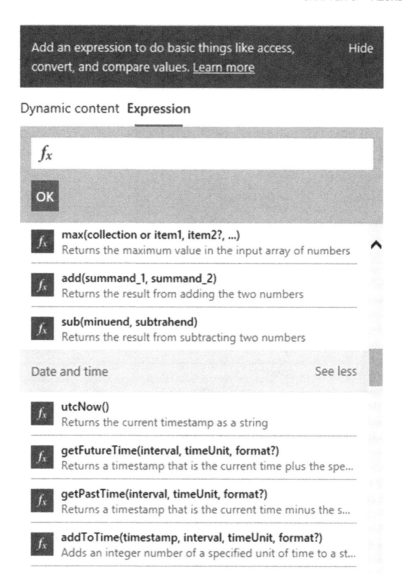

Figure 6-34. *Dynamic expressions*

Now that you have developed the logic app, the finished solution will look like Figure 6-35.

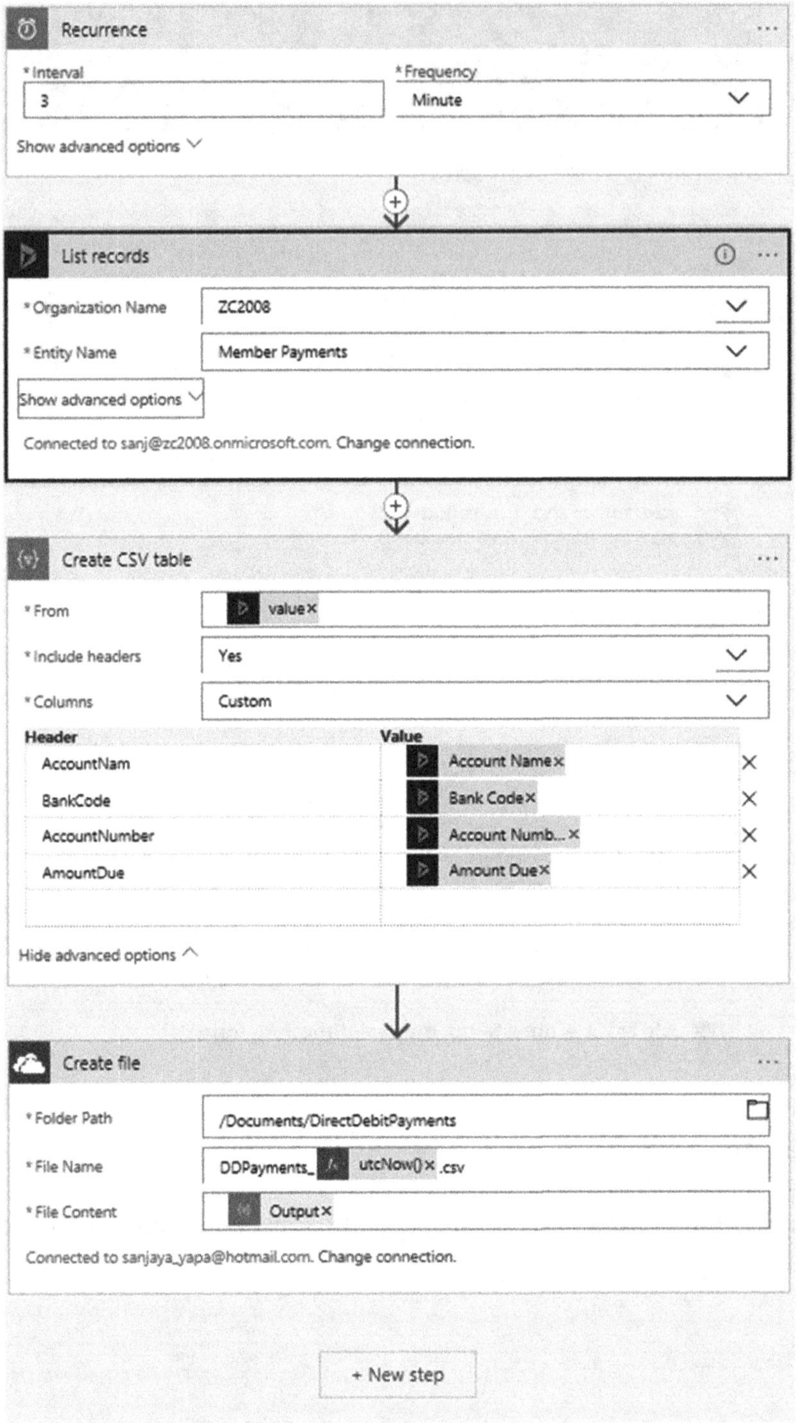

Figure 6-35. Completed workflow

Deploying the Project

Let's publish the workflow. Right-click the logic app project and click the Deploy option; you will be prompt with the window shown in Figure 6-36. Also note that, in this window, you will have to create a resource group, so make sure to log into your Azure account first.

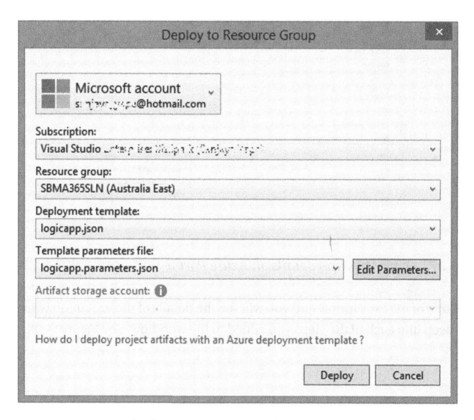

Figure 6-36. *Logic app deploy settings*

Once the app is deployed successfully, you will be able to see the application under Azure Logic Apps. You can run the application by clicking the Run button, and at the bottom of the window, the application execution details will be listed. It is easy to troubleshoot the workflow. See Figure 6-37.

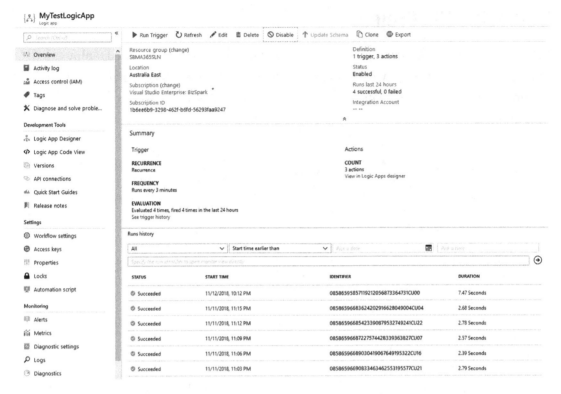

Figure 6-37. *Logic Apps app details on Azure Portal*

Click one of the executions, and you will see the details of the execution where you can drill deep into each of the steps you added to the workflow. See Figure 6-38.

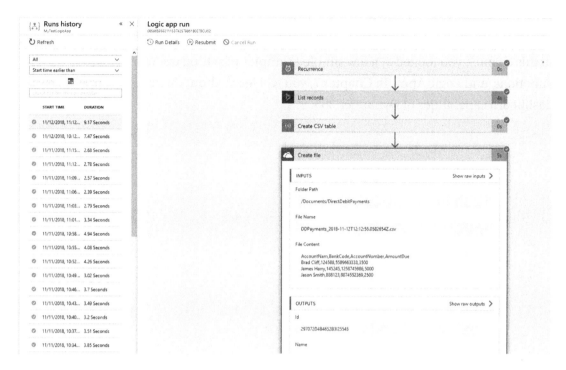

Figure 6-38. *Execution steps and details*

Figure 6-39 shows the file created in the given OneDrive location.

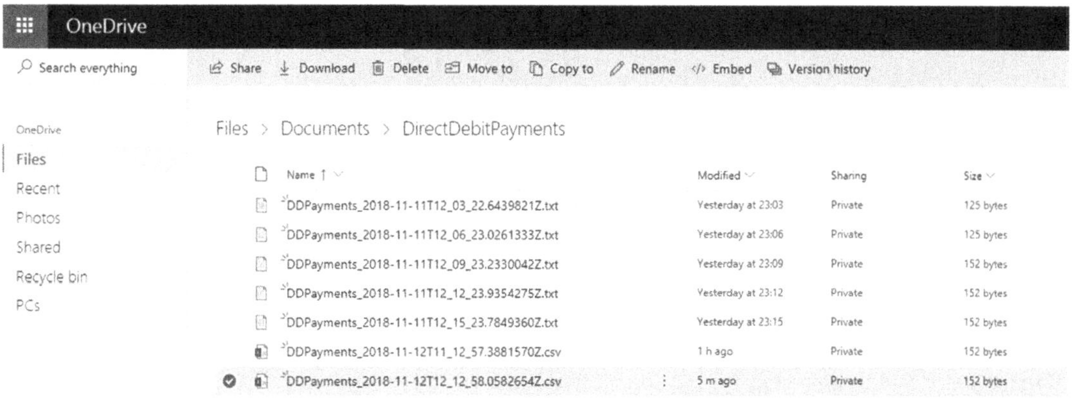

Figure 6-39. *Logic Apps app output created at the provided OneDrive location*

Summary

In this chapter, you looked at a few simple examples of setting up Azure WebJobs, Functions, and Logic Apps. In Chapter 7, you will learn about the reporting and dashboard capabilities of Dynamics 365.

CHAPTER 7

Reports

In every organization, decision-makers rely on various reports to drive the business to success. Therefore, with every software development project there is always a requirement to develop reports, and Dynamics 365 is equipped with state-of-the-art reporting capabilities. These reports range from simple queries to more advanced reports with complex queries. Also, one of the key features of the Dynamics 365 is its dashboard capability, which provides some nice data visualizations with drill-down capabilities.

In this chapter, you'll learn how to create simple queries with Advanced Find views. Also, Dynamics 365 comes with a report editing wizard that enables power users to create reports with moderate complexity. If users require reports with more advanced queries, then they have the option to use Fetch XML–based reports. In addition, Dynamics 365 supports integration with Power BI and extends its dashboard capabilities. We will discuss all these and show examples of them in this chapter.

Grid Filters

Grids in Dynamics 365 provide valuable information. That is, in every area of the application all the records in the system can be viewed via grids. In the grid columns, you will see an icon that looks like a funnel indicating a filter can be applied to the column. Click the icon, and a small pop-up window will appear where you can specify the filter. As shown in Figure 7-1, you even have the option to combine two filters. End users have the option utilize these filters to extract the data they want.

© Sanjaya Yapa 2019
S. Yapa, *Customizing Dynamics 365*, https://doi.org/10.1007/978-1-4842-4379-4_7

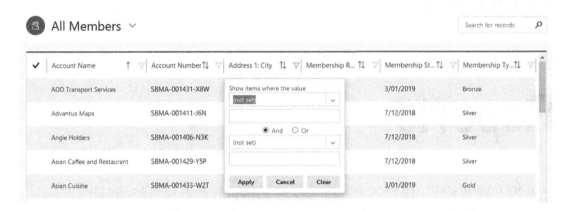

Figure 7-1. *Grid filters*

In addition to the grid filters, each grid is equipped with index filtering. This feature is available at the bottom of the grid, as shown in Figure 7-2.

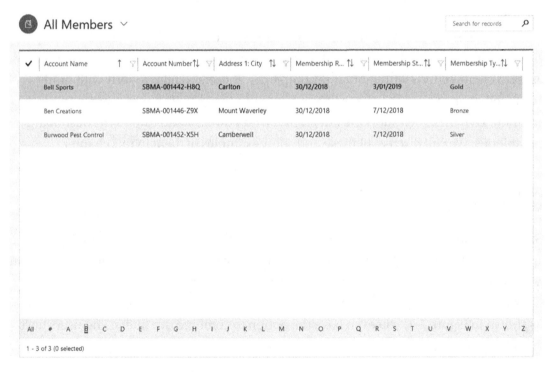

Figure 7-2. *Index filtering*

As you can see, the arrow on each column indicates that the column can be sorted. In the previous example, the results are filtered in ascending order on the account name, identified by the arrow directing upward. The other columns show two arrows; one is pointing up, and the other is pointing down, meaning the column is not sorted yet.

All these features can be considered as the simplest form of reporting. Let's take reporting to the next level by looking at Advanced Find views.

Advanced Find Views

Advanced Find views are the simplest form of reporting in Dynamics 365. They are useful when customers or users come to you and ask for a certain set of data based on some given criteria. The majority of these queries are for supporting daily tasks and can be implemented with Advanced Find views easily. This section will demonstrate how to create an Advanced Find view and share it with users. Let's assume a scenario where, in our sample solution, the membership manager wants to know the upcoming subscriptions where the membership type is Silver and the subscription status is Pending. You can easily extract this information using Advanced Find.

To create the view, navigate to the Member Subscription entity and click the filter button on the main title bar of Dynamics 365. This displays the Advanced Find editor. Here you can add the conditions to filter the data. See Figure 7-3.

Figure 7-3. *Advanced Find editor*

For this scenario, you must use the conditions shown in Figure 7-4. You simply pick them up from the drop-down lists available.

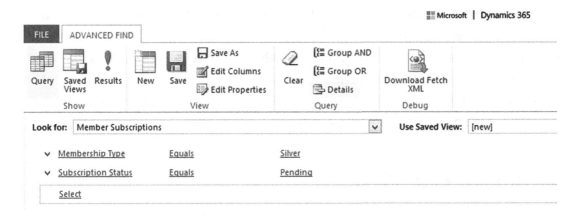

Figure 7-4. Adding filter criteria to an Advanced Find view

When you click the lookup button next to the filter, you will be directed to the Look Up Records window to select a specific value. See Figure 7-5.

Look Up Records   ×

Enter your search criteria.

Look for	Membership Type ☑
Look in	Membership Type Lookup Vie ☑
Search	Search for records 🔍

☐	Name	Created On	↻
☑	Silver	18/11/2018 9:21 ...	
	Bronze	18/11/2018 9:21 ...	
	Gold	18/11/2018 9:22 ...	

1 - 4 of 4 (1 selected)   ◀◀ ◀   Page 1   ▶

Selected records:

🔺 Silver

| Select |
| Remove |

| New | | Add | Cancel |

Figure 7-5. Selecting the lookup values

It's the same for the option set values; in other words, when you click the button next to the value field of the filter, you will be taken to a Select Value pop-up to select the option set values. After configuring the filters, the next step is to add the required columns. If there are any requirements to use multiple filters, then right-click the row and click the Select Row option. See Figure 7-6.

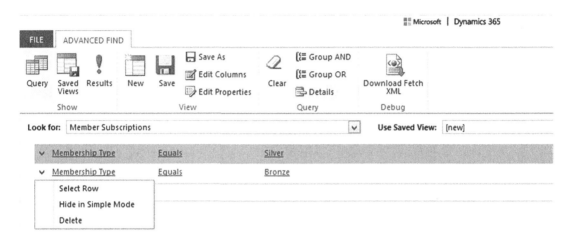

Figure 7-6. *Selecting filter rows*

After that, you can group your conditions using either the Group AND or Group OR option available on the ribbon. Figure 7-7 illustrates the two conditions combined with Group OR. Figure 7-8 shows XXX.

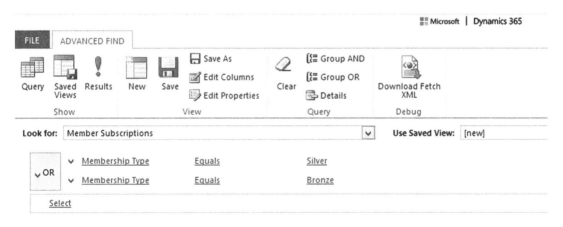

Figure 7-7. *Condition grouping*

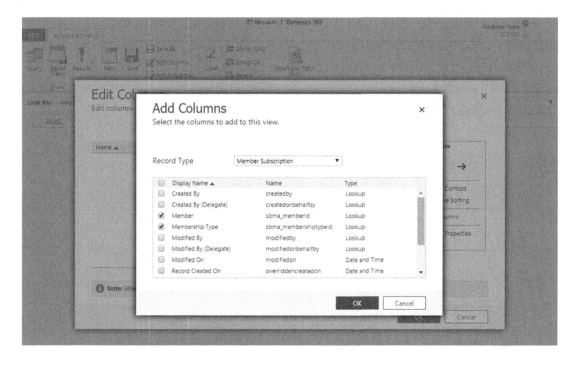

Figure 7-8. *Adding the required columns*

Based on the content of the column, the default length may not be enough to view the content, meaning that when the query is executed, the content will be truncated. To increase the column width, click Change Properties. See Figure 7-9.

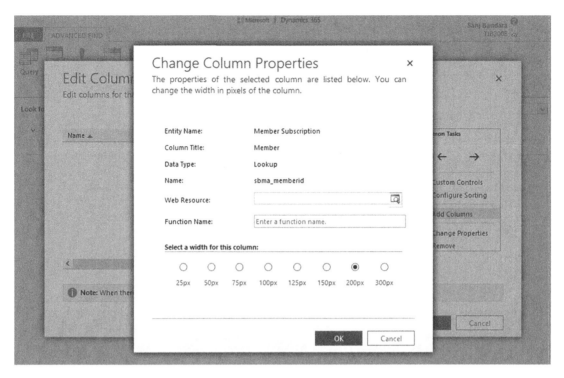

Figure 7-9. *Changing the column properties*

For Advanced Find views, you also can add the columns from the related entities that you have used in the query. The related entities are listed by record type. To view the output of the report, click the Results button on the ribbon. See Figure 7-10.

	Member	Name ↑	Membership Type	Subscription Due Dat...	Subscription Status	Subscription Fee (Me...	
	Advantus Maps	SUB-01000-20181128113642	Silver	5/12/2018	Pending	$2,500.00	
	Angle Holders	SUB-01001-20181128113744	Silver	5/12/2018	Pending	$2,500.00	
	Asian Caffee and Restaurant	SUB-01002-20181128113747	Silver	5/12/2018	Pending	$2,500.00	
	DSHD Compter Repairs	SUB-01003-20181128113749	Bronze	5/12/2018	Pending	$1,500.00	
	Eldon Accounting	SUB-01004-20181128113749	Bronze	5/12/2018	Pending	$1,500.00	
	Hamilton Stationaries	SUB-01007-20181128113749	Bronze	5/12/2018	Pending	$1,500.00	
	Office Refrigerators and Air C...	SUB-01010-20181128113749	Bronze	5/12/2018	Pending	$1,500.00	
	Plymouth Rubber Products	SUB-01011-20181128113749	Silver	5/12/2018	Pending	$2,500.00	
	Avery 52 transpotation Services	SUB-01012-20181128113750	Silver	5/12/2018	Pending	$2,500.00	
	Holmes HEPA Air	SUB-01014-20181128113750	Bronze	5/12/2018	Pending	$1,500.00	
	Cardinal Slant	SUB-01017-20181128113750	Silver	5/12/2018	Pending	$2,500.00	
	SANFORD Builders	SUB-01020-20181128113750	Silver	5/12/2018	Pending	$2,500.00	
	COSAF Commercial Wire Shelvi...	SUB-01023-20181128113750	Bronze	5/12/2018	Pending	$1,500.00	
	The Photographers Club	SUB-01027-20181128113750	Bronze	5/12/2018	Pending	$1,500.00	
	Xerox 198 Coppiers	SUB-01028-20181128113750	Bronze	5/12/2018	Pending	$1,500.00	

1 - 15 of 15 (0 selected)   Page 1

Figure 7-10. *Advanced Find results*

The next task is to share the view with stakeholders. After creating the view, you must save it. Click the Save As button in the ribbon and give a meaningful name to the view so that the users can easily locate it. Once the view is saved, the saved view will appear in the Use Saved View drop-down, as illustrated in Figure 7-11.

Figure 7-11. *Saved views*

Click Saved Views in the ribbon, and you will be directed to list of saved views. Select the view you want share, click the Share button in the ribbon, and click Add User/Team on the left pane of the Share Saved View window. The list of users will be displayed, and you can share the view with target users. See Figure 7-12.

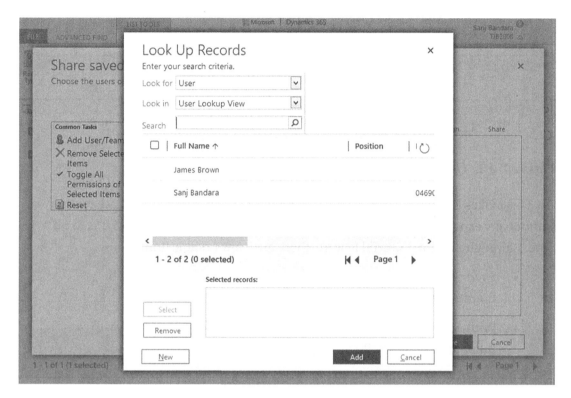

Figure 7-12. *Sharing the view with target users*

Now that the view is shared with the target users, they can view it in the list of views. These Advanced Find views are capable of querying related entities as well. As shown in Figure 7-13, you can build the query by drilling down to the related records.

Figure 7-13. Querying related records

This makes Advanced Find views a powerful tool to build quick and easy reports without any expertise. Especially power users can easily build a query like this in no time. Although this is a powerful feature, there are a few notable limitations.

- Even though you could query related entities, grouping cannot be done across the entities in the query.

- With Advanced Find views, you can query only related entities with inner joins but not with outer joins.

In the next section, we will discuss how to create reports with the Dynamics 365 Report Wizard.

Creating Reports with the Dynamics 365 Report Wizard

In scenarios where the stakeholders come up with complex reporting needs, you can use the Dynamics 365 Report Wizard. With it, you can easily create reports such as SQL Server Reporting Services reports within Dynamics 365. You can create reports with charts, tables, drill downs, and grouping capabilities. You can even share the reports with the colleagues. There are two types of reports in Dynamics 365.

- **SQL Server Reporting Services reports**: To build these reports, you can use SQL queries and filtered views, but this is not supported in Dynamics 365 online since you won't have access to the SQL database.

- **Fetch XML reports**: To build these reports, you must use Fetch XML queries to retrieve data from Dynamics 365. Reports that you create using the Dynamics 365 Report Wizard are Fetch-based reports.

When it comes to report security, all reports from the filtered views will filter the data based on the user's security role. If the person executing the report does not have permission to view the report, then the user can't view the report. By default, when the report is created, it can be used only by the owner of the report, unless it is shared. There are two settings available; the report is visible either to the organization or to the individual. *Organization* means that any user who is authorized to see reports within the organization can view the report, and *individual* means the report will be visible based on the user's security role. For instance, if user A belongs to Business Unit A and the scope of the report is set to Individual, then any user in Business Unit A who has read privileges to the report would be able to view the report. But someone from Business Unit B who has the same privileges would not be able to see the report.

The other cool thing about reports is that they can be included in a solution, which extends the visualization capabilities of Dynamics 365. Keep in mind that the reports owned by an organization can be included in a solution. In this section, you will learn how to create a simple report for the SBMA system. The stakeholders want to view the credit card payments that are paid for a given period.

So, let's navigate to Reports in the Marketing section of Dynamics 365. See Figure 7-14.

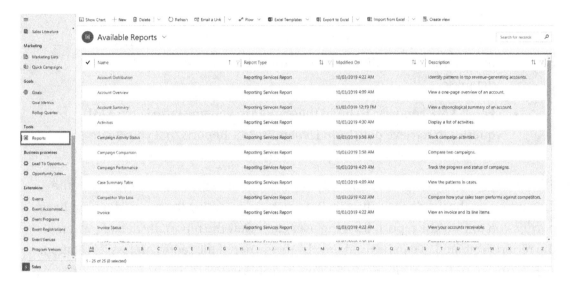

***Figure 7-14.** Dynamics 365 reports*

In the New Report window, make sure that Report Wizard Report is selected from the "Report type" drop-down. Under this field, click the Report Wizard button. You will be directed to the Get Started page where you must select the Start New Report option and click Next. In the Report Properties window, give the report a name, select the primary record type and the related record type, and click Next. Figure 7-15 shows the screen for adding the filters to select the required records.

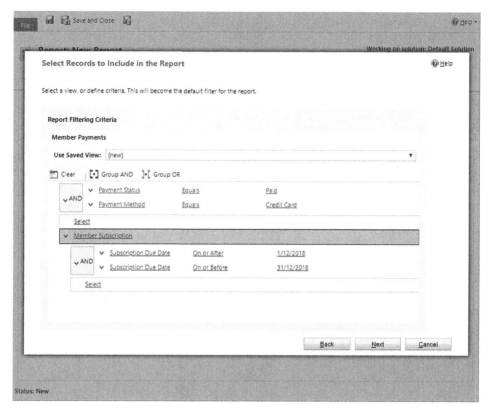

Figure 7-15. *Report filter settings*

As you can see, we have grouped the conditions using AND. First the query filters the payments and then it selects them by the related subscription due date. Once the filters are completed, on the next wizard page you can add the required columns to the report. As per the example, you must add the columns from the member payments first (see Figure 7-16).

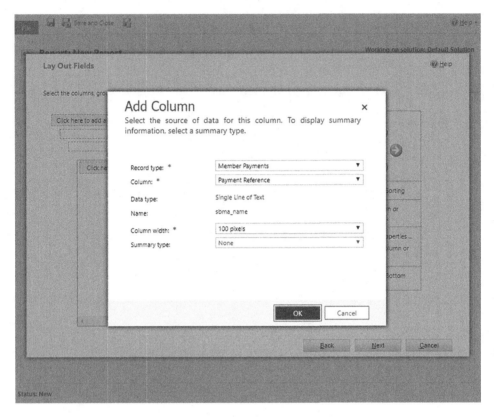

Figure 7-16. *Adding columns to a report*

Next add the columns from the Member Subscription entity. You can find the entity in the "Record type" drop-down. See Figure 7-17.

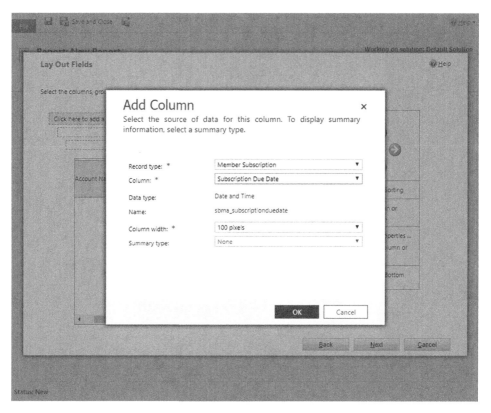

Figure 7-17. *Adding columns of the related entities*

After adding the columns, the next step is to group the records. On the same screen, click the "Click here to add a grouping." A pop-up to define the grouping will be displayed. See Figure 7-18.

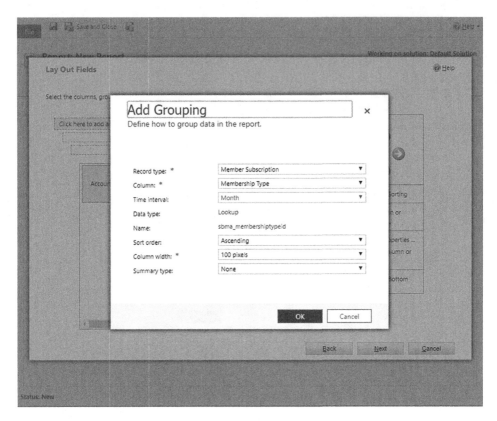

Figure 7-18. *Adding a grouping to the report*

As per the requirements, the stakeholders want to group the results by the type of membership. Once the grouping is completed, the settings will look like Figure 7-19.

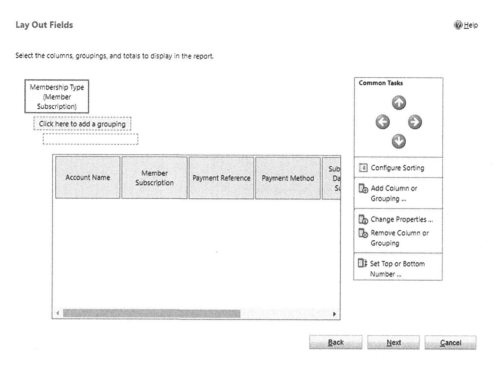

Figure 7-19. *Report data grouping completed*

Click the Next button to move to the next step to decide on the format of the report. For this example, we will be using the "Table only" format. See Figure 7-20.

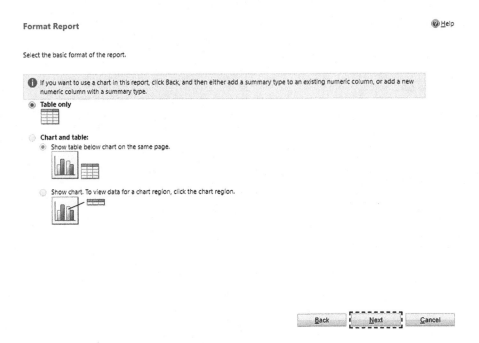

Figure 7-20. *Selecting the format of the report*

Click the Next button, and the report summary will be displayed. Click the Next button, and the report will be created. The system will display a notification if the report is successfully created. Click Finish to complete the configuration, and the report details will be displayed. See Figure 7-21.

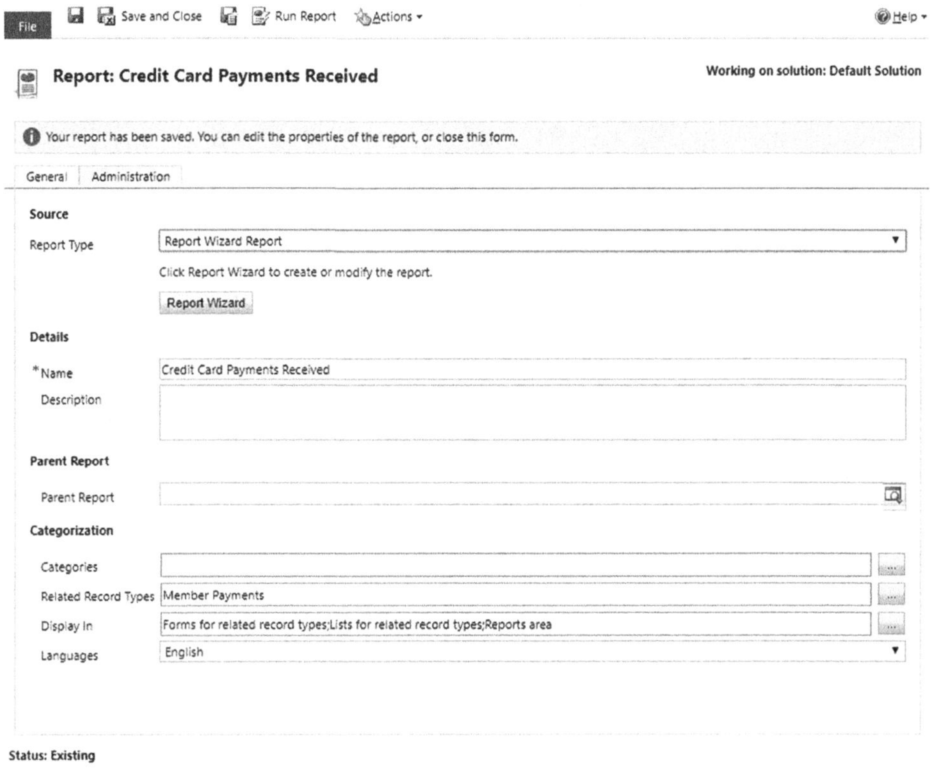

Figure 7-21. *Report details*

You can click the Run Report button with the lightning icon on the toolbar of the window, and the final output will be displayed, as shown in Figure 7-22.

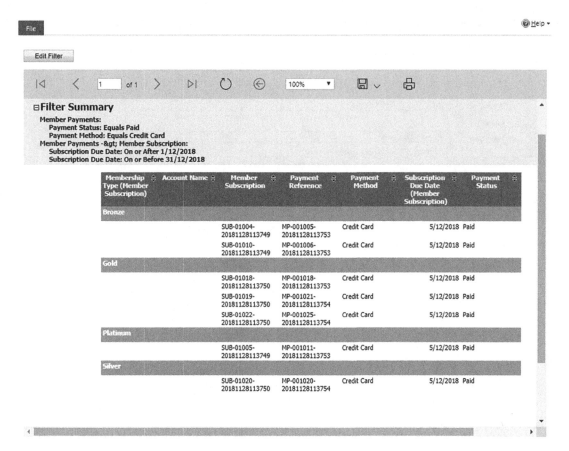

Figure 7-22. *Final output of the report*

If the stakeholders require any charts, it is just a matter of selecting the format of the report. Similar to the steps explained earlier, create the report, and for the step where the wizard asks you to select the report format, select the "Chart and table" option. You can see that this option is available only if your query has a summary field defined. For instance, if you want to show the sum of the amount due, then you can define the summary type at the point where you add the column, as shown in Figure 7-23.

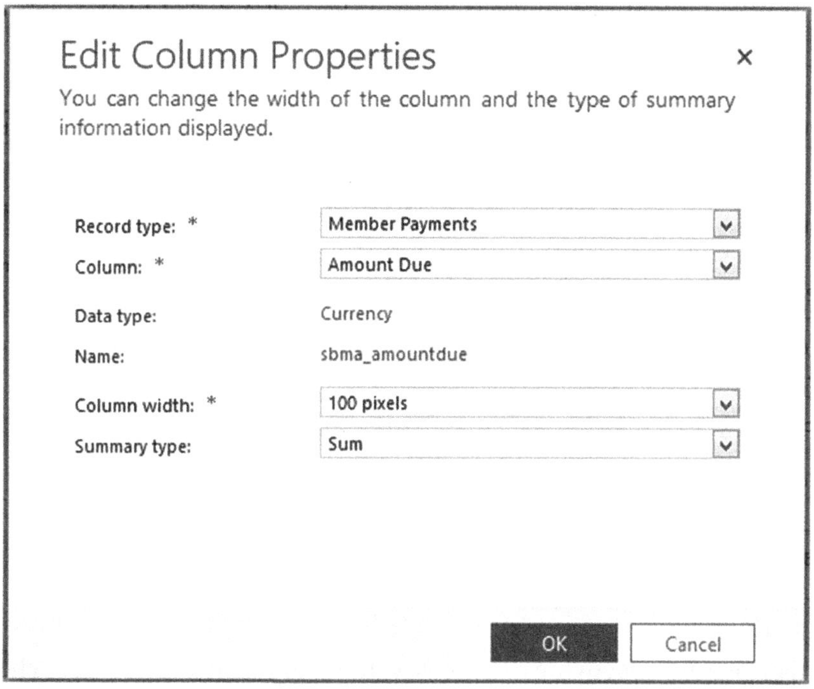

Figure 7-23. *Selecting the summary types*

As you can see, there are two options: "Show table below chart on the same page" and "Show chart." To view data for a chart region, click the chart again. See Figure 7-24.

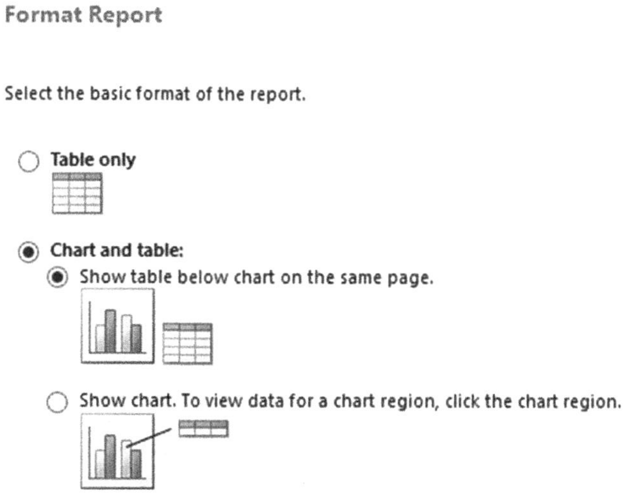

Figure 7-24. *Selecting the report format*

Like any other chart wizard, in the next step, select the chart type. For this example, a pie chart is selected. See Figure 7-25.

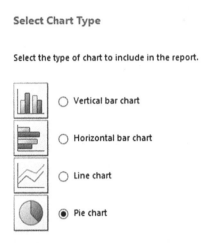

Select Chart Type

Select the type of chart to include in the report.

○ Vertical bar chart

○ Horizontal bar chart

○ Line chart

● Pie chart

Figure 7-25. *Selecting the chart type*

The final page is for specifying the slices, values, and labels. After specifying them, click the Next button. See Figure 7-26.

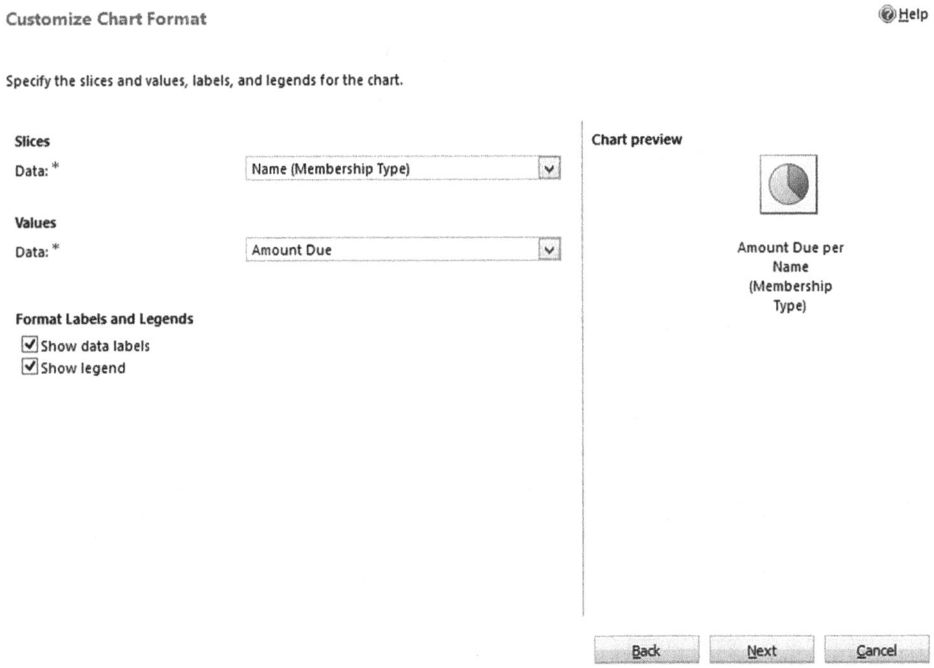

Customize Chart Format   ⓘ Help

Specify the slices and values, labels, and legends for the chart.

Slices

Data: *   [Name (Membership Type)   ▼]

Values

Data: *   [Amount Due   ▼]

Format Labels and Legends
☑ Show data labels
☑ Show legend

Chart preview

Amount Due per
Name
(Membership
Type)

[Back]   [Next]   [Cancel]

Figure 7-26. *Setting slices, values, and data*

The subsequent wizard page shows the progress of the report. Finally, the output will look like Figure 7-27.

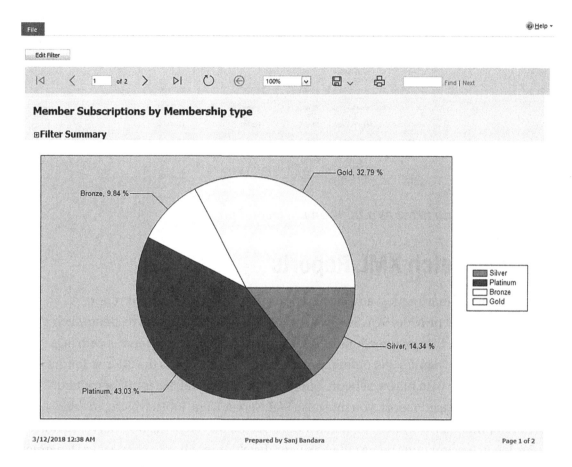

Figure 7-27. *Pie chart completed*

As per the initial settings, since the report is configured to display both the chart and the report, the data will be listed on the second page. See Figure 7-28.

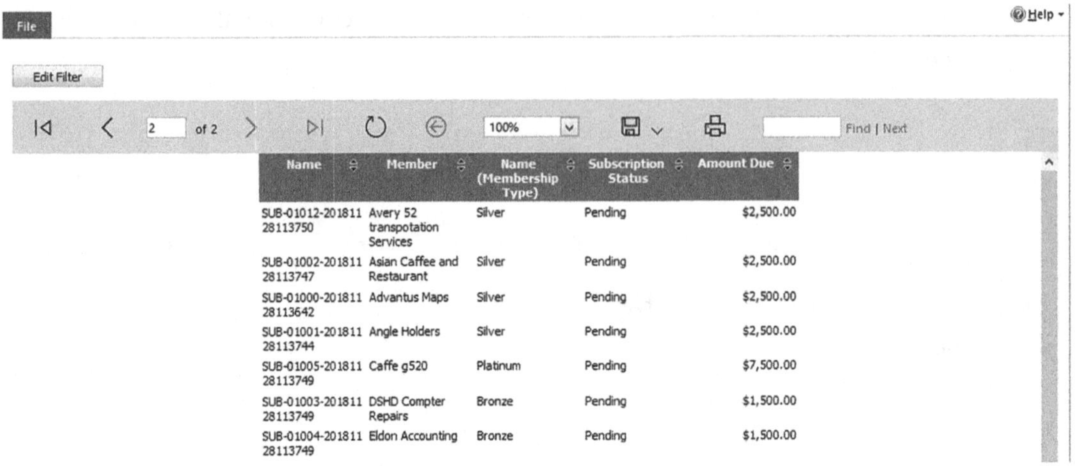

Name	Member	Name (Membership Type)	Subscription Status	Amount Due
SUB-01012-201811 28113750	Avery 52 transpotation Services	Silver	Pending	$2,500.00
SUB-01002-201811 28113747	Asian Caffee and Restaurant	Silver	Pending	$2,500.00
SUB-01000-201811 28113642	Advantus Maps	Silver	Pending	$2,500.00
SUB-01001-201811 28113744	Angle Holders	Silver	Pending	$2,500.00
SUB-01005-201811 28113749	Caffe g520	Platinum	Pending	$7,500.00
SUB-01003-201811 28113749	DSHD Compter Repairs	Bronze	Pending	$1,500.00
SUB-01004-201811 28113749	Eldon Accounting	Bronze	Pending	$1,500.00

Figure 7-28. *Data listed as a table on the second page*

Creating Fetch XML Reports

Sometimes users may request advanced reports that the out-of-the-box report capabilities do not provide. SQL Server Report is the preferred option to create such advanced reports. Previous versions of CRM supported SQL Server reports with SQL Queries. But on Dynamics 365 online, you must use Fetch XML as the queries for the data sets, because with online version, querying the SQL Database is not permitted. To create an advanced report, you must use SQL Server Data Tools, which provides the development environment in Visual Studio. As the first step, the SQL Server Report Authoring Extension must be installed on your development box to connect to Dynamics 365 as the data source.

This is where the issue pops up. That is, if you have Visual Studio 2017, then an error will display when installing the extension. The primary reason for this issue is that Visual Studio does not support the extension at the time of writing the book. The only way to overcome this issue is with Visual Studio 2015 as per the documentation: `https://www.microsoft.com/en-us/download/details.aspx?id=50375`. In the System Requirements section, you can see the highest Visual Studio version is Visual Studio 2015. Therefore, install Visual Studio 2015, then Business Intelligent Development Studio, and finally install SQL Server Report Authoring Extension.

Let's look at a quick example of listing members and subscriptions categorized under each membership type. Create a report project, and in the Reports folder of the solution, right-click the folder and click Add New Report. This example will be developed by using the Report Wizard, but you can create the report manually. See Figure 7-29.

Figure 7-29. *Adding a report file*

To start with, create a report using the Dynamics 365 Report Wizard and download the RDL file. This is a best practice that will give you a good starting point. As shown in Figure 7-29, add the RDL file to the solution as an existing file after copying it to the solution folder. This approach will automatically set the data source and the data set. Open the Data Source Properties window by double-clicking the data source. On the General tab, make sure that Type is Microsoft Dynamics 365 and Fetch is selected for the "Embedded connection" option. The organization URL as the connection string is automatically set. Click the Credentials button on the left of the Connection String pane and provide the credentials to access the Dynamics 365 instance. This example is for Dynamics 365 online; therefore, select "Use a specific user name and password" and click OK.

Next open the Dataset Properties window by double-clicking the data set. In this window, you can update the Fetch query as per the requirements. See Figure 7-30.

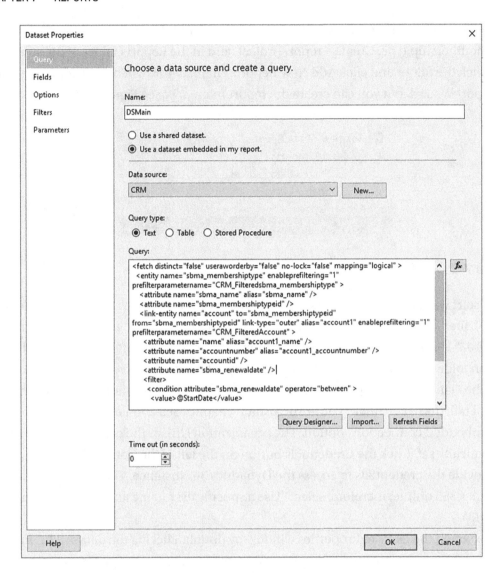

Figure 7-30. *Creating the Fetch XML query*

The simplest way to create a proper Fetch XML is to use the Fetch XML Builder plugin in XrmToolBox. Once the query is created, paste it in the Query string box in the form shown in Figure 7-30 and click OK to save the data set settings. Next you can alter the grouping, as shown in Figure 7-31. Double-click the highlighted grouping to alter the grouping as per your requirements. For this example, we added the grouping when we first created the report in the report wizard.

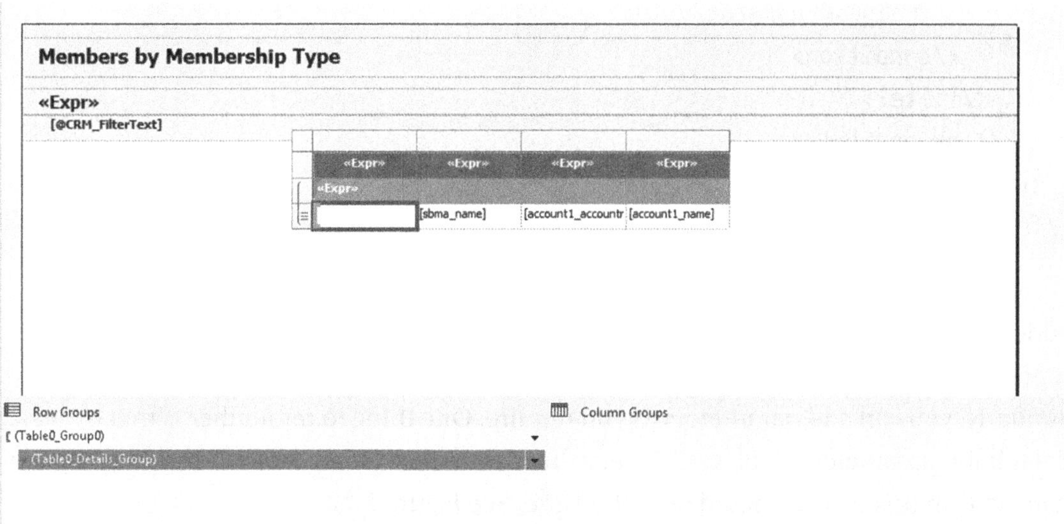

Figure 7-31. *Grouping and designing the table*

As shown in Listing 7-1, we have added two parameters to filter the report data. These are the parameters that are passed into the query when the user enables them to decide the scope based on the member's renewal date.

Listing 7-1. Fetch XML with Parameters

```
<fetch distinct="false" useraworderby="false" no-lock="false"
mapping="logical" >
  <entity name="sbma_membershiptype" enableprefiltering="1"
    prefilterparametername="CRM_Filteredsbma_membershiptype" >
    <attribute name="sbma_name" alias="sbma_name" />
    <attribute name="sbma_membershiptypeid" />
    <link-entity name="account" to="sbma_membershiptypeid"
       from="sbma_membershiptypeid" link-type="outer" alias="account1"
      enableprefiltering="1" prefilterparametername="CRM_FilteredAccount" >
      <attribute name="name" alias="account1_name" />
      <attribute name="accountnumber" alias="account1_accountnumber" />
      <attribute name="accountid" />
      <attribute name="sbma_renewaldate" />
      <filter>
        <condition attribute="sbma_renewaldate" operator="between" >
          <value>@StartDate</value>
```

231

```
        <value>@EndDate</value>
      </condition>
    </filter>
  </link-entity>
  </entity>
</fetch>
```

When you update and save the Fetch XML to the data set, these parameters are added in the Parameters folder in the Report Data pane. So, when you execute the report, these two report parameters are available for the user to select the date range. Similarly, you can add parameters as you require. One thing to remember is that by default the parameter "Data type" is set to Text. You must change it to the appropriate data type; in this case, it should be Date/Time. See Figure 7-32.

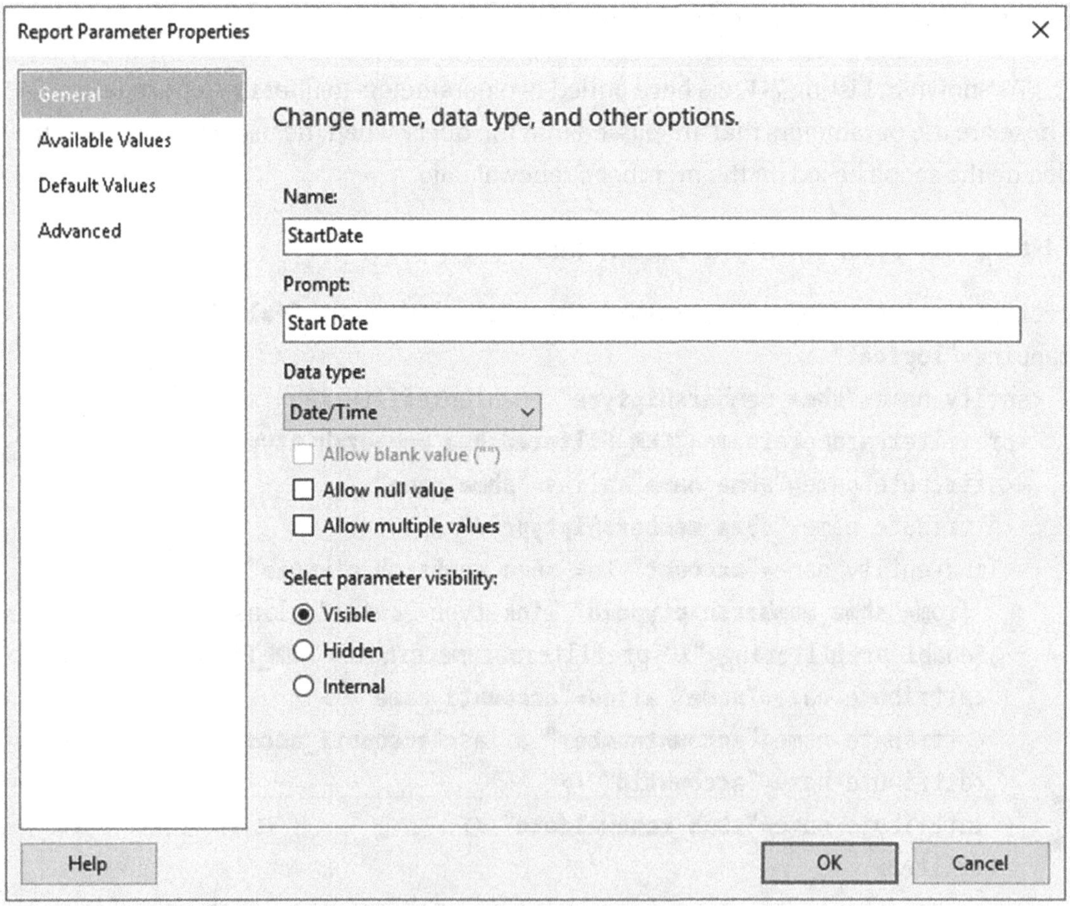

Figure 7-32. *Changing the data type of the parameter*

Once all the configuration is completed, you can import the RDL file to the report in Dynamics 365, as shown in Figure 7-33. Since we have created a report as the starting point, you can go into edit mode and upload the RDL file to the report.

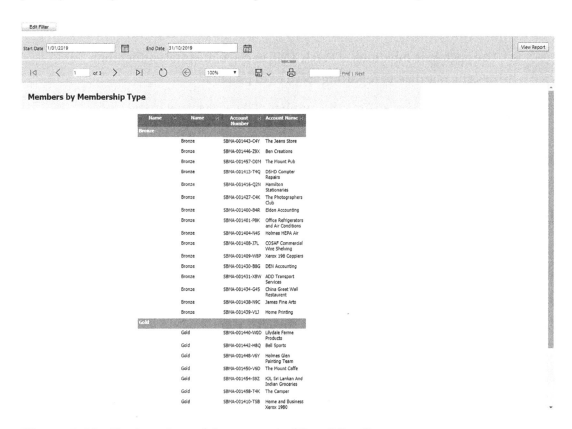

Figure 7-33. *Design view of the report in Visual Studio*

One of the powerful features of Dynamics 365 reporting is subreports. To keep it simple, this book will give a helicopter view of the feature. Let's assume a scenario where SBMA wants to print a receipt for the members who consume different membership products of the club. So, the invoice would contain details such as the company logo, ID, member details, and so on. Plus, it will list all the membership products as the line items on the report. To accomplish this demand, you should use subreports. How it works is that the main report will have the logo, invoice ID, member details, and so on, and the subreport will contain all the membership products as the line items. First create the parent report and then create the subreport and remember to select the parent report in the Parent Report field. With this approach you can execute the report on single records as well as multiple records.

Report consumers will always complain about the performance of the report. What can you do to improve the performance of the report?

- Scope the data set to a specific time period.

- Prefilter the report to limit the data set.

- Use aggregate functions of Fetch XML to calculate totals rather than passing raw data to reporting services to process.

- Take all measures to limit the number of data sets used in the report.

Applying prefilters makes your report perform well. Let's take a quick look at how to apply the prefilters to your report.

Apply Prefilters

It is a known fact that reports that query larger data sets suffer from performance issues. This will continue over time since an organization's data is growing on a daily basis. To improve the performance of the reports, you can use prefiltering in your reports, which will make your reports context sensitive by consolidating the report scope to query more relevant data. This will also make the report filtered using the Advanced Find feature.

You must keep in mind that only automatic prefiltering is supported on fetched-based reports. To enable prefiltering, you must set the value of enableprefiltering to 1, as shown in Listing 7-2. Prefiltering can be applied to both the primary and linked entities in your Fetch query. When you create a report through the wizard and use the RDL file to build your report, these prefilters are automatically added.

Listing 7-2. Fetch XML with Parameters

```
<fetch distinct="false" useraworderby="false" no-lock="false"
mapping="logical" >
  <entity name="sbma_membershiptype" enableprefiltering="1"
  prefilterparametername="CRM_Filteredsbma_membershiptype" >
    <attribute name="sbma_name" alias="sbma_name" />
    <attribute name="sbma_membershiptypeid" />
    <link-entity name="account" to="sbma_membershiptypeid"
      from="sbma_membershiptypeid" link-type="outer" alias="account1"
      enableprefiltering="1" prefilterparametername="CRM_FilteredAccount" >
```

For more information on prefiltering, please refer to `https://docs.microsoft.com/en-us/dynamics365/customer-engagement/analytics/improve-report-performance-by-using-filters`.

Dashboards

Among the out-of-the-box personalized reporting options, Dynamics 365 dashboards are the best because they can be developed without the help of the experts and are available to all users. The dashboards are a visual representation of the data in your Dynamics 365 instance. Primarily, a dashboard consists of views and charts, and these visualizations are interactive. That is, the end users can quickly jump into individual records from the dashboard. The primary benefit of dashboards is the aggregation of a wide array of data into a single page or a view. Plus, you have the option to control the access to the dashboards based on the end users' security roles.

For instance, the owner of the dashboard can decide who will get to see it by just sharing it with specific users or teams. Also, you can create dashboards that suit different roles of the organization. For example, information requirements are different for the sales team and the customer services team. So, each team can have their own dashboards to carry out their daily duties. Let's look at a quick example of a dashboard.

As with any other development work, the first step is to design the dashboard, which means draw a simple sketch of the dashboard and define where the user wants to see information and in what format, whether it is a chart or a view. Before creating the dashboard, you must first create the required views and charts. Once the foundation is set, you can start to create the dashboard. Open the solution and navigate to the dashboard under the solution components. Click the New button to add the dashboard. See Figure 7-34.

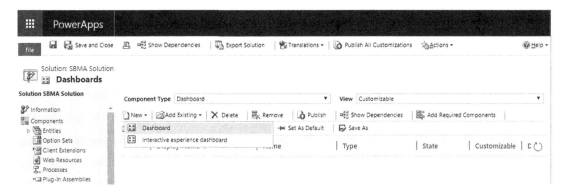

Figure 7-34. *Creating a new dashboard*

The next window is for selecting the appropriate layout for the dashboard. This is where the initial design is important because it will guide you to select the layout. See Figure 7-35.

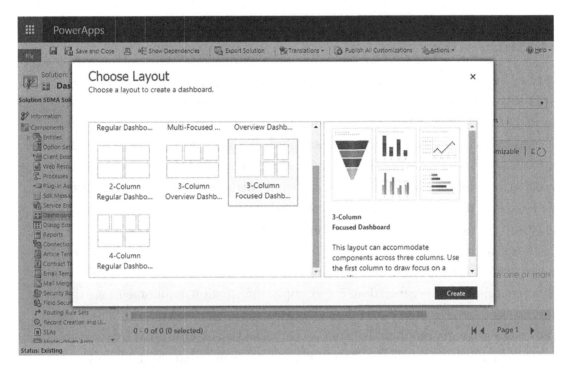

Figure 7-35. *Selecting the dashboard layout*

Click Create, and the dashboard will be created. In the dashboard editing window, when you click the small icon in the middle of each component in the dashboard, you can select the view or the chart to add to each component. See Figure 7-36.

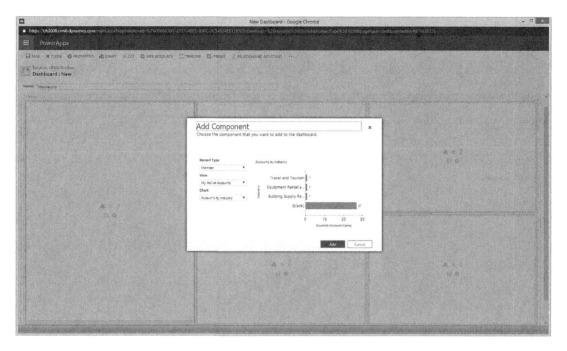

Figure 7-36. *Adding components to the dashboard*

After setting up all the required components, save the dashboard by providing a meaningful name. The newly created dashboard will be listed with the other dashboards. See Figure 7-37.

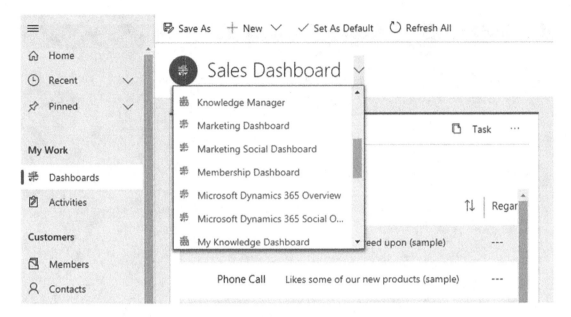

Figure 7-37. *New dashboard listed*

Select the dashboard from the list, and you will be directed to the dashboard. See Figure 7-38.

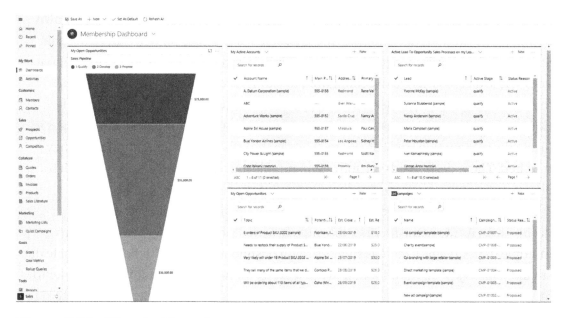

Figure 7-38. *New dashboard*

These dashboards can be easily shared with other users. On the dashboard click Share Dashboard on the command bar, and the rest of the process is similar to sharing an Advanced Find view, which we discussed earlier in this chapter. One important thing to know is that there are two types of dashboards: system and user dashboards.

System dashboards are created by the users with system administrator or system customizer user roles. These are created in the Settings area and must be published to be visible. Although they can be visible to everyone in the organization, they can also be hidden using the security roles of the users. The system administrator or the system customizer who creates the dashboard can set it as a default dashboard, making it the one every user can see when Dynamics 365 loads. System dashboards are useful in scenarios where the information is required at a broader scope across the organization.

On the other hand, user dashboards are created by the user under the user's work area such as Sales, Services, or Marketing. These are not required to be published to be visible, and they are visible only to the users who create them, although the owner can share them with other users. User dashboards are more suitable for quick information requirements within the team, and the users can create the dashboard and share it within the team or specific users.

The following link provides more details about dashboards: `https://docs.microsoft.com/en-us/dynamics365/customer-engagement/customize/create-edit-dashboards`.

In addition to these standard dashboards, there is new form of dashboards known as *interactive dashboards*. They provide an intuitive customer service experience that you will find within Dynamics 365 for Customer Engagement and the Customer Services hub. These dashboards can be configured to extract more relevant information for the customer service representatives to perform their job effectively and efficiently. Customer service representatives no longer have to navigate through so many pages to locate the information because interactive dashboards provide the information they required. These dashboards are fully configurable and security role sensitive, which always ensures they are exposing the relevant information to the right person.

Interactive dashboards come in two flavors: multistream and single-stream dashboards. As the name implies, the multistream dashboards present data from multiple data streams, whereas single-stream dashboards present data from a single data stream. This is just an introduction to the feature; for more information, please refer to `https://docs.microsoft.com/en-us/dynamics365/customer-engagement/customize/configure-interactive-dashboards`.

The next section is dedicated to creating more complex dashboards using Power BI.

Dynamics 365 and Power BI

Sometimes, the senior stakeholder, board of directors, external stakeholders, or even customers might require rich and sophisticated dashboards to use in the decision-making process. Microsoft Power BI is just the tool that can be utilized in such scenarios because it is the platform that can be easily integrated with Dynamics 365 and provide additional reporting capabilities to Dynamics 365. For more information, visit `https://docs.microsoft.com/en-us/dynamics365/customer-engagement/analytics/reporting-analytics-with-dynamics-365`.

The following section covers just the tip of the iceberg of the Power BI space. It explains how to establish a connection with Dynamics 365 from Power BI, create a dashboard, and publish it to Dynamics 365. First you must sign in with Power BI. Use your global administrator credentials and sign up. During the process, you can nominate other users who might be using the platform to produce state-of-the-art dashboards. See Figure 7-39.

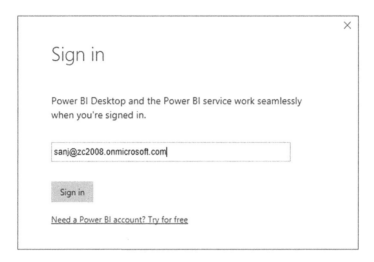

Figure 7-39. *Signing in to Power BI*

To establish the connection, you need to copy the link in Instance Web API URL. To develop the examples in this section, we will be using the Power BI desktop. On the ribbon, click Get Data and then More at the bottom of the pop-up menu; this will load the connection wizard, as shown in Figure 7-40.

Figure 7-40. *Establishing the connection with Dynamics 365*

In this window, select the Online Services option, and you will see all the online services available. From this list, click Dynamics 365 (online) and click Connect. This action will then ask you to enter the Web API URL. See Figure 7-41.

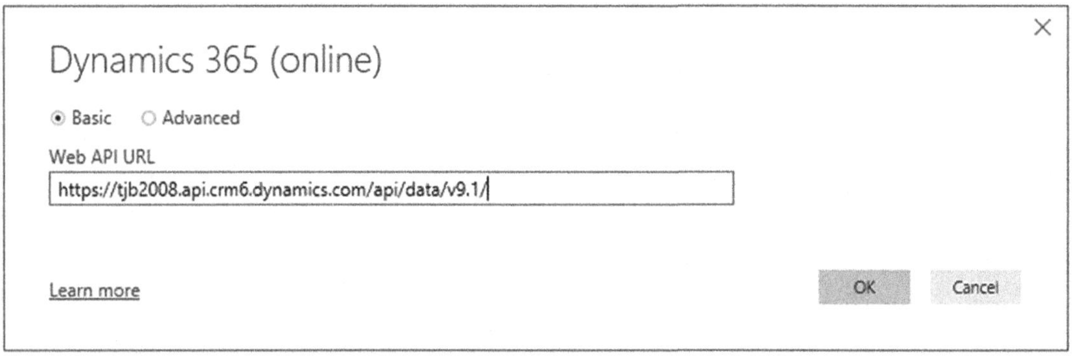

Figure 7-41. *Connecting to Power BI*

Once you're successfully connected, the list of available entities will be displayed, as shown in Figure 7-42. Keep in mind that when you select the entity, all the columns of the entity will be selected as well. We will discuss how to limit the query to select only the required columns later in this section. You can see a subset of data on the screen.

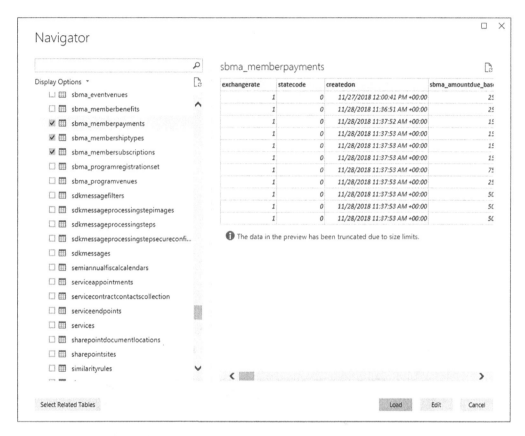

Figure 7-42. *Selecting entities for the query*

After selecting the entities and clicking the Load button, the tool will load the entities, which will take a few minutes depending on the number of entities you have selected. By default, this will load all the columns, and you must edit the data set and select only the required columns.

The most important thing to remember here is to prefilter your data. If not, then by default, it will retrieve all the data in entities you have selected for the query. In a scenario where you are querying a large data set, you should filter the data for performance and security reasons. Generally, if the data set is large, then Power BI will take several minutes to pull all the required records, which is frustrating to the consumer.

Therefore, you must always ensure to include the require data in your data set. For this book we are using a small data set. If you have a larger data set, the following URL explains how to use Fetch XML to create a query and filter data: `https://crmchartguy.com/2017/09/30/use-fetchxml-in-power-bi-with-dynamics-365-customer-engagement/`. See Figure 7-43.

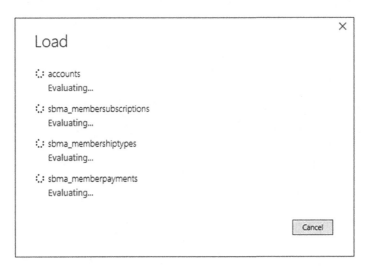

Figure 7-43. *Loading selected entities*

Once the entities are loaded, you can see the entities and the fields underneath each entity on the right side of the desktop tool. See Figure 7-44.

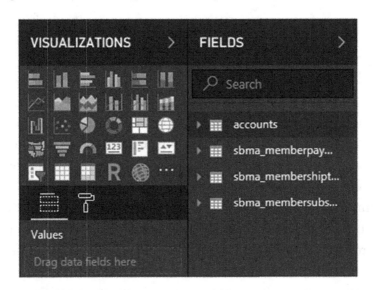

Figure 7-44. *Entities and fields*

When you expand the tree, the columns are listed, and to edit the columns, you must open the Power Query Editor to add/remove the fields and apply any filters to the query. Select the entity you want to edit, and from the pop-up menu, select the Edit Query option to open the Power Query Editor. See Figure 7-45.

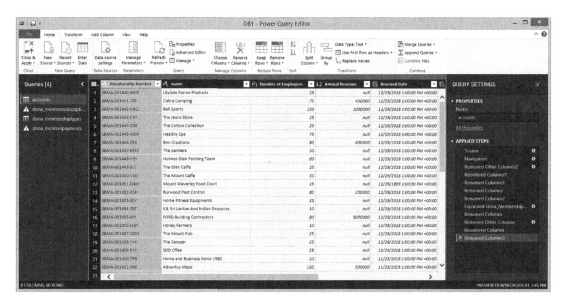

Figure 7-45. *Power BI Query Editor*

On the ribbon of this screen, click the Choose Columns button to select the columns that you want. As you can see, the column names have been renamed to a more readable format. You can do this just by right-clicking and selecting the Rename option from the pop-up menu. See Figure 7-46.

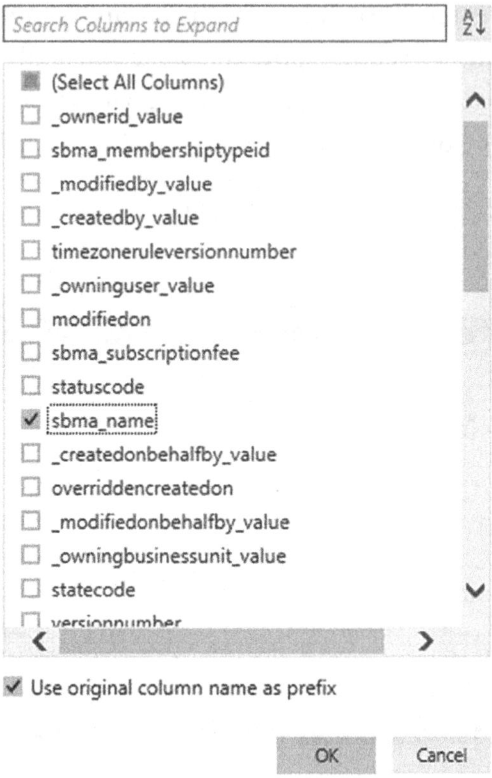

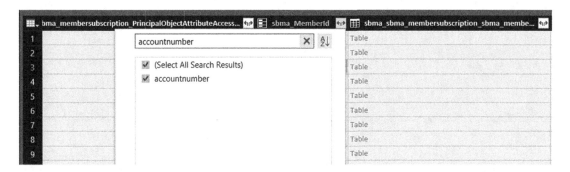

Figure 7-46. *Selecting the columns*

When there are related entities, by default the word *Record* is displayed, which is not useful for the end users. Next to the column header there is a button with two arrowheads, and when you click this button, the lookup entity columns are displayed. You can select the column that lists a meaningful name. For instance, instead of displaying a GUID, you could select the name, which will display the name of the member. See Figure 7-47.

Figure 7-47. *Setting up the lookup records*

As you can see in Figure 7-48, the query completed after adding all the changes.

		Membership Number		name		Renewal Date		Start Date		Payment Method		Membership Type	
1		SBMA-001440-W0D		Lilydale Farme Products		12/29/2018 1:00:00 PM +00:00		12/7/2018 5:53:00 AM +00:00		646150000		Gold	
2		SBMA-001441-T8F		Cobra Camping		12/29/2018 1:00:00 PM +00:00		12/7/2018 6:45:00 AM +00:00		646150000		Silver	
3		SBMA-001442-H8Q		Bell Sports		12/29/2018 1:00:00 PM +00:00		12/7/2018 6:43:00 AM +00:00		646150001		Gold	
4		SBMA-001443-C4Y		The Jeans Store		12/29/2018 1:00:00 PM +00:00		12/7/2018 6:01:00 AM +00:00		646150001		Bronze	
5		SBMA-001444-C6X		The Cotton Collection		12/29/2018 1:00:00 PM +00:00		12/7/2018 6:00:00 AM +00:00		646150001		Platinum	
6		SBMA-001445-W0V		Healthy Spa		12/29/2018 1:00:00 PM +00:00		12/7/2018 5:48:00 AM +00:00		646150001		Platinum	
7		SBMA-001446-Z9X		Ben Creations		12/29/2018 1:00:00 PM +00:00		12/7/2018 6:44:00 AM +00:00		646150001		Bronze	
8		SBMA-001447-M3S		The painters		12/29/2018 1:00:00 PM +00:00		12/7/2018 6:17:00 AM +00:00		646150000		Platinum	
9		SBMA-001448-V6Y		Holmes Glen Painting Team		12/29/2018 1:00:00 PM +00:00		12/7/2018 5:49:00 AM +00:00		646150001		Gold	
10		SBMA-001449-B7J		The Glen Caffe		12/29/2018 1:00:00 PM +00:00		12/7/2018 6:01:00 AM +00:00		646150001		Platinum	
11		SBMA-001450-V6D		The Mount Caffe		12/29/2018 1:00:00 PM +00:00		12/7/2018 6:02:00 AM +00:00		646150001		Gold	
12		SBMA-001451-D4M		Mount Waverley Food Court		12/29/1899 1:00:00 PM +00:00		12/7/2018 6:01:00 AM +00:00		646150000		Silver	

Figure 7-48. *Finalized Power Query Editor*

Click the Close and Apply buttons in the ribbon, and your changes will be submitted to the query. It is now ready to be used in producing the dashboard. Just drag and drop the columns to the canvas. By default, the details are listed as a table. See Figure 7-49.

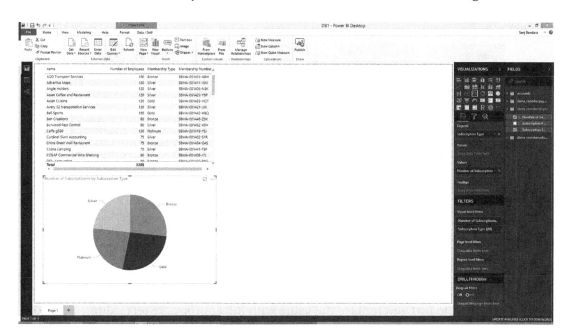

Figure 7-49. *Power BI dashboard canvas*

To apply the chart visualizations, you must first prepare the data. In the visualization shown in Figure 7-49, the pie chart displays the memberships based on the membership type. For this, you must go to the query that pulls the membership type data, and in the column that illustrates the relationship between the membership type and the members, click the button next to the column heading. In the pop-up menu, select the Aggregate option, and it will list all the available options. These options include Sum and Count options. For this example, select "#Count of accounted," which will count the accounts under each type. After completing the query, then add the changes, add the table to the canvas, and select the type of visualization required. The changes will be applied immediately.

When it comes to querying option sets and status fields, by default it will display only the integer value stored. But if you use the Common Data Service, you do not have to write any additional queries to retrieve the label. The following URL will guide you through the process of creating such a connection and adding option sets: `https://community.dynamics.com/crm/b/crminogic/archive/2018/10/19/connect-to-the-power-bi-using-common-data-service-cds`. If you are not using the Common Data Service, then you can also follow the steps defined in this article: `https://nishantrana.me/2018/10/06/dealing-with-optionset-inside-powerbi-in-dynamics-365-ce/`. See Figure 7-50.

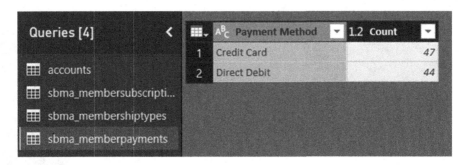

Figure 7-50. *Replacing option set values*

As per the query editor, the member payments are grouped under Payment Type, but the issue is that the payment type is an option set, and the numbers will be displayed instead of the name values. The workaround used here is to change the data type of the payment method to text and replace the value with the appropriate text value.

Also, you can insert custom columns on the Add Column tab on the ribbon. In the editor window, you can combine the columns and develop the formula. The custom column is calculated by multiplying the subscription fee by the number of subscriptions under each subscription. See Figure 7-51.

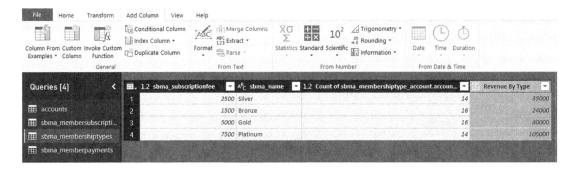

1.2 sbma_subscriptionfee	A^B_C sbma_name	1.2 Count of sbma_membershiptype_account.accoun...	Revenue By Type
2500	Silver	14	35000
1500	Bronze	16	24000
5000	Gold	16	80000
7500	Platinum	14	105000

Figure 7-51. *Inserting custom columns*

As shown in Figure 7-52, you can add these to the canvas, and the final output contains all the components you have configured.

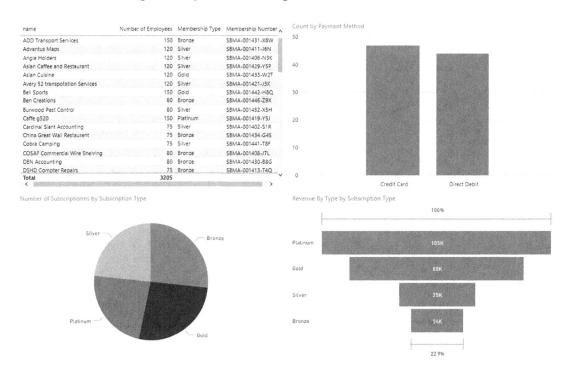

Figure 7-52. *Completed Power BI dashboard*

Next we will quickly publish our dashboard to Dynamics 365. First, you must enable Power BI visualizations for your organization. Under Settings ➤ Administration ➤ System Settings, click the Reporting tab, and select "Allow Power BI visualization embedding." You must avoid adding Power BI visualizations to system dashboards because it is not supported at the time of writing this book.

Next publish the dashboard to the Power BI workspace. Select File ➤ Publish, and select Publish to Dashboard. See Figure 7-53.

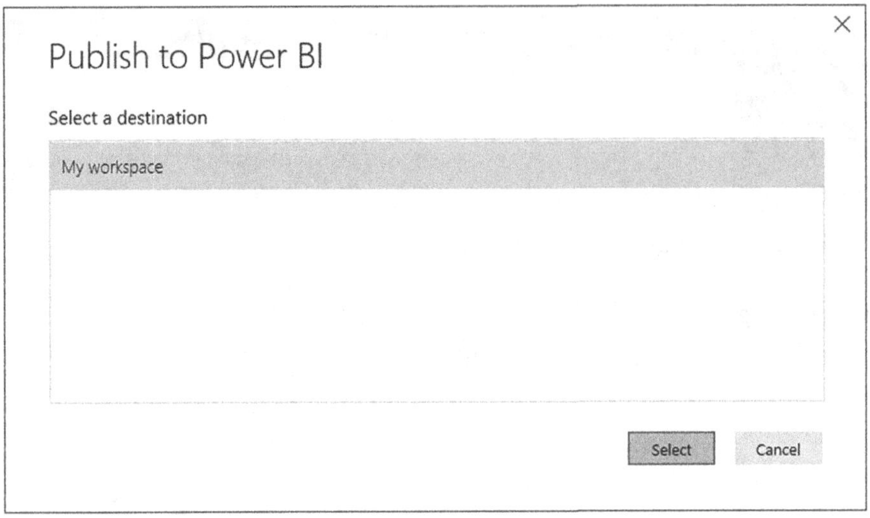

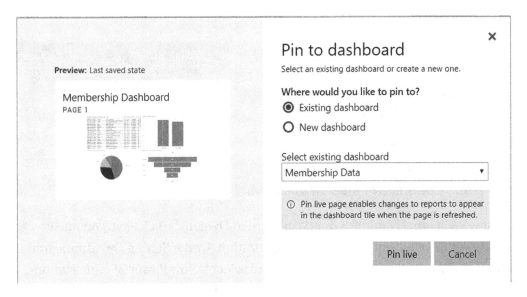

Figure 7-53. *Selecting the Power BI workspace*

Keep in mind that when you publish the dashboard, it will be published as a report. You must select the report on the Reports tab of the workspace and then click Pin to Live Page. There are two options, so select the one appropriate. See Figure 7-54.

Figure 7-54. *"Pin to dashboard" option*

The option will now be available in the Dashboard section, which means it can be reached from Dynamics 365. From the Dynamics 365 instance, click the New Dashboard icon and select the Power BI Dashboard option. It is amazing to see that the pop-up will give you a quick view of the dashboard you have selected. See Figure 7-55.

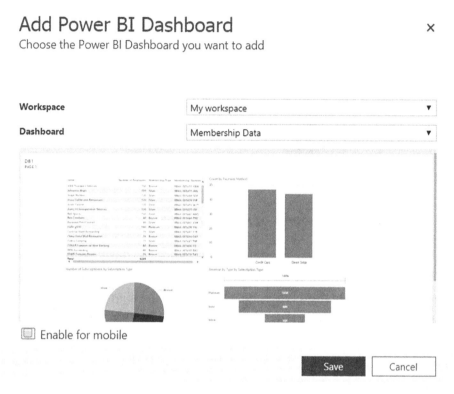

Figure 7-55. *Add Power BI Dashboard pop-up window*

Once you save the selection, the dashboard will be rendered to Dynamics 365, as illustrated in Figure 7-56.

Figure 7-56. *Dashboard rendered in Dynamics 365*

Even these visualizations can be added to Dynamics 365 dashboards. In the dashboard editor, click the Power BI icon to select the component on the dashboard. If you want to share the dashboards with the users within the team, you must configure the sharing options in both Power BI and Dynamics 365 for Customer Engagement. Also keep in mind that the user group must have the same access rights on both services. For more information about sharing, please refer to `https://tjb2008.crm6.dynamics.com/ main.aspx?forceClassic=1#579876531`.

You could also find more details about the security implications via `https://docs. microsoft.com/en-us/dynamics365/customer-engagement/basics/add-edit-power- bi-visualizations-dashboard#privacy-notice`. See Figure 7-57.

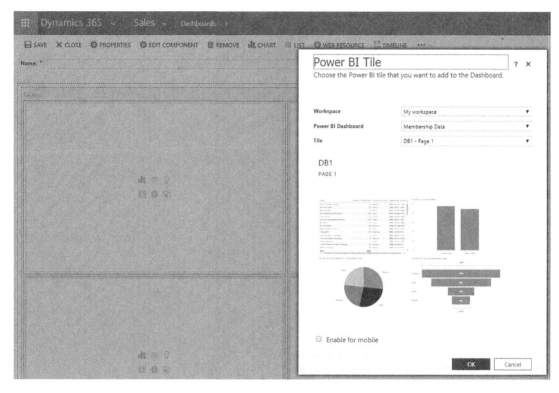

Figure 7-57. *Adding Power BI to the Dynamics 365 dashboards*

As mentioned earlier, this is just the tip of the iceberg of what you can do with Dynamics 365 and Power BI integrations. One such approach is to use the Data Export Services, which is a much faster approach when you have to query huge volumes of data. You can find additional information at `https://docs.microsoft.com/en-us/power-bi/service-connect-to-microsoft-dynamics-crm`.

Summary

This chapter covered the simplest data reporting to more advanced reporting options available in Dynamics 365. It started with Advanced Find views and gradually moved to the Dynamics 365 Report Wizard and then to Fetch XML reports. Finally, we covered the big beast, Power BI integration.

CHAPTER 8

An Introduction to Dynamics 365 Portals

The primary purpose of a portal is to provide access to someone external or sometimes internal to the client's organization. Why is this level of access required? Providing a Dynamics 365 license for the users outside of the organization is not economically viable, and operationally it is not required because some users might execute only a few actions such as opening a case, logging an online application, or registering for an event. In such situations, the portals provided as an add-on to Dynamics 365 for Customer Engagement are an ideal tool. There are many options when it comes to developing portals; the most versatile and recommended approach is to use the portal add-on provided with Dynamics 365.

You could use other content management systems to develop portals or even use ASP.NET MVC to develop a portal from scratch. But these strategies would require extensive development and experienced developers. The primary benefit of using the portals available for Dynamics 365 for Customer Engagement is that there is no hardware provisioning or maintenance. If your client has access to a Dynamics 365 Enterprise subscription, then you will have at least one portal license available.

Selecting the right fit for your client is up to you. In this chapter, we will be just scratching the surface of the portals feature for Dynamics 365 for Customer Engagement; we will provide references for additional reading because this particular area will not fit into a single chapter. The primary objective of this chapter is to give you a starting point.

Dynamics 365 Portals

First you need to configure the portal, which is a simple task. You must navigate to the Dynamics 365 Administration Center page and select the Applications tab. See Figure 8-1.

© Sanjaya Yapa 2019
S. Yapa, *Customizing Dynamics 365*, https://doi.org/10.1007/978-1-4842-4379-4_8

Figure 8-1. *Dynamics 365 Administration Center*

Select Portal Add-On and click the Manage icon. You will be directed to the configuration page. You could also use the Power Platform admin center (which was announced in September 2018) to get to this point. The role of this new admin center is to consolidate all the administration tasks of the environments in one view rather navigating to several locations. As you can see in Figure 8-2, all the environments are listed on one page so the administrators can manage them easily. Please note that at the time of writing this book, the Power Platform admin center is in preview. Microsoft will continue to add new features, and ultimately this will become the go-to station for administrators. See Figure 8-3.

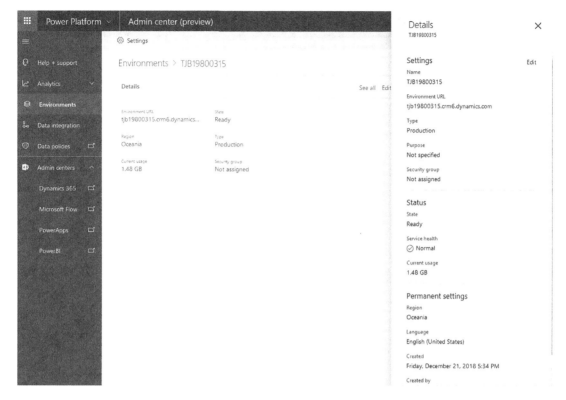

Figure 8-2. *New Power Platform admin center*

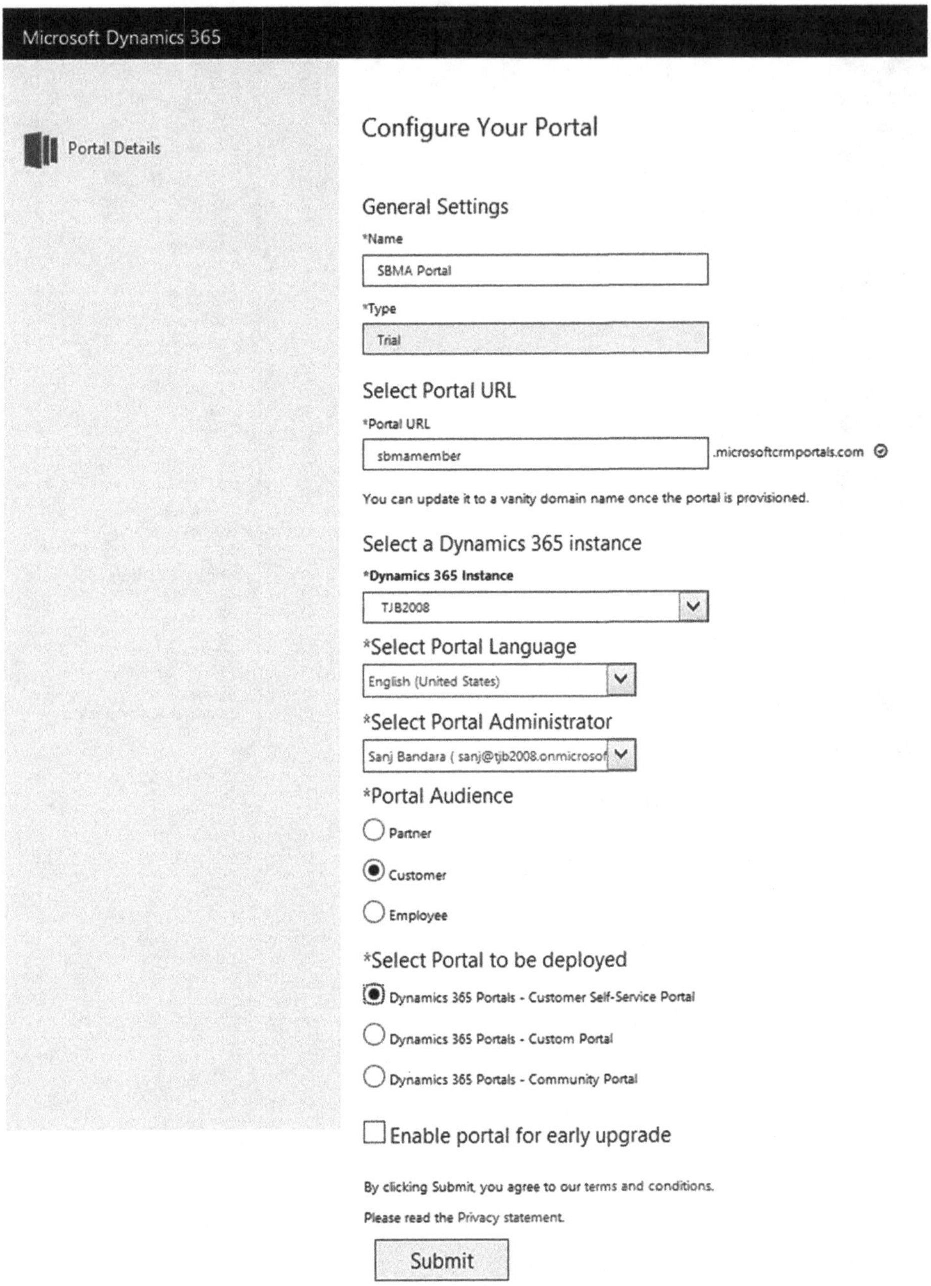

Figure 8-3. *Portal configuration*

Once you click Submit, it will take some time to complete the configuration. Once this process completes, click the URL, and it will commence provisioning of the portal. See Figure 8-4.

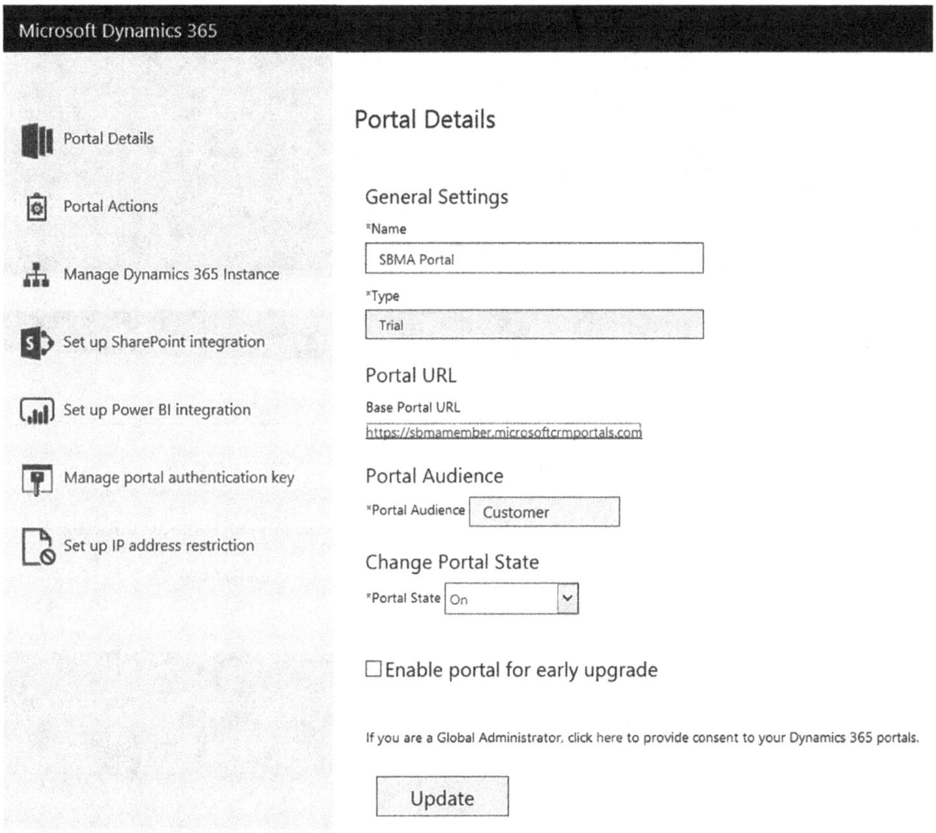

Microsoft Dynamics 365

Portal Details

Portal Actions

Manage Dynamics 365 Instance

Set up SharePoint integration

Set up Power BI integration

Manage portal authentication key

Set up IP address restriction

Portal Details

General Settings

*Name

SBMA Portal

*Type

Trial

Portal URL

Base Portal URL

https://sbmamember.microsoftcrmportals.com

Portal Audience

*Portal Audience   Customer

Change Portal State

*Portal State   On

☐ Enable portal for early upgrade

If you are a Global Administrator, click here to provide consent to your Dynamics 365 portals.

Update

Figure 8-4. *Portal settings completed*

When click the URL, you will be directed to the provisioning page, which indicates the process will take a while to complete. Once completed, the portal is created. For this demo, we have used the self-service portal. As per the SBMA requirements, members can log cases related to memberships using this portal. It is obvious that the amount of work that is required to get to this stage is minimal. After configuration, a fully functioning portal is created for you. It is that simple. See Figure 8-5.

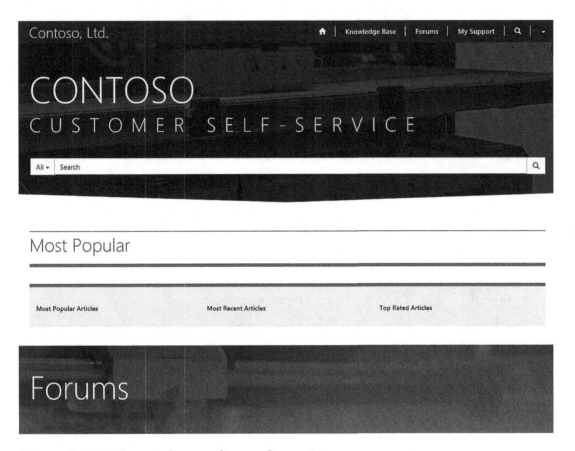

Figure 8-5. *Web portal soon after configuration*

The portals feature in Dynamics 365 comes with a web editor where you can easily modify the web pages. To modify a web page, you must log in with the user role who has the web admin role. At the point when you set up the portal, a System Administrator account will be created. In Dynamics 365 portals, an authenticated portal user is created and associated with either a contact or a system user. The default configuration is contact-based authentication. So, to log in to the portal, the contact must have the appropriate authentications granted. Except for unauthenticated users, portal users must be granted the appropriate web role. The latest authentication comes in two flavors.

- **Local authentication**: This is the common forms-based authentication that uses the Dynamics 365 contact; to extend this, developers can use the ASP.NET Identity API.

- **External authentication**: In this approach, account credentials and password management are handled by third-party identity providers.

You can find more information from the following URLs:

- `https://docs.microsoft.com/en-us/dynamics365/customer-engagement/portals/configure-portal-authentication`

- `https://docs.microsoft.com/en-us/dynamics365/customer-engagement/portals/set-authentication-identity`

Open the contact, and the users are created as contacts. You can assign web roles from the web roles page. Please note that when you setup Portals, a Dynamics 365 Portals app which is a Unified Interface Application and it will be istalled to MyApps section of Dynamics 365. See Figure 8-6.

Figure 8-6. *Assigning web roles*

After you log in, just hover your cursor over the areas you want to modify, and the Edit option will be displayed. When you click the link, the WYSWYG editor for that section will open. See Figurc 8-7.

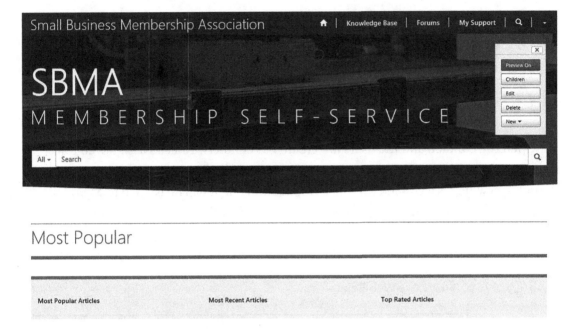

Figure 8-7. *Classic editor*

As you can see, the web editor is displayed on the right side of the page. There are a few functions that you can perform. When you click the Children button, you can see the list of child pages of this portal and the actions that can be performed on each page. See Figure 8-8.

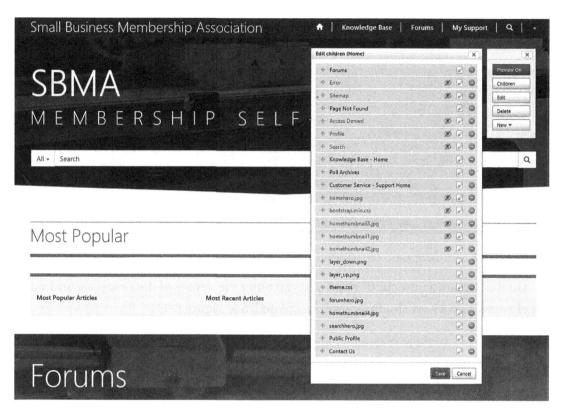

Figure 8-8. *Editing child pages*

Click the Edit button to open the page settings page where you can perform general editing. See Figure 8-9.

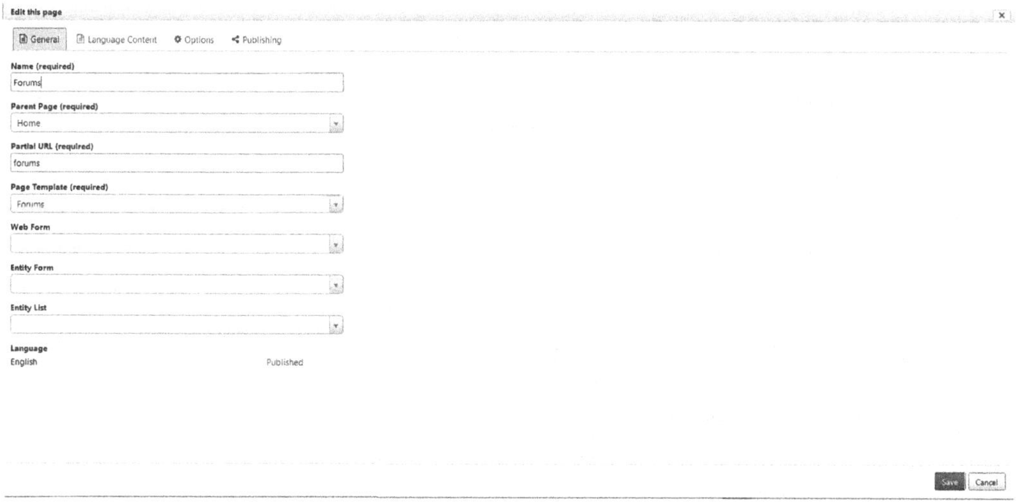

Figure 8-9. *Page settings*

After completing the changes, you can save the changes by just clicking the Save button. You can even add more child pages from this editor. See Figure 8-10.

Figure 8-10. *Adding new child page, file, forum, and shortcut*

On the "Create a new child" page, you can enter the details of the new page and save the changes, and a new child page will be created. See Figure 8-11.

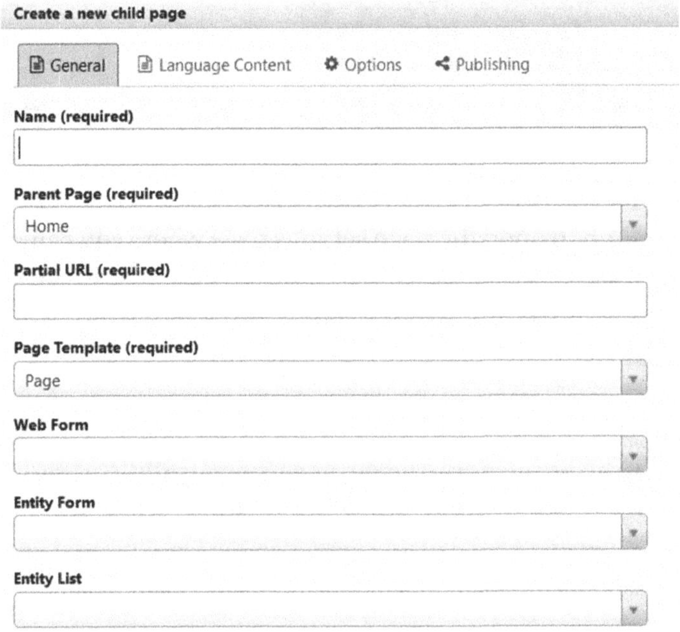

Create a new child page

📄 General   📄 Language Content   ⚙ Options   ◀ Publishing

Name (required)

Parent Page (required)

Home

Partial URL (required)

Page Template (required)

Page

Web Form

Entity Form

Entity List

Figure 8-11. *"Create a new child" page*

When you navigate to the My Support page, the members will be directed to the Support query list. On this page, when the member clicks the Open a New Case button, they will be directed to the form to enter the case details and submit them, which will create an entry in Dynamics 365. See Figure 8-12.

Small Business Membership Association   🏠 | Knowledge Base | Forums | My Support | 🔍 | ▾

Home > **Support**

Support

🔍 What can we help you with?

| ✖ | e.g. User login is failing | 🔍 |

▤ My Open Cases ▾   Search   🔍   Open a New Case

| Case Number | Case Title | Case Type | Subject | Origin | Customer | Status Reason | Created On ↓ |

There are no records to display.

Figure 8-12. *Support section*

So far, we have discussed the classic web editor, but there is also a new editor available. For online instances, on the top of the browser, a message is displaying "A new and simplified content editor is available for portal customization." Click the Try New Editor button, and you will be directed to the new web editor. See Figure 8-13.

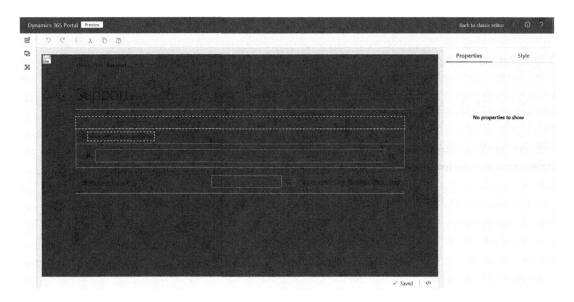

Figure 8-13. *New support section*

In the top-right corner there is a link to switch back to the classic editor, which was discussed at the beginning of this chapter. Many configuration and settings are available for further customizing the portal. These rich functionalities are available in the Portals menu. See Figure 8-14.

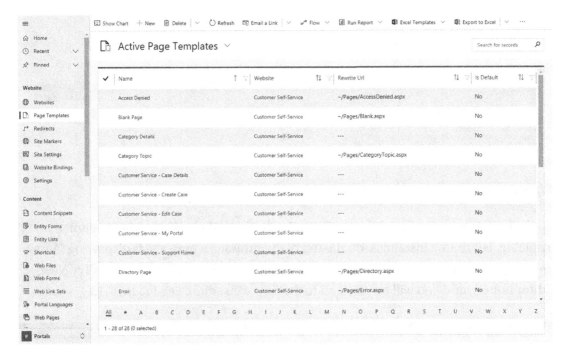

Figure 8-14. *Portals menu*

When you navigate to a web site, all the configuration and settings related to the site are available; in the scenario in Figure 8-14, it is the customer's self-service portal. For instance, the configuration details about the Home page can be found under the Root Pages section of the form. See Figure 8-15.

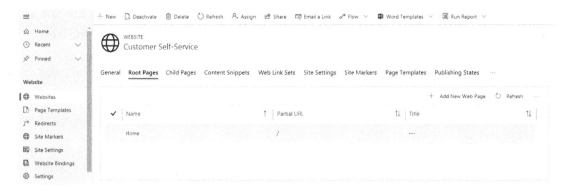

Figure 8-15. *Root Pages section*

In the Child Pages section, all the child pages are listed, and you can edit and configure these child sites by navigating to them individually. All these settings are basically records in Dynamics 365 instance, and they are arranged hierarchically. When you open the Home page record, then you can see the list of child pages under the Child Pages tab. See Figure 8-16.

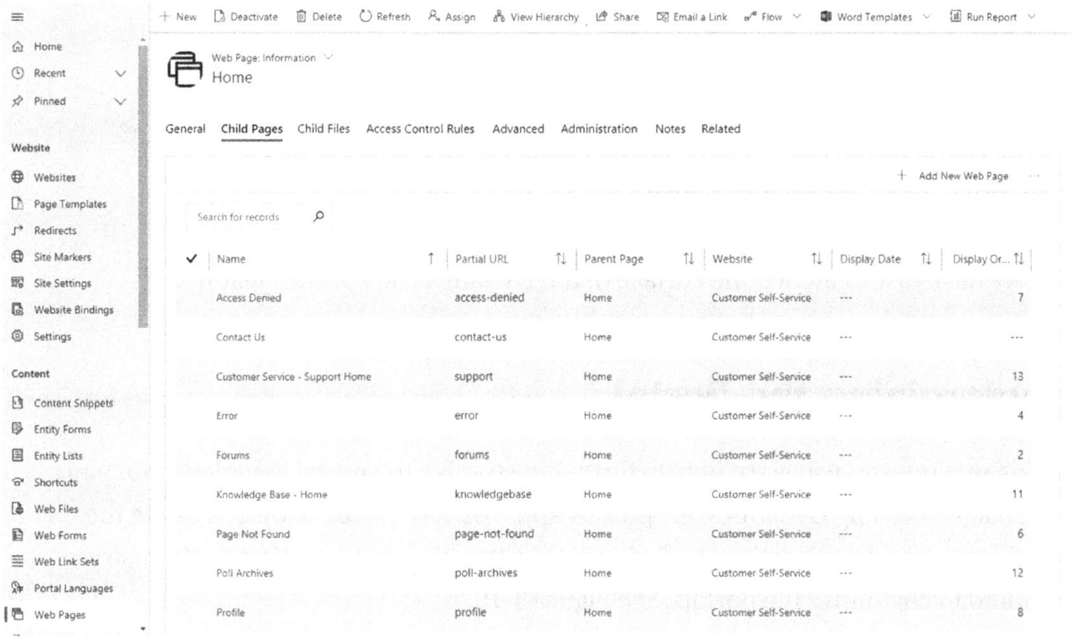

Figure 8-16. *Child Pages section*

Many other configurations are available under each section, which makes the portal add-on more flexible and extensible. You can even define the permissions for the web site. Dynamics 365 portals have facilities to add custom JavaScript and CSS files as advanced portal customizations. See Figure 8-17.

Figure 8-17. *Other web site settings*

We have just scratched the surface of the Dynamics 365 portals feature.

Customizing the Portal

In this section, you will learn how to further customize the portal experience for your external users using Dynamics 365 portals app. You also have the option to use the classic web interface, but this Unified Interface Portals app becoming the industry standard to customize the portals. See Figure 8-18.

Figure 8-18. *Dynamics 365 portal app in Unified Interface*

As you can see from the navigation menu of the portal, we have few web pages here. Let's add a new one for event registration. When the user navigates to this page, it should list all the current active events. On the app, navigate to Websites ➤ Child Pages and click + Add New Web Page on the grid toolbar. See Figure 8-19.

Figure 8-19. *Adding a new web page*

On the next screen, you can enter the web page details such as the name, web site, parent page, page template, publishing state, and so on, as shown in Figure 8-20. All this metadata basically describes the structure and the location of the new web page.

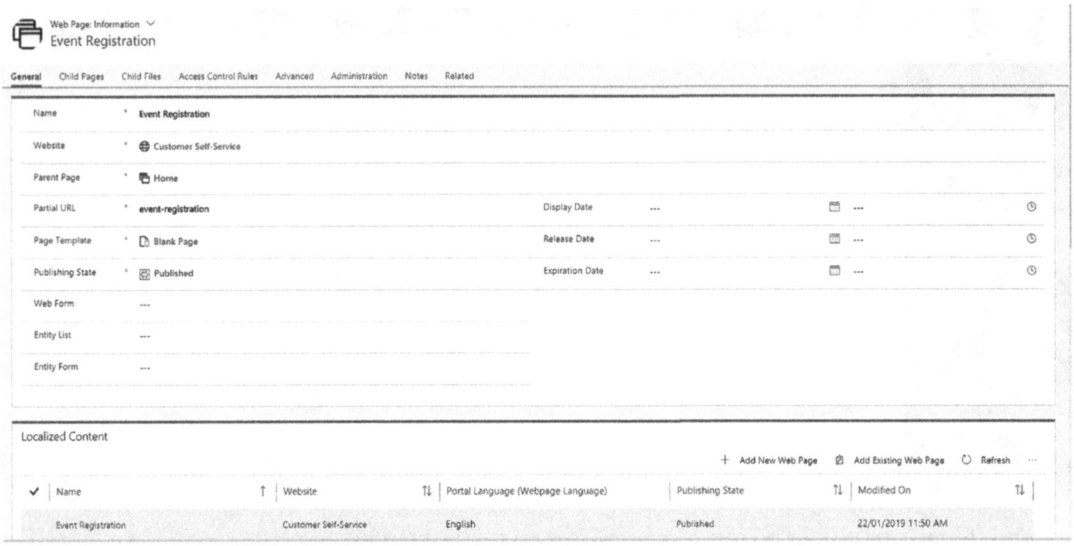

Figure 8-20. *Web page details*

As the next step, let's add the newly created web page to the navigation. Log in to the portal as a web administrator so that you can edit the navigation. Click the Edit option for navigation, and you will be prompted with the options to edit the navigation. For more information about using web pages, visit `https://docs.microsoft.com/en-us/dynamics365/customer-engagement/portals/add-webpage-render-list-records`. See Figure 8-21.

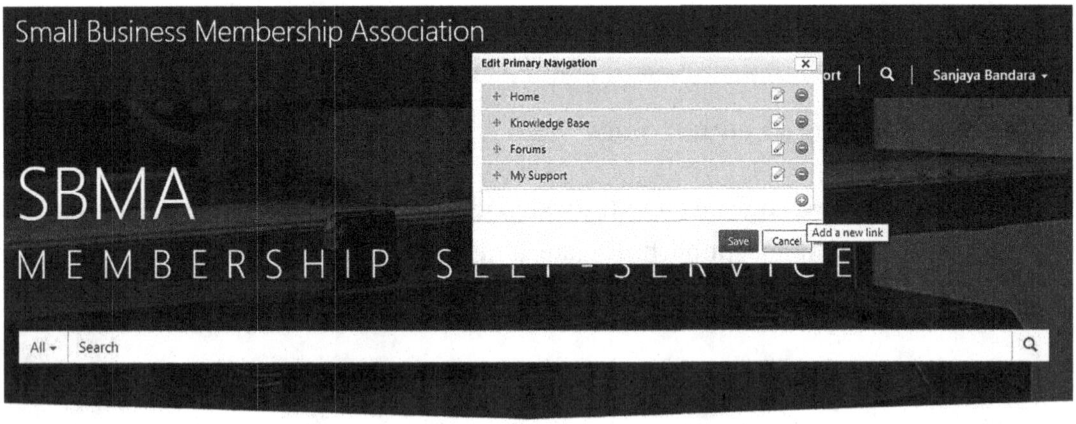

Figure 8-21. *Navigation editor*

Click the small green + icon on the menu to add the new link to the Event Registration page. As shown in Figure 8-22, your page will be listed in the Page drop-down of the "Add a new link" window.

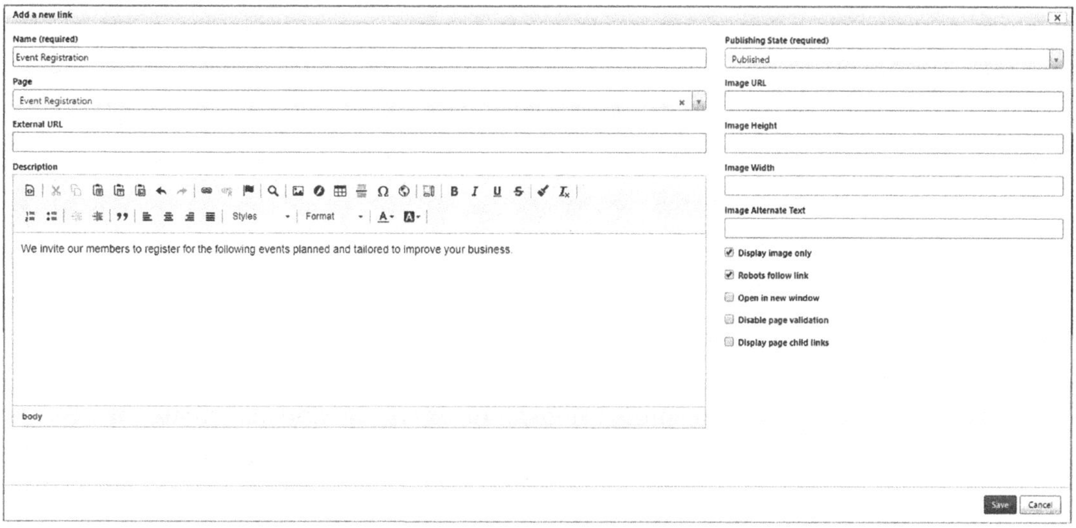

Figure 8-22. *Adding a new link*

After entering all the settings, click the Save button of this window, which will redirect you back to the Edit primary navigation menu, and click Save in the menu. The navigation to your page will be added. See Figure 8-23.

Figure 8-23. *New menu added to the navigation*

As per the requirements, you must show the list of events in the system so that the members can select it for registration. Therefore, you must open the web page created and add an entity list, which will be bound to the view of the Events entity. When you click the Entity List search box, if the entity list is already created, you can search for it and select it or click + New to create a new one. See Figure 8-24.

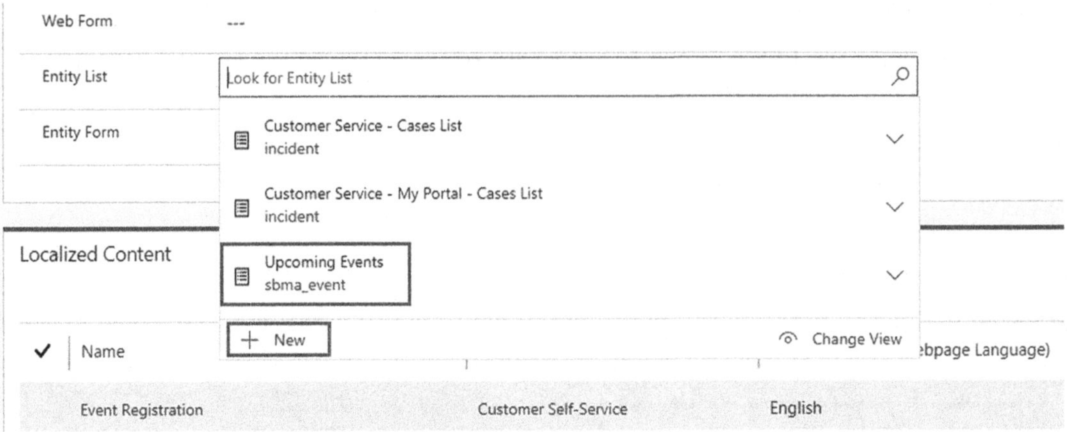

Figure 8-24. *Adding a new entity list*

Or, you could navigate to the entity list from the left navigation and create the new entity list. When creating the entity list, you must select the entity and the view you want to display to the client. In this scenario, it is the events entity and the Active Events view. See Figure 8-25.

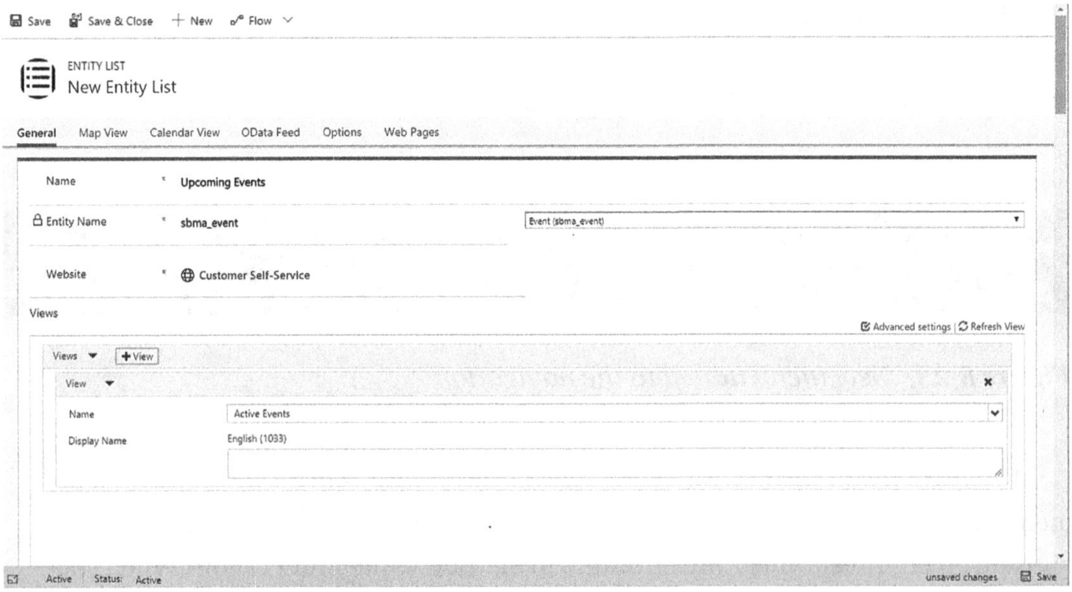

Figure 8-25. *New entity list*

You must also make sure you have configured the entity permission so that the user can see the data. To add permissions, you could open the entity permissions from the left navigation and create a new one by adding the required permissions, as shown in Figure 8-26. You can learn more about entity permissions at `https://docs.microsoft.com/en-us/dynamics365/customer-engagement/portals/assign-entity-permissions`.

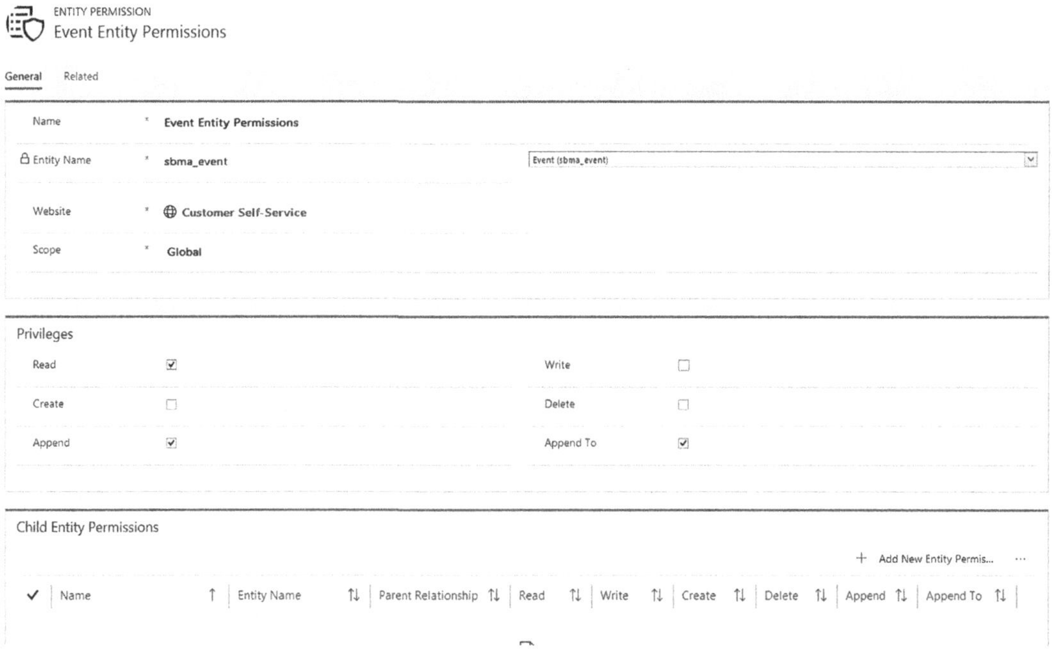

ENTITY PERMISSION
Event Entity Permissions

General   Related

Name	*	Event Entity Permissions	
Entity Name	*	sbma_event	Event (sbma_event)
Website	*	Customer Self-Service	
Scope	*	Global	

Privileges

Read	☑		Write	☐
Create	☐		Delete	☐
Append	☑		Append To	☑

Child Entity Permissions

＋ Add New Entity Permis...   ···

| ✓ | Name | ↑ | Entity Name | ↑↓ | Parent Relationship | ↑↓ | Read | ↑↓ | Write | ↑↓ | Create | ↑↓ | Delete | ↑↓ | Append | ↑↓ | Append To | ↑↓ |

Figure 8-26. *Entity permissions*

Once all these are set up, when you refresh the Events page, you can see the list of upcoming events. See Figure 8-27.

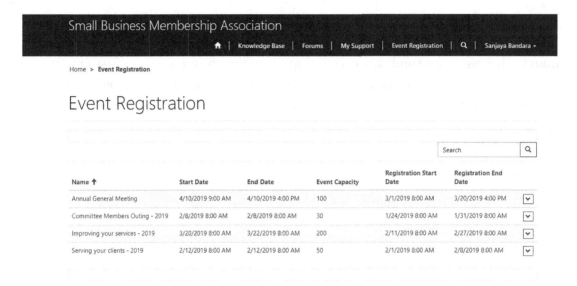

Figure 8-27. *Events list*

To see the details of each event in a pop-up window, you can easily configure it. Navigate to Entity Form in the left navigation, click + New, and enter the settings, as shown in Figure 8-28.

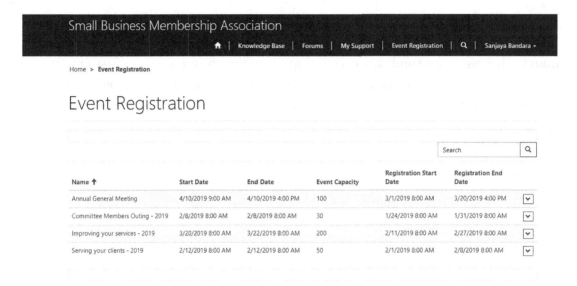

Figure 8-28. *Event form*

You can find more information about entity forms at `https://docs.microsoft.com/`
`en-us/dynamics365/customer-engagement/portals/entity-forms-custom-logic`.

Now you must link this entity form to the entity list. Select the entity list from the left
navigation, open the entity list, navigate to the Options tab, and scroll down to the Grid
Configuration section. Click the + Details button, and specify the form to display when
clicking the record on the grid. See Figure 8-29.

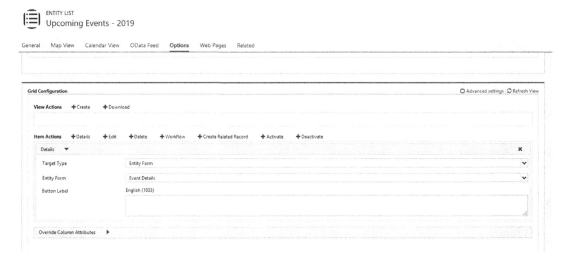

Figure 8-29. *Configuring the Event Details form*

Now when you navigate to the Events page of the portal and click the event name,
the event details will be displayed. See Figure 8-30.

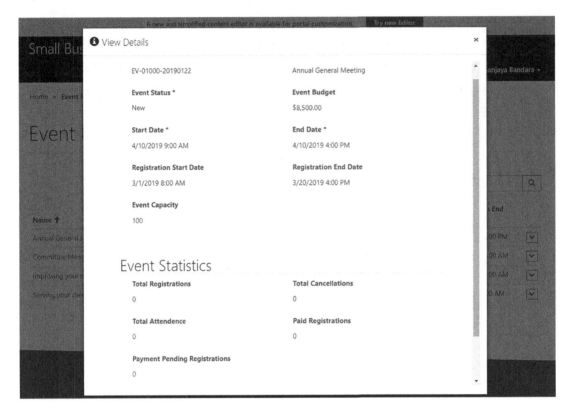

Figure 8-30. *View Details window*

Web Forms

When it comes to improving the user experience, web forms play a big role because they are designed to provide an intuitive end-user experience. Web forms support creating a step-by-step or wizard-like experience for data entry. Mainly power users can implement web forms without the intervention of developers. Web forms support both single and multiple steps with conditional logic. The following URL provides more details: `https://docs.microsoft.com/en-us/dynamics365/customer-engagement/portals/web-form-properties`.

Liquid Templates

So far we have discussed how power users can extend the user experience without a developer's expert knowledge. But there could be scenarios where you have to implement complex and custom business logic. This is not possible because the

Dynamics 365 portal is a SaaS application and developers do not have access to its server-based source code. To overcome this barrier, Dynamics 365 portals use an open source template engine known as Liquid, which enables developers to create custom templates without needing to access the server-side source code.Liquid was created by Shopify using Ruby and was later ported to .NET under the DotLiquid project. For more information about the project, visit `https://github.com/dotliquid/dotliquid`. You can learn even more about Liquid from the Shopify documentation at `http://shopify.github.io/liquid/`.

This section is just a starting point to Liquid templates; for more information, refer to `https://docs.microsoft.com/en-us/dynamics365/customer-engagement/portals/custom-templates-dynamic-content`.

Other Portal Technologies

As discussed, the purpose of developing a portal is to extend the capabilities of Dynamics 365 to external users. It is obvious that Dynamics 365 Portals is the best solution out there, but still there are other portal technologies available that can be connected with Dynamics 365.

- As a traditional approach, you could develop a portal from scratch using ASP.NET MVC.

- You could use a content management system such as Orchard to develop a portal.

- Sitecore is another popular CMS that has a built-in Dynamics 365 connector.

All these approaches will require specialized knowledge, which is quite rare to find and might be expensive. Unless properly designed, these portals might cause maintenance overheads in the future. Therefore, it is always the best approach to use Dynamics 365 Portals.

Summary

In this chapter, you learned about the client portals available for Dynamics 365 for Customer Engagements. We specifically looked at configuring the portal add-on and some power user customizations. For advanced customizations, the chapter has introduced the Liquid templates. This was just an introduction Dynamics 365 Portals, and many references were given.

CHAPTER 9

Data Migration

In this chapter, you will explore one of the daunting tasks of Dynamics 365: data migration. The majority of projects that you will undertake will require some level of data migration mainly because your clients will have been working with some legacy system and they will want the legacy data on the new system in order to continue their operations effectively and efficiently. In most cases, the success of the project depends on the data migration. That is, it is only after you migrate the data that you will get to see how the system that you designed and developed is performing. Needless to say, this activity impacts every stakeholder, from the development team to the end users.

Since this is a sensitive task, it must be preplanned so you can allocate resources accordingly. For instance, some clients might provide you with data dumps in a certain format, such as XML or CSV. To begin with, experts will have to analyze these formats carefully. In other scenarios, you will get access to your customer's back-end data stores or databases to extract the data. Before doing any data analysis or extraction, you must first design and develop a proper strategy for the data migration, and the scope of the strategy will depend on the complexity of the data migration. Let's look at how you can do this.

Data Migration Strategy

At this point, you know the destination, which is Dynamics 365. There are a few key steps that you must take into account when performing this activity.

1. Assemble a team of experts. For this tedious task, based on the scope and the complexity, you must assemble a task force of experts including database administrators, database developers, testers, analysts, and so on.

© Sanjaya Yapa 2019
S. Yapa, *Customizing Dynamics 365*, https://doi.org/10.1007/978-1-4842-4379-4_9

2. Format the data provided to you. As mentioned earlier, the data provided will be some form of file format, or you will be given access to the legacy system's data stores. Based on this, you will have to decide on the data analysis phase.

3. Identify the data required. In most scenarios, all the data in the data dump is not required, and a thorough analysis of the existing data is a must. During this, you must identify the master data and the transaction data.

4. Once the data analysis is over, you must create a data map that illustrates where the source data should be at the Dynamics 365 destination.

5. Apply any transformation required. Sometimes you will have to transform the data before you put it into Dynamics 365. This involves converting data into a format that is acceptable by Dynamics 365.

6. Decide on the technology or the mechanism to move the data. There are many options available, and we will discuss them at a high level in this chapter. Since you are migrating to Dynamics 365 online, you cannot use SQL scripts. But the most popular and stable option is to use SQL Server Integration Services. There are third-party tools such as KingswaySoft, Scribe, and CozyRoc that are ideal for this task.

7. Develop the scripts to migrate the data. If you are using a third-party package like KingswaySoft, there are Dynamics 365 connectors that you can use and easily create the connections from source to destination, meaning that there are several different sources and destinations.

8. You should also give top priority for executing and business process–related workflows. That is, if there are any workflows that need to be triggered on the transaction data, decide when to execute them. These SSIS packages are capable of executing workflows on data.

9. Finally comes the testing cycle. This is where the testers can find bugs in the implementation. Your developers should be available for fixing any issues identified by the testers.

With these steps you can successfully develop a data migration strategy, but if you are migrating from a Dynamics CRM on-premise instance, you need to follow a different path. Based on the system that you are on, you need to move to Dynamics 365 on-premise by applying the relevant upgrades. Only then can you move the on-premise instance to the online version. This is known as Microsoft FastTrack for Dynamics 365. In the next section, I will give a brief introduction to this process.

Microsoft FastTrack for Dynamics 365

Microsoft FastTrack for Dynamics 365 is a guided process to move from a CRM on-premise to online, and it enables customers to identify the unsupported customizations and fix them. This process also provides tools that will facilitate platform-level transformations. This migration tool is hosted in the cloud through the Lifecycle Service Portal, which provides a guided mechanism to perform the following steps:

1. Move the on-premises CRM to the Azure infrastructure.

2. Apply the updates and convert it to a state acceptable for Dynamics 365.

3. Push the CRM instance to the Dynamics 365 for Customer Engagement organization.

The following are few factors you should keep in mind:

- This tool and process will support databases up to SQL Server 2012.

- You can migrate only the managed solution; therefore, if you have any unmanaged solutions, you must convert them.

- Facilitate user migrations and audit log migrations.

- The tool also performs security vulnerability check in the databases and with associated extensions.

- This tool will not solve any upgrade issues, and keep in mind that the upgrade is a multistep process.

- You cannot do any selective data migration, and it will not solve any third-party integrations.

- It will also not fix any security issues.

For instance, if you are migrating from Dynamics CRM 2011, the path would be as follows:

1. Provision the CRM instance in Azure.

2. Apply the validation services.

3. Promote the instance to CRM 2013.

4. Promote the instance to CRM 2015.

5. Promote the instance to CRM 2016.

6. Perform a database validation process.

7. Push to Dynamics 365 online.

You must go through a set of steps like these based on the on-premise version that you are in. The FastTrack approach is guided and managed through FastTrack or solution architecture CXP teams. Nominations for the FastTrack program are accepted through the FastTrack portal: `https://www.microsoft.com/microsoft-365/partners/fasttrack`. Once the nomination is approved, a FastTrack engineer will be assigned to you, and they will work with you through the end of the migration process. You can find more about the program at `https://docs.microsoft.com/en-us/previous-versions/dynamicscrm-2016/admins-customizers-dynamics-365/mt812191(v=crm.8)`.

In the sections to follow, you will look at some of the other options available to migrate data to Dynamics 365.

Import Wizard

Dynamics 365 is equipped with a Data Import Wizard that can be used to import data into your Dynamics 365 instance. It accommodates simple data imports and supports the `.csv`, `.xml`, `.txt`, and `.xlsx` file types. It also allows zipped files, which include the previous file types. Let's look at a simple example where you can use the Data Import Wizard. Figure 9-1 shows a CSV file consisting of a list of members. Note that the Membership Type field is a lookup field, and the Payment Method field is an option set in your destination system. Also on the first line of the data dump are the field names.

A	B	C	D	E	F	G
Account Name	Renewal Date	Suburb	Post Code	Membership Type	Payment Type	Phone Number
Eldon Accounting	19/11/2019	Mount Waverley	3149	Bronze	Credit Card	125988743
Office Refrigerators and Air Conditions	19/11/2020	Glen Waverly	3150	Bronze	Credit Card	325633214
Cardinal Slant	19/11/2021	Mulgrave	3170	Silver	Direct Debit	321547789
R380 Pest Control	19/11/2022	Mulgrave	3170	Gold	Credit Card	211455885
Holmes HEPA Air	19/11/2023	Blackburn	3130	Bronze	Direct Debit	214333566
G.E. Longer Electricians	19/11/2024	Glen Waverly	3150	Silver	Direct Debit	441123553
Angle-D Binders with Locking Rings, Label Holders	19/11/2025	Mount Waverley	3149	Silver	Direct Debit	121234547
SAFCO Mobile Desks	19/11/2026	Burwood east	3151	Gold	Credit Card	224545777
COSAF Commercial Wire Shelving	19/11/2027	Burwood east	3151	Bronze	Direct Debit	465322263
Xerox 198 Coppiers	19/11/2028	Mulgrave	3170	Bronze	Direct Debit	243543547

Figure 9-1. *List of member accounts to upload*

Now navigate to the Settings and in the Data Management section select Import Data. See Figure 9-2.

Figure 9-2. *Data Management section*

On the Upload Data File screen, browse and select the CSV file to upload the data and click Next. You can also drag and drop the files from the source to the window. See Figure 9-3.

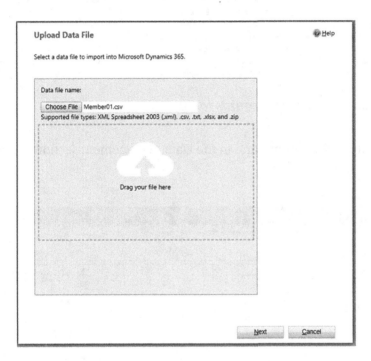

Figure 9-3. Selecting the data file to import

On the next screen, you can review the file upload summary that displays the number of files, the file size, and the delimiter settings. As you can see, we have selected the "First row contains column headings" check box. See Figure 9-4.

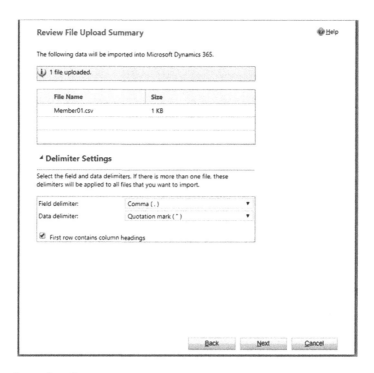

Figure 9-4. *File upload summary*

On the next screen, you must select the data map before the import. If you have created a data map and imported it into the Dynamics 365, then you can select it from here. For this example, we will select the default option and will map the source and destination field names manually. See Figure 9-5.

Figure 9-5. *Selecting the data map before import*

Next, select the record type; in this example, it is the member record. See Figure 9-6.

Figure 9-6. *Selecting the record type*

As the final step, you will map the fields. As mentioned earlier, select the "Look up" field and the option set value. Map them as shown in Figure 9-7.

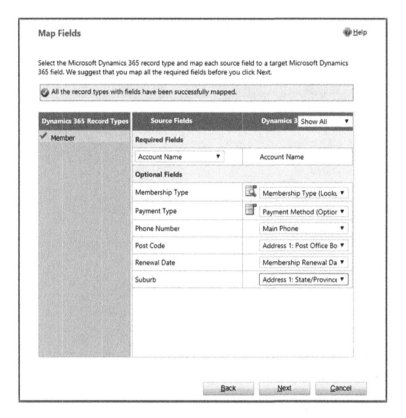

Figure 9-7. *Mapping fields with the source and the destination*

Click Next, and on the last screen click the Submit button to submit the data for import. Once you click Submit, you will see the progress when you refresh the list. When the import is successfully completed, you will see the number of records successfully imported and the failures. See Figure 9-8.

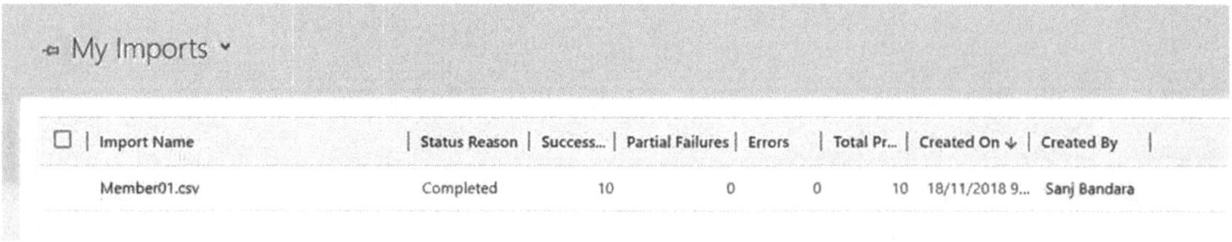

	Import Name		Status Reason	Success...	Partial Failures	Errors		Total Pr...	Created On ↓	Created By	
☐	Member01.csv		Completed	10	0	0		10	18/11/2018 9...	Sanj Bandara	

Figure 9-8. *Data import progress*

When import completes, you can navigate to the Members list and see the actual data that has been imported, as illustrated in Figure 9-9.

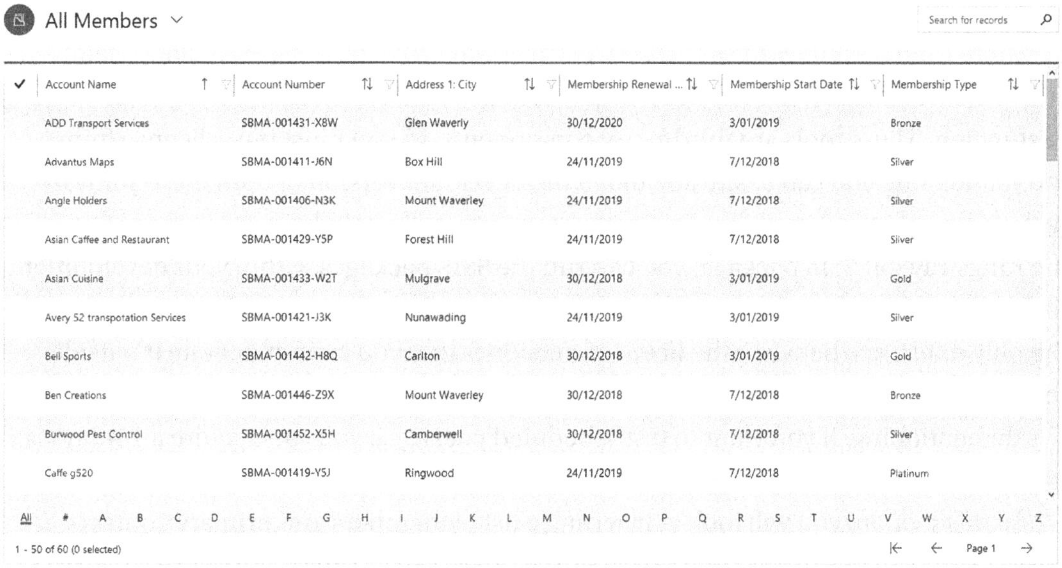

Account Name		Account Number		Address 1: City		Membership Renewal ...		Membership Start Date		Membership Type	
ADD Transport Services		SBMA-001431-X8W		Glen Waverly		30/12/2020		3/01/2019		Bronze	
Advantus Maps		SBMA-001411-J6N		Box Hill		24/11/2019		7/12/2018		Silver	
Angle Holders		SBMA-001406-N3K		Mount Waverley		24/11/2019		7/12/2018		Silver	
Asian Caffee and Restaurant		SBMA-001429-Y5P		Forest Hill		24/11/2019		7/12/2018		Silver	
Asian Cuisine		SBMA-001433-W2T		Mulgrave		30/12/2018		3/01/2019		Gold	
Avery 52 transpotation Services		SBMA-001421-J3K		Nunawading		24/11/2019		3/01/2019		Silver	
Bell Sports		SBMA-001442-H8Q		Carlton		30/12/2018		3/01/2019		Gold	
Ben Creations		SBMA-001446-Z9X		Mount Waverley		30/12/2018		7/12/2018		Bronze	
Burwood Pest Control		SBMA-001452-X5H		Camberwell		30/12/2018		7/12/2018		Silver	
Caffe g520		SBMA-001419-Y5J		Ringwood		24/11/2019		7/12/2018		Platinum	

All # A B C D E F G H I J K L M N O P Q R S T U V W X Y Z

1 - 50 of 60 (0 selected)

Figure 9-9. *Member data imported*

Even though this is an easy solution for data imports, there are a few limitations with the Data Import Wizard.

- There is a file size limitation; the maximum file size for .zip files is 32 MB and for other file types such as .csv is 8 MB.

- You can link records that have only 1:N relationships where the lookup fields are present on the entity you are importing data for.

- Data changes or transformations must be added manually, which leads to errors during the data import.

- You can apply only basic mappings. Mappings such as calculations and complex business logic cannot be mapped with this tool.

- There are no scheduled imports; it is on demand.

For more complex data imports, you should consider using SQL Server Integration Services. In the next section, you will take a quick look at the options available.

Data Importing with SSIS

Using SQL Server Integration Services is a great way to migrate data from different sources to Dynamics 365. The KingswaySoft (`https://www.kingswaysoft.com/products`) and CozyRoc (`https://www.cozyroc.com/products`) SSIS toolkits enable you to create effective and efficient scripts that move data from the source to the destination. These tools are third-party components, so you must buy a license from the vendor. But, you can easily download the developer version of both these software without any cost and try them. For instance, when you install the developer version of the KingswaySoft SSIS package, you can run the SSIS packages within your development tools such as Visual Studio. The tool is fully functional under the developer license, and the only difference between the licensed version is that you cannot operate it outside the developer tools, for instance scheduled execution. But there is an exception that is worth mentioning. If you want to test scheduled packages, you can acquire a 14-day trail license that will revert to a developer license after 14 days.

In this section, you will look at inserting a list of members and primary contacts into Dynamics 365. First, you must install SQL Server Data Tools for Visual Studio 2017. Visit this link to find out more details: `https://docs.microsoft.com/en-us/sql/ssdt/download-sql-server-data-tools-ssdt?view=sql-server-2017`. Next, download and install the SSIS components from the Kingsway Soft product page. Then, create the project to include the data migration scripts. Under New Project, select Business Intelligence and select the Integration Service Project template. Give the project a meaningful name and save it.

When the project is loaded, the SSIS Toolbox will also be loaded, and you can see the components. As the first step of creating the script, you must insert a component such as the Data Flow task on the Control Flow tab. The Data Flow task defines the data from a source to a destination and defines the transformation while moving data. Within the Control Flow tab of the package, you can have multiple data flow tasks and manipulate them using the containers such as the For Loop, Foreach, and Sequence containers. When you double-click or click the Data Flow tab, you can define the actions to perform for that particular data flow task.

Creating the Connection Manager

For this example, you will use four data flow tasks. Add the data flow task and connect them with the green arrow. Select the first task and open the Data Flow tab. Since you are going to read the data from the CSV file, you must create a connection to the file. At the bottom of the screen, you can see the Connection Managers tab. Right-click the view and select New Connection, and from the list of connections, select Flat File Connection and click Add. This will open the configuration window. See Figure 9-10.

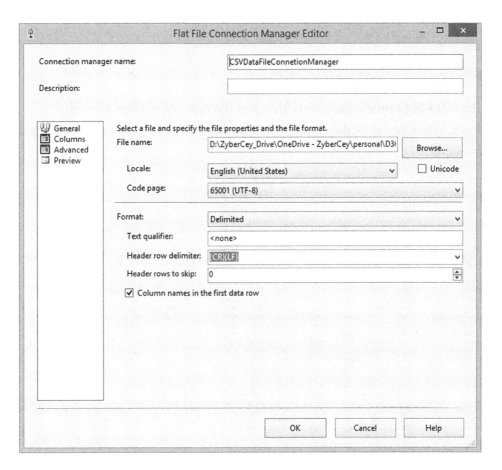

Figure 9-10. *Configuring the flat-file connection*

In this window, you will be selecting the location of the file and leaving the other settings as they are. One important thing to mention here is to check the "Column names in the first data row" option if the first row contains column names. Click OK, and the new connection will appear on the Connection Managers tab.

Configuring the Source

Now, select Flat File Source in the toolbar. See Figure 9-11.

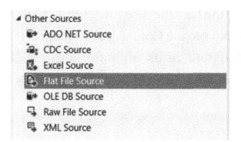

Figure 9-11. Selecting Flat File Source

In the Flat File Source editor, you can select the new connection from the drop-down. When you click the Preview button, you can see a preview of the data that is to be loaded. See Figure 9-12.

Account Name	Renewal ...	Suburb	Post Code	Members...	Payment...	Phone N...	Contact First Name	Contact Last Name	Email Ad...	Telephone	Job Title
Eldon Accounting	19/11/2...	Mount ...	3149	Bronze	Credit C...	125988...	Barry	French	Barry.Fr...	125988...	CEO
Office Refrigerators and Air Conditions	19/11/2...	Glen Wa...	3150	Bronze	Credit C...	325633...	Clay	Rozendal	Clay.Roz...	325633...	MD
Cardinal Slant	19/11/2...	Mulgrave	3170	Silver	Direct D...	321547...	Carlos	Soltero	Carlos.S...	321547...	Director
R380 Pest Control	19/11/2...	Mulgrave	3170	Gold	Credit C...	211455...	Carl	Jackson	Carl.Jac...	211455...	Business...
Holmes HEPA Air	19/11/2...	Blackburn	3130	Bronze	Direct D...	214333...	Monica	Federle	Monica.F...	214333...	Business...
G.E. Longer Electricians	19/11/2...	Glen Wa...	3150	Silver	Direct D...	441123...	Dorothy	Badders	Dorothy...	441123...	CEO
"Angle-D Binders with Locking Rings	Label H...	19/11/2...	Mount ...	3149	Silver	Direct D...	121234547	Neola	Schneider	Neola.Sc...	121234...
SAFCO Mobile Desks	19/11/2...	Burwoo...	3151	Gold	Credit C...	224545...	Carlos	Daly	Carlos.D...	224545...	Director
COSAF Commercial Wire Shelving	19/11/2...	Burwoo...	3151	Bronze	Direct D...	465322...	Claudia	Miner	Claudia...	465322...	Branch ...
Xerox 198 Copiers	19/11/2...	Mulgrave	3170	Bronze	Direct D...	243543...	Neola	Schneider	Neola.Sc...	243543...	Business...
Home and Business Xerox 1980	19/11/2...	Glenroy	3046	Gold	Credit C...	454654...	Allen	Rosenblatt	Allen.Ro...	454654...	Director
Advantus Maps	19/11/2...	Box Hill	3128	Silver	Credit C...	445887...	Sylvia	Foulston	Sylvia.F...	445887...	Director
Holmes Agriculture Labs	19/11/2...	Carlton	3053	Gold	Direct D...	545454...	Fong	Chun	Fong.Ch...	545454...	MD
DSHD Compter Repairs	19/11/2...	Mitcham	3132	Bronze	Credit C...	554422...	Henry	Peters	Henry.P...	554422...	MD
Wilson Jones Contractors	19/11/2...	Mulgrave	3170	Platinum	Credit C...	221555...	Anne	Jhones	Anne.Jh...	221555...	MD
Ultra Commercial windows	19/11/2...	Carlton	3053	Platinum	Direct D...	546689...	Jim	Radford	Jim.Radf...	546689...	MD
Hamilton Stationaries	19/11/2...	Mount ...	3149	Bronze	Direct D...	623147...	Ben	Stacks	Ben.Sta...	623147...	CEO
Readers Dimension Books	19/11/2...	Glenroy	3046	Silver	Direct D...	321569...	Carlos	Soltero	Carlos.S...	321569...	CEO
Lesro Sheffield furniture	19/11/2...	Mitcham	3132	Gold	Direct D...	125874...	Carl	Ludwig	Carl.Lud...	125874...	CEO
Caffe g520	19/11/2...	Ringwood	3134	Platinum	Credit C...	213265...	Don	Miler	Don.Mile...	213265...	CEO
Morning Mind Breakfast and Coffee	19/11/2...	Burwoo...	3151	Gold	Direct D...	213285...	Annie	Cyprus	Annie/C...	213285...	Business...
Avery 52 transpotation Services	19/11/2...	Nunawa...	3131	Silver	Credit C...	216985...	Carl	Ludwig	Carl.Lud...	216985...	Branch ...
Plymouth Rubber Products	19/11/2...	Camber...	3154	Silver	Direct D...	653241...	Carlos	Soltero	Carlos.S...	653241...	CEO
GBC Heavy Printing	19/11/2...	Carlton	3053	Platinum	Direct D...	635285...	Grant	Carroll	Grant.C...	635285...	MD
Max Norman Home Shopping	19/11/2...	Forest Hill	3131	Gold	Credit C...	326688...	John	Richardson	John.Ric...	326688...	MD
Newel 335 Electronics	19/11/2...	Glen Wa...	3150	Platinum	Credit C...	444523...	Emaly	Young	Emaly.Y...	444523...	CEO
SANFORD Builders	19/11/2...	Box Hill	3128	Silver	Credit C...	222258...	Karen	Hearts	Karen.H...	222258...	Sales Ma...
The Photographers Club	19/11/2...	Camber...	3154	Bronze	Direct D...	774522...	Bob	Dean	Bob.Dea...	774522...	Sales Ma...
TenX Person Project Systtems	19/11/2...	Blackburn	3130	Gold	Credit C...	445236...	Samson	Andrews	Samson...	445236...	CEO
Asian Caffee and Restaurant	19/11/2...	Forest Hill	3131	Silver	Credit C...	415878...	Richard	Gates	Richard...	415878...	Head of ...

Figure 9-12. Flat file data preview

In this window, you can see that all the columns were loaded. For the first step, you are planning to load the contacts only. Therefore, from the Columns tab, select the columns you want. See Figure 9-13.

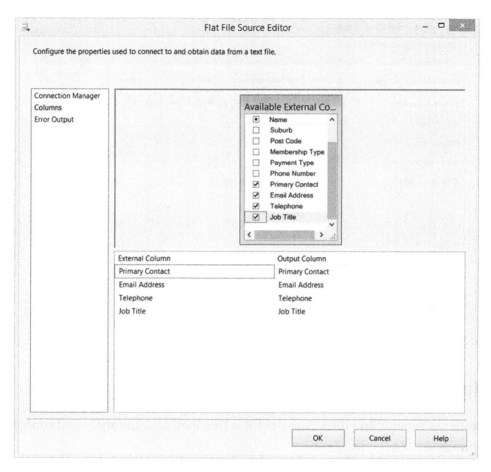

Figure 9-13. *Selecting the columns to use*

You've established the source connection, and the configuration has been completed. Since there is no transformation is required, you will simply use the Dynamics CRM destination. Before that, you are going to set up the connection manager for the Dynamics CRM destination. As previously explained, select the Dynamics CRM connection manager from the SSIS Connection Manager. When you provide the details of your Dynamics 365 instance, it should look something like Figure 9-14.

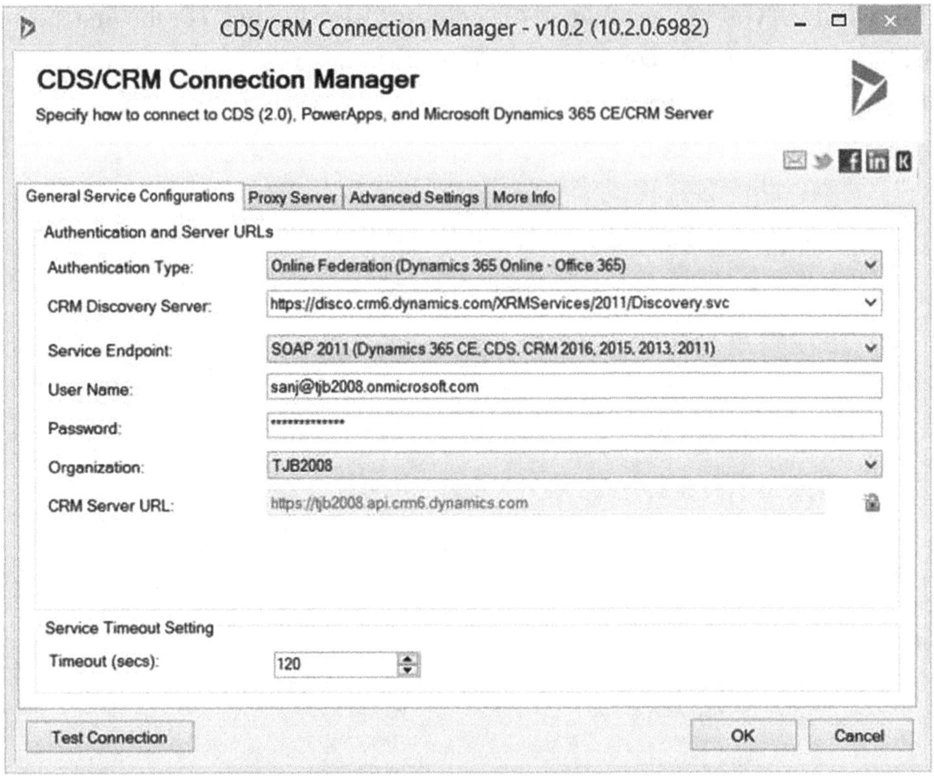

Figure 9-14. *Dynamics 365 Connection Manager settings*

Configuring the Destination

Now, from the Toolbox add the Dynamics CRM Destination component and configure.
See Figure 9-15.

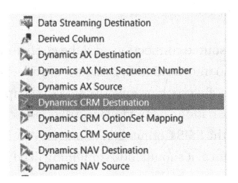

Figure 9-15. *Dynamics 365 Destination component*

As shown in Figure 9-16, set the destination settings. As you can see, we have selected the connection manager that we created. The action is set as Upsert, which is a great way of performing an insert and an update at the same time. What does this mean? As per this example, you are importing the contacts, and if a contact exists, the destination component will go and update existing contact. If the contact does not exist, it will create a new one. This action is determined by the upsert/update settings you specify. There are few options available here. For the purposes of this example, you will be manually specifying the matching criteria, and if there are any multiple matches, you will raise an error. See Figure 9-16.

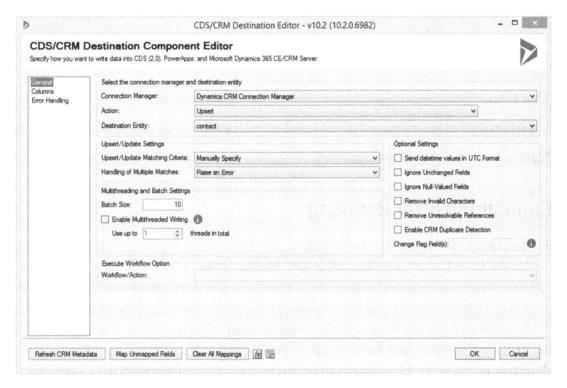

Figure 9-16. *Dynamics 365 Destination Component Editor*

On the Columns tab of this window, we have selected the required columns to be updated for the contact record at the destination instance. As you can see in Figure 9-17, three columns have been selected as key columns. This where the Upsert/Update Matching Criteria field is configured, which means based these fields, the package will look for any matching records.

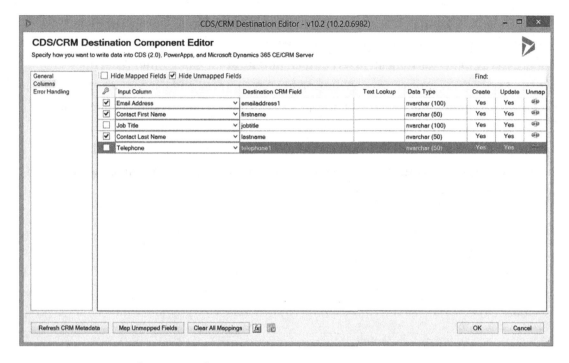

Figure 9-17. *Configuring columns*

Configuring Error Handling

Now it's time to configure error handling.

On the Error Handling page, choose the "Redirect rows to error output" option in the "Choose error-handling mechanism" section to direct any duplicate rows to be written to a flat file so that you can examine them, correct the errors, and re-upload them.

Sometimes if you did not give much consideration to the data types and the size of the fields, you will end up in failures during the migration, which makes it difficult to troubleshoot. To make the matters worse, you might end up rolling back data, which will result in incomplete records or data inconsistencies. This is important at the time of transformation. That is, you must take all the measures you can to make the data types and field size match the target system's field data types and sizes. Ideally, the output fields from the transformation should match the target system's fields exactly. This can be detected with error handling, but you should try to avoid this type of issue in the first place. See Figure 9-18.

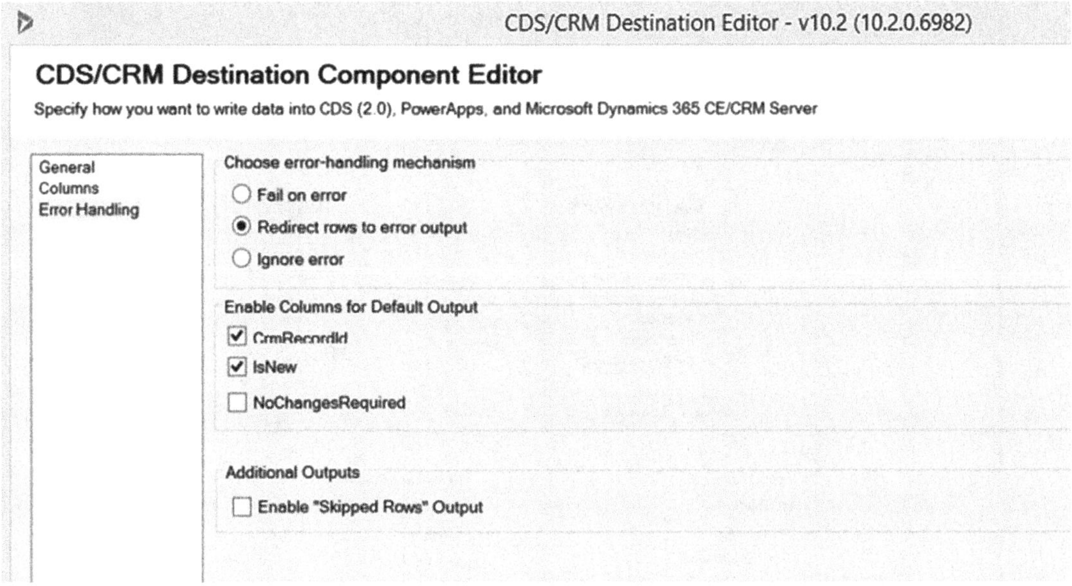

Figure 9-18. *Configuring the error handling mechanism*

Add another flat-file destination with a new flat-file connection manager and map the error fields as illustrated in Figure 9-19 to ensure the errors are written to a new file.

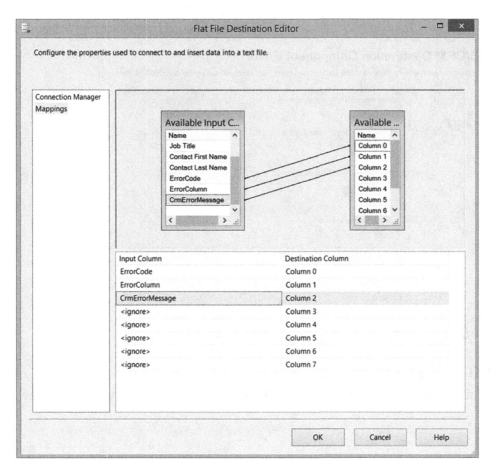

Figure 9-19. *Mapping error to an error file*

Once everything is set up, your data flow task should look something like Figure 9-20. When connecting the Dynmics CRM destination to the flat-file destination for error logging, make sure you select the red line, which defines the error pipeline.

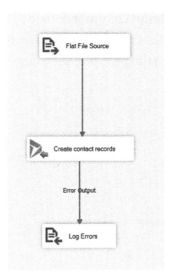

Figure 9-20. *Loading the contacts data flow task*

Data Transformation

Now that you have created the first data flow to load the contacts, let's create the next data flow to insert the member records. Again, you will read the same CSV file to retrieve the member details, and therefore you will add the flat-file source and set the connection like you did in the previous step. As shown in Figure 9-21, there is a new component added to the flow. It is a script component that you can code with C#. Within this component, you have transferred the renewal date to a date-time value.

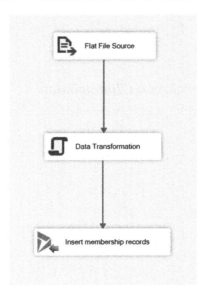

Figure 9-21. *Completed data flow to insert members*

When you double-click the script component named Data Transformation, a settings window will appear. In this window, on the Input Columns tab, you can define which columns should be pushed down the pipeline. See Figure 9-22.

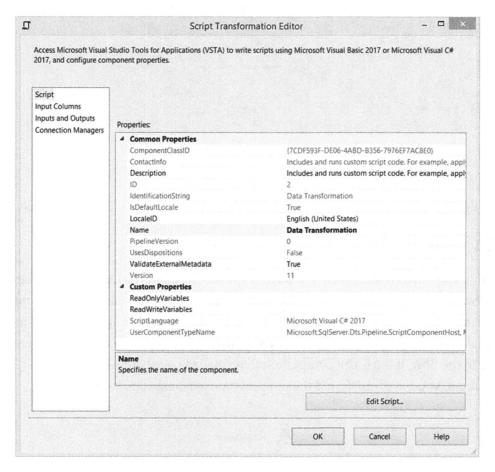

Figure 9-22. *Script Transformation Editor window*

At the bottom of the window, click the Edit Script button to load the C# editor. For this example, you have simply converted the renewal date in string format to a date-time format. During a transformation there are three events: Pre Execute, Post Execute, and Transformation. As per the comments in the code, the Pre Execute event is triggered once before processing the rows, and Post Execute will be triggered once after processing all the rows. All the transformation is carried out within the `Input0_ProcessInputRow` method. The parameter `Input0Buffer` contains all the rows that you are passing to the script component. The nice thing about this method is that all the records in the input buffer will be iterated and processed. See Figure 9-23.

Figure 9-23. *Script component C# editor*

Configuring the Dynamics CRM destination is the same as discussed earlier. But for the demonstration purposes, there are slight differences in the settings. After completing the membership update, the next configuration is to update the contact record with the company details or the member company. This one is a bit more complex than what you did in the previous two tasks. See Figure 9-24.

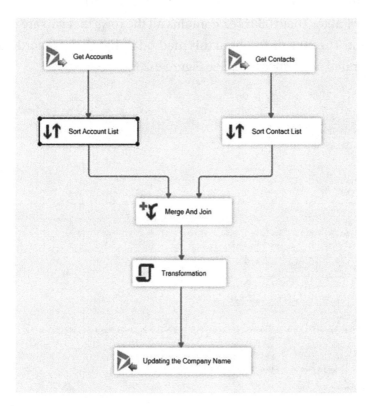

Figure 9-24. *Updating the contact details*

As per the requirements, you have selected both accounts and contacts using two separate Dynamics CRM data sources. Your plan is to merge the outputs together. To do this, you have to sort the data sets separately, and you can use the Sort component from the toolbox. Sorting is a must for merging records. In the Sort Transformation Editor window, you specify the name (member name) as the sorting field. The same setting was applied to the contact list retrieved as well.

Note   This merge and join scenario might not work for extremely larger data import scenarios. This is primarily because SSIS will create a temporary data store to perform the merge and join. It would be a better option to create a Fetch XML query with the join and then filter the records. In the previous example, the Dynamics CRM source component is configured to directly query the entity. As shown in Figure 9-25, when you change Source Type to FetchXML, you can enter the Fetch XML query. You can use the Fetch XM Builder tool in XrmToolBox to build your Fetch XML query. See Figure 9-26.

Figure 9-25. *Fetch XML option for Dynamics CRM source component*

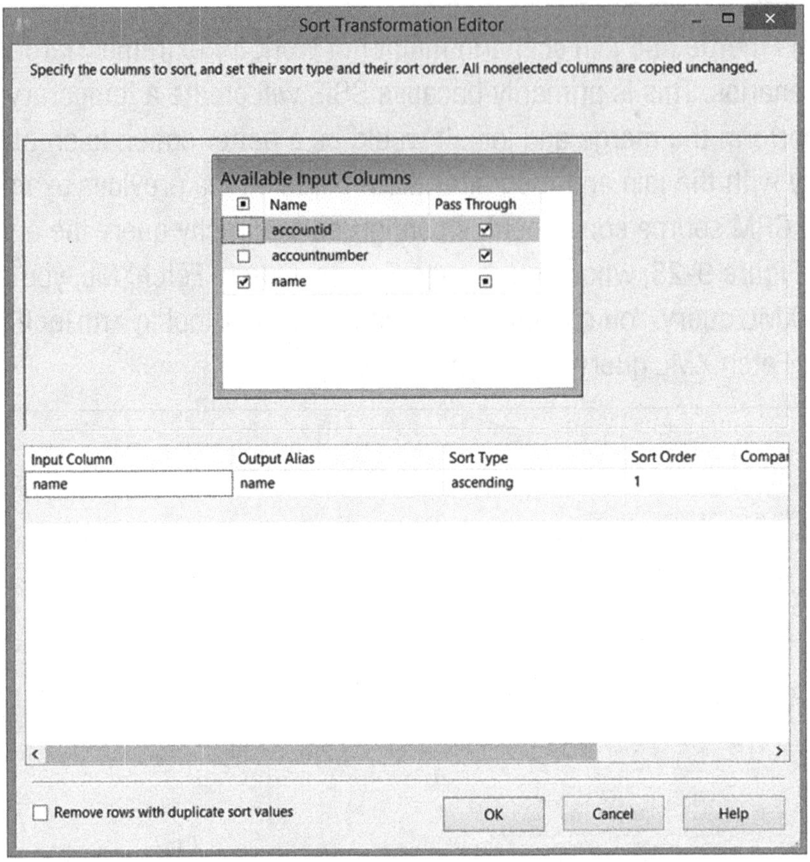

Figure 9-26. *Sort Transformation Editor, setting the available input columns*

Configuring the transformation and the destination is the same process as you did earlier. For the final step, the membership record must be updated with the primary contact; we have used the contact record that was created in the first step. See Figure 9-27.

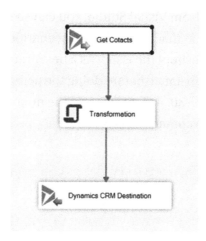

Figure 9-27. *Updating the primary contact of the membership record*

For this task, you retrieve the contacts and select the company name and the contact ID. The company name is used to match the account. Again, the configuration and transformation are the same as earlier. The final outcome of all the data flow tasks will be something similar to the one illustrated in Figure 9-28. The check mark indicates that each step has executed successfully. If there are any errors, you will see a red X on the component that failed.

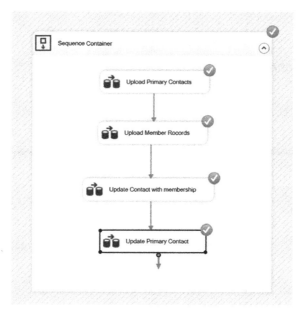

Figure 9-28. *Data flows executed successfully*

When you run a package from Visual Studio, you can see the progress, and if any step fails, the execution stops at that point. In such scenarios, you can open the Progress tab of the package and troubleshoot the issue. As a best practice, it is always good to try the package against a test instance before doing the actual migration. As you can see in Figure 9-29 and Figure 9-30, the contact and the membership record have been successfully updated with the contact details.

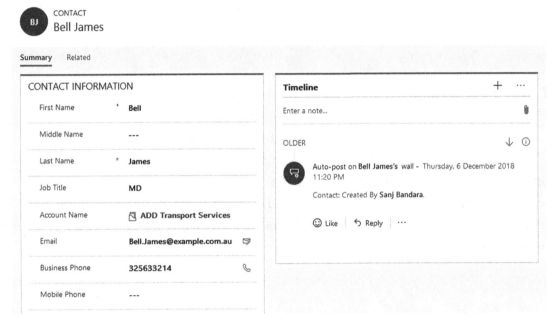

Figure 9-29. *Contact record*

Figure 9-30. *Membership record*

Not only for data migration tasks, these SSIS packages are ideal for bulk data updates and scheduled processes. Since the updates are done using the SDK through the destination components, you will have full traceability as well. CozyRoc is similar to KingswaySoft components with minor differences and with pricing differences as well. You have the option to select the tool that best fits your client's specific scenario.

Summary

In this chapter, you learned about moving data from your legacy system to Dynamics 365. At the beginning of the chapter, a good explanation was given to highlight the importance of setting up a strategy. Next you took a quick peek into the Microsoft FastTrack program, and finally you looked at the out-of-the-box tools and the custom tools that can be used to facilitate the tedious task of data migration.

Index

A

Advanced Find views
    columns, add, 211
    filter, 208–209
    grouping, 209
    limitations, 214
    look up records, 208
    member subscription, 207
    saved view, 212
    target users, 213
Automating business processes
    actions
        arguments, 125–128
        creation, 124
        definition, 123
    business process flows
        application review process, 110
        creation, 111
        data fields, 113
        definition, 110
        designer window, 112
        enabling entity, 112
        unified interface, 115
        workflow, 114
    check conditions, 122
    Microsoft flow
        creation, 130
        definition, 129

Dynamics 365 Settings, 129
        external database, 133
        scenarios, 129
        triggers and connectors, 131
        Twilio connection, 132
    workflows
        check conditions, 122
        condition configuration, 119–120
        creation, 117
        definition, 115
        membership registration, 116
        properties, 118, 121
Auto Number Manager
    configuration window, 81–83
    definition, 79
    Event entity setting, 84
    XrmToolBox, 80
Azure Active Directory (AAD), 157
Azure app service, 167
Azure DevOps, 4–5
Azure functions, 174–175
    CORS, 181
    creation
        app, 176
        Azure subscription, 179
        HTTP trigger, 177
        properties, 178
        templates, 177
        testing, 180

Printed in the United States
By Bookmasters